Birkenhead

Garston

RIVER DEE

RIVER MERSEY

ris

Conway

Abergele

Rhyl

Mostyn

Parkgate

Aber

Rhyddlan

Holywell

Mooton

Trefriw

St Asaph

Flint

Caerwys

Connahs Quay

Sandycroft

CHES

bor

Denbigh

Llanynys

Mold

Buckley

Hawarden

Salthey

CHESTER

Wax

Llanrwst

Nerquis

Treuddyn

Hope

Holt

Capel Curig

Cyffylliog

Ruthin

Minera

T

Llanberis

Bettws-y-Coed

Bryn

Wrexham

Elston

Snowdon

Pentre Voelas

Llanelidan

Marchwiel

Malp

Beddgelert

Penmachno

Bryn Eglwys

Ruabon

Worthen

Cary-y-draidion

Llangwm

Llangollen

Erbistock

Festiniog

Corwen

Cefn

Overton

Whitt

Maentwrog

Glyn Ceiriog

Martins

Duddleston

Hanmer

adoc

Bala

Martins

Whixe

Trawsfynydd

Llandrillo

Ellesmere

Welsh

arlech

Llangower

Dyffryn Ceiriog

Whittington

Hampton

Llanuwchllyn

Cockshutt

anbedr

Pennant

Oswestry

Aston

Loppington

landdwye

Llanrhaiadr

West

Felton

Middle

Llangynog

Porthywen

Knockin

Llanaben

Llangedwin

Puyton

Llanymowddy

Hirnant

Llangyllin

Llanymynech

Fitz

Dolgelly

Llanwddyn

Llansaintffraid

Capel Orthog

Dinas Mowddwy

Meifod

Llandrinio

Griggion

SHREWSBURY

Llanfihangel

Mallwyd

Garthbibio

Guilsfield

Woolaston

SHREWSBURY & WELSH

ngelynin

Cemmaes

Llangeniew

Butlington

Westbury

Hanwood

POOL R

Llanwrin

Darowen

Llanfair

Welshpool

Condo

yn

Pennal

MACHYNLLETH

Worthyn

Minsterley

Fro

rdovey

Machynlleth

Trelystan

Chirbury

Shelve

Leebotw

Llanbrynmair

Llanwyddelan

Montgomery

Stretton

Llancynfelin

Carno

Tregynon

Llanwnog

Llandyssil

Hyssington

Church

Planlimmon

Trefeglws

Llandinam

Newtown

Bishops

Castle

Norbury

Acton

Scott

MILFORD

Kerry

Diddleburr

Capel Banger

Llanidloes

Craven Arms

Col

Llangwrig

Old Chapel

Bettws-y-Crwyn

Clun

Culm

Ispay Cynfyn

Devils Bridge

Llanbadarn

Fynydd

Onibury

The Neath and Brecon Railway

A History

NEATH AND BRECON RAILWAY — DISTRICT MAP—1871.

National Archives

THE NEATH AND BRECON RAILWAY

A HISTORY

Gwyn Briwnant Jones
Denis Dunstone
and
Tudor Watkins

Gomer

First impression – 2005

ISBN 1 84323 452 1

Printed in Wales at
Gomer Press, Llandysul, Ceredigion

CONTENTS

The winter sun casts an eerie light as a dining-car excursion winds its way up the Dulais valley, in February 1979.

John Davies

FOREWORD

It is very surprising that the Neath & Brecon Railway (N & B) has had to wait so long for its first full-length history. It may not have been among the largest of the pre-grouping companies of south Wales in terms of mileage or receipts; it may not have yielded such impressive dividends as the Taff Vale in its heyday, nor carried such an intensive mineral traffic as the Barry, but few lines of its size have been associated with such a variegated and interesting assortment of characters or operated in such wonderful scenery.

The N & B originated as a typical contractor's railway. The brains behind the scheme was the flamboyant Scottish contractor, John Dickson – and 'flamboyant' has to be the word to describe someone with Dickson's taste in trousers. He was hand in glove with William Lawrence Banks, the first vice-chairman and later chairman, a true railway enthusiast if ever there was one, but highly eccentric and totally impractical. They were followed by the diligent liquidator, Thomas Cave, who sorted out the financial mess that Dickson and Banks had left behind them, and Colonel Laurie who steered the company to a modest prosperity in the early twentieth century.

It is widely known that the first Fairlie locomotives in the world worked on the N & B. What is still not clear is how this came about. Without doubt it indicates collaboration between Dickson and his fellow Scot, Robert Fairlie, but which one of them took the initiative and why? If only evidence had survived to make it possible to explore their relationship; if only, too, we had a time machine to go back to 1867 and watch *Progress* or *Mountaineer* as they struggled up the 1 in 50 from Colbren towards Penwyllt – and by all accounts they would have been struggling. Penwyllt, the station serving that wild and isolated quarry hamlet, later came to enjoy the regular patronage of the still not fully forgotten Victorian 'diva', Madame Adelina Patti, and acquired the name of Craig-y-nos from the nearby mock castle that she made her home.

For most of its existence the N & B pursued an uneventful life, content just to stay solvent and meet the needs of the farmers of southern Breconshire and the collieries of the Dulais valley, but there were times when it seemed as though it might enjoy a more prominent place in the national network. Dickson's vision for the N & B was that it should form part of a trunk route from south Wales to the Midlands and in pursuit of this he cultivated the London & North Western. That company had other plans, but the Midland was glad to offer its patronage to the struggling N & B, although the result was hardly a major trunk route. In 1889 Edward Watkin of the Manchester, Sheffield & Lincolnshire tried to lure the N & B into his camp as part of a pan-Wales network. He did not succeed in this but his efforts resulted in the sort of stand-off that might have been expected of the swashbuckling companies of the 1840s but hardly of the grown-up railways of the late Victorian era.

I am delighted that the rich history of the N & B has now finally been addressed, and that it is Gwyn Briwnant Jones and Denis Dunstone who have tackled it. The success of the previous histories of the Vale of Neath Line and of the LMS in South Wales, together with the specialized knowledge and enthusiasm of Tudor Watkins for all things N & B, makes them ideally placed to handle the subject. Their thoroughly researched and well-illustrated account helps us to understand the history of the N & B and of the characters who were associated with its formation and development, and also to enjoy once again, if only in our imagination, the vision of a steam-hauled train on the side of Fan Gyhirych or in the fertile farmland of the Usk valley. For the present reader, and I suspect the same will be true of many others, this account also brings on a deep sense of regret – and that not for the first time – that I never had the opportunity to make that journey. I welcome this history as the next best thing.

Paul Reynolds, Librarian,
University of Swansea

Pannier tank engine No. 3706 trundles its short freight train from Neath to Brecon across the lattice girder bridge over the Usk. 7 May 1958.

J. Spencer Gilks/Tudor Watkins Coll.

PREFACE

This book combines the work of three writers, Tudor Watkins having joined the established partnership of Jones and Dunstone and bringing a probably unique knowledge of the Neath and Brecon as an operating railway. Others have assisted very generously with written material and with the loan of photographs. These include John Davies of Swansea, Bob Grant of Neath, Alan Jarvis of Cardiff, Glyn Powell of Sennybridge and Peter Treloar of Calne; also, Ray Burrows and David G. Eldard for ticket information. The Rev. Dr. Martin Connop Price of Shiplake, Oxfordshire and Paul Reynolds of Swansea University have been enthusiastic supporters and advisers.

Some might feel that the Neath & Brecon hardly merits a whole volume. It is one of the last of the independent railways in Wales to be without a historical record. Yet it was particularly notable for its relationship with the Midland and for its financial shenanigans. Possibly it was the complexity of the financial affairs which deterred earlier railway historians, more interested in boilers than balance sheets. Unfortunately, the financial history which played such an important part in the early days is not clearly or consistently documented and it has been necessary to piece it together from disparate records. Although it has proved impossible to discover precisely, pound by pound, how the company came so seriously to grief, sufficient circumstantial evidence has been uncovered for it to be possible to make some informed deductions. As a result the story hangs reasonably well together.

But there are other reasons for this book. The route of the railway was picturesque and it traversed contrasting countryside, coalmines, bare mountainsides and the pastoral Usk valley. But, above all, people gave it a personality unlike other minor mineral lines. This book is about them as much as about business and transport.

Our increasing awareness of the correct form and spelling of Welsh place-names makes it difficult to perpetuate the errors initially instigated by the railways. Consequently, the earlier idiosyncratic 'railway' forms are confined to references in documents, timetables or to stations; the more modern and correct form is generally used elsewhere. Thus, both *Colbren* and *Coelbren*, for example, are acceptable within the appropriate context.

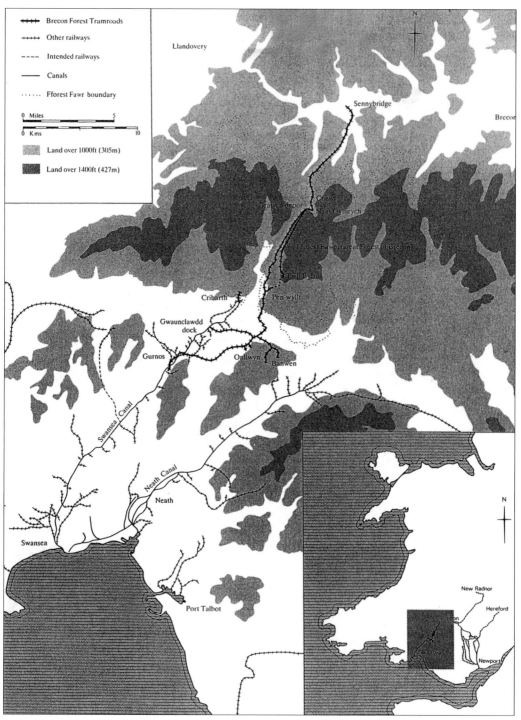

General plan of the Brecon Forest Tramroad and canal connections.

Courtesy Stephen Hughes

Chapter 1

BEFORE THE RAILWAY

Brecon and Neath have little in common and indeed little commercial interest in one another, and it was something of an accident of history that caused a railway to be built between them. Brecon has for centuries been a centre of trade associated with agriculture, while Neath has been largely industrial. Brecon is well inland, sheltered by mountains, while Neath lies close to the sea. But they share a long history; Brecon had a priory and Neath an abbey and both had castles founded in the early Middle Ages. In the nineteenth century both were for a time served by railway companies with their names in the titles. At Brecon there were the Brecon and Merthyr (B & M) and the Hereford, Hay and Brecon (HH & B), while at Neath there were the Vale of Neath (VoN) and the Swansea and Neath (S & N). Common to both was the Neath and Brecon (N & B). Oddly, Brecon never saw a railway along the most obvious route, up the Usk valley from Abergavenny and on over the pass to Llandovery. Its railways approached over hilly or mountainous terrain along routes as attractive and interesting as any in the whole of Britain. Brecon was on

No. 8732 labours up the grade, in the vicinity of Craig-y-nos, quite oblivious of the grandeur of the scenery. July 1962.
John Davies

The already bleak terrain of Onllwyn is transformed by a fall of snow to represent a vista from outer space as two Class 37 diesels work an 'up' excursion. February 1979.

John Davies

the Midland and later LMS route from Birmingham to Swansea and effectively at the crossing point with a north-south route from the north-west of England to Merthyr Tydfil. Neath was on the GW main line from London to Swansea and eventually had two other routes to Swansea, the S & N already mentioned, and the Rhondda and Swansea Bay. The broad gauge VoN reached Aberdare and Merthyr.

Between Brecon and Neath lies the mountain range known as Fforest Fawr or the Great Forest of Brecon. This open moorland country links the still higher ground of Carmarthen Fan on the west to the Brecon Beacons on the east and is the catchment area for the river Tawe which flows into the Bristol Channel at Swansea (Abertawe). In 1870, three years after the N & B was opened across these mountains, *Murray's Handbook* described the route as offering some of the most beautiful scenery in Wales, first in the upper reaches of the river Usk and then amidst the mountains of what were then called 'the Breconshire and Caermarthenshire Beacons'.

Across this open moorland rising in parts to over 2,500ft, ancient highways had been driven for centuries. Part of the Sarn Helen Roman road from north to south Wales through Brecon and ending at Neath, ran between the Usk valley and the Vale of Neath, just to the east of where the railway was to run. Nearby standing stones bear witness to Bronze Age occupation. The 13ft high monolith Maen Madog testifies to the fact that this wild and desolate country was home to man in the fifth century AD. The turnpike road from Brecon to Swansea ran from a junction with the present A470 Brecon to Merthyr road, over the mountains, down the Llia valley to

Ystradfellte, and then down the Vale of Neath. *Cliffe's Guide Book to South Wales*, published in 1848, spoke of the magnificent solitude of this high and lonely place where local people recalled the sighting of groups of fairies dressed in white, borne by miniature white horses. Many attested to the truth of these reports. The guidebook also mentioned the regrettable rumour that a railway was being mooted.

Summer sunshine can transform most places, but the area surrounding Pantyffordd Halt retains its shorn appearance. 1963.

Alan Jarvis

However, the idea of a railway in these parts was not as improbable as it may seem as there were already tramroads. Indeed, part of the Brecon Forest Tramroad (BFT) which ran over much of the northern part of what was to become the N & B was first laid in 1821. The story of this tramroad is relevant to the history of the railway and it is therefore worthy of closer examination. Not only did it act as a precursor, but it also experienced some of the economic problems which confronted the later railway company. It may be a matter of some surprise that so early in British industrial history a tramroad should even be mooted across such hostile terrain. The reasons were not purely commercial. Fforest Fawr had been Crown land, having once been the hunting territory of a Norman baron. In 1812, the government was in need of funds to finance the war against Napoleon and sold some 5,000 hectares of the Forest to a Scotsman, John Christie. He had made a fortune importing indigo and other dyes from India and planned to improve the area as agricultural land. He saw the band of limestone lying across the southern boundary of his estate as a source of lime. In order to move the limestone to kilns on his land he constructed a tramroad.

Mountain scenery, Fan Gyhirych, Bwlch Bryn-rhudd and Crai reservoir, looking south.
DD

View along the railway, looking north towards Craig-y-nos with the ruined brickworks on the right. 1978.
M. Lloyd

Approaching Craig-y-nos station, looking north. 1959.
G.H. Platt

Heading north from Craig-y-nos. 1961.

R.M. Casserley

Approaching the summit. 1959.

G.H. Platt

Beyond the summit, Crai reservoir loomed into view.

G.H. Platt

As originally conceived, the tramroad was to run northward continuously downhill from a limestone source 1,500ft up on the south-west side of Fan Gyhirych, high above and to the east of the source of the Tawe. It was to end on the Usk at what is now Sennybridge. However, the difficulty of such a route was soon realised and it also emerged that this would not provide access to any coal reserves. Instead, the tramroad was laid from quarries lower down in the Tawe valley and then over the 1,267ft pass known as Bwlch Bryn-rhudd (Red Hill Pass), still ending at the Usk. However, it now entailed hauling loaded trams uphill to the pass, a practice normally avoided wherever possible.

The view from a north-bound train as it made for the summit at Bwlch Bryn-rhudd. 1959.

G.H. Platt

It was completed in 1824 but already in 1822 it seems that Christie had doubts about the economic viability of this scheme. Not only had he made no provision for sourcing coal for his limekilns, but he also realised that the distances, the height and the volume of potential traffic were going to limit earnings. Hauling materials northward to relatively poor agricultural country was of doubtful economy; the commercial future lay in sending materials down to the ironworks in the Tawe valley or to the sea for export. He accordingly invested in coal-mining, opening the Drum Colliery that year, and building an extension of the tramroad down to the Swansea Canal at Gwaun-clawdd where he invested also in a then declining colliery. He also invested in 24 canal boats and three sailing vessels. This was more than the business could sustain and at the end of 1827 he was bankrupt. In 1831 the tramroad came under the control of a creditor, a Lincolnshire banker named Joseph Claypon, and he built a new arm of the tramroad from its southern end to the Swansea Canal at Gurnos. He also invested in limekilns and an improved depot at Sennybridge.

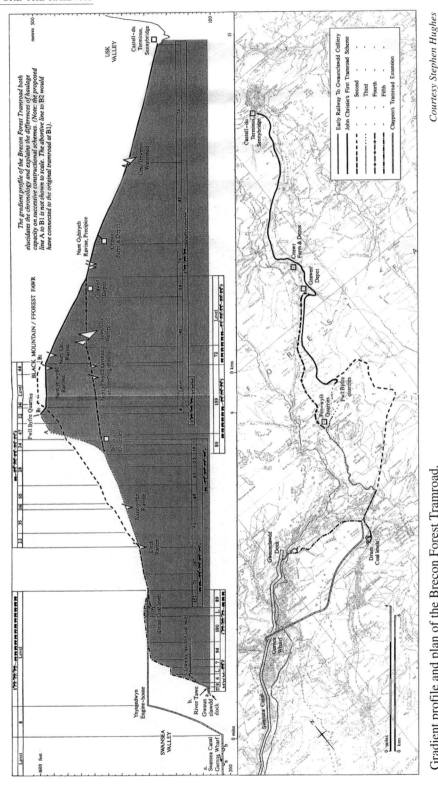

Courtesy Stephen Hughes

The gradient profile of the Brecon Forest Tramroad both
elucidates the chronology and explains the differences of haulage
capacity on successive constructional schemes. (Note: the proposed
line A to B1 is not shown to scale. The abortive line to B2 would
have connected to the original tramroad at B1).

Gradient profile and plan of the Brecon Forest Tramroad.

While the Brecon Forest Tramway wound its way around the contours, the railway was more direct. Here, a Great Western pannier tank slips through the mountain landscape on its way towards Cray. August 1960.

Alan Jarvis

Ynysgedwyn Iron and Tinplate Works site some time after closure.   *J.E. Martin*

The new line was known as the Brecon Forest Branch Tramroad or more simply as Claypon's Tramroad Extension and is of interest in the general history of railways as it was laid by a team of 500 'navigators' to a higher specification than that used hitherto for tramroads, though, like the rest of the tramroad, it was a plateway with a gauge of 3ft 6ins. Although it ended in an inclined plane with a gradient of 1:5 at its steepest part, locomotive haulage may have been considered for the main part of the line and it has even been thought that it was intended to carry passengers. However, it is almost certainly fanciful to imagine it being used for anything other than the unofficial carriage of tramroad workers. It was completed in 1834. The successor to Christie, the Brecon Forest Tramroad Company, operated this line and used it to haul goods northward from the Swansea Canal. The tramroad was advertised as a part of the route for general goods from Bristol and Swansea to mid Wales. However, it still suffered from insufficient traffic, especially in coal. Other tramroads in the area such as the Hay Railway and those between Abergavenny and Hereford carried a much higher proportion of coal, upon which the operating margins were higher. Furthermore, the market in the Usk valley to the east was already served by the Brecon & Abergavenny Canal, while westward in Carmarthenshire, coal was being supplied to the upper Tywi valley by road from Brynaman.

That industrial activity rather than agriculture offered the best prospects for traffic growth was made apparent by the growth of iron-ore furnaces in the Swansea valley. These furnaces saw a peak of production beween 1830 and 1860. Ystalyfera and Ynysgedwyn in the Tawe valley were the largest. In 1856, for instance, the Ystalyfera furnaces peaked at nearly 30,000 tons. For a time this became the largest tinplate works in the world but by the 1860s the ironworks were declining as the reserves became exhausted and as a result of competition from imported iron ore and the more economic furnaces set up near the ports.

As for the other products, after the opening of the Extension in 1834, a new source of income was developed southward, but little new traffic was capable of being developed northward into the agricultural market. For instance, in 1835 the traffic in coal on the tramroad to the rural north was 3,250 tons and in lime and limestone 6,200 tons, whereas in 1843 export trade in coal reached 24,500 tons. Even back in 1827 Christie had shipped 21,500 tons at Gwaun-clawdd on the Swansea Canal.

Stone sleeper blocks of the Brecon Forest Tramroad, looking south towards Fan Gyhirych. *Courtesy Stephen Hughes*

A development of significance for the future N & B was the opening of coal and anthracite production and the building of iron furnaces in the Onllwyn area. This is a plateau of high ground lying at the head of the Dulais valley between the Tawe valley and the Vale of Neath. It is a mile south of Capel Coelbren which was destined to be the location of an important junction on the railway, once the lines from Swansea and from Neath to Brecon were built. An area of higher ground called Mynydd y Drum, lay to the west between the plateau and the Tawe valley. Christie had bought what was called Drum Colliery on the eastern side of Mynydd y Drum in order to create traffic for the tramroad and to supply coal for his kilns. After a number of disappointments and the construction of an incline as steep as 1:8 up to the Extension Tramroad, anthracite was moved to export down the Swansea Canal and to the Ynysgedwyn furnaces. From a total of 5,000 tons in 1837, by 1843, as was noted above, this amounted to 24,500 tons a year. However, this traffic ceased in 1844 when iron furnaces were installed at the Onllwyn Colliery. Thereafter the traffic on the tramroad would have consisted of the pig-iron produced and the raw material feed of limestone and iron ore. In 1848, only 4,200 tons were produced. There followed a period of instability and in 1851 iron production ceased altogether. There was a revival after 1859 when William Parsons of Pontardawe took over and evidence to a Commons Committee in 1864 from the Onllwyn Ironworks suggests that production of iron was at some 8,000 tons and capable of more if better communications were in place.

In addition, Mynydd y Drum was investigated from the south by the Ystalyfera company, but a report in 1839 recommended taking coal down the Dulais valley rather than over the BFT and the Swansea Canal. Reference was made to a projected railway down the Dulais valley. This may have been the project put forward by George Tennant as early as 1819 to link the Dulais valley coal deposits to his canal; this proposal foundered on the rival interest of Lewis Weston Dillwyn in protecting his own coal interests.

The sinuous route of the tramroad, north of Coelbren, contrasts with the more direct route of the subsequent railway. This view also shows the upper reaches of the Tawe valley.

Courtesy Stephen Hughes

The Dulais valley runs southward from the Drum plateau to join the Vale of Neath at Aberdulais and in 1825 this project was revived, leading in 1826, to the authorisation by Parliament of a tramroad down the Dulais valley to join the Tennant Canal at Aberdulais. In the Victoria Tower of the Houses of Parliament a vellum role records in a stylish hand the terms of the Aberdulais Railway Act of 1826. This Act authorised the building and operation of a tramroad to carry minerals, coal and iron ore, from Cwm Dulais down to the canals in the Neath valley at Aberdulais. Although promoted by Tennant whose canal linked Neath and Swansea, and supported in the House of Lords by Lord Jersey who was a powerful local voice, it seems unlikely that the proposal ever got beyond the planning stage. There is no evidence of it ever having been built.

Nevertheless, the subject of communication down the Dulais valley was a live issue over the next 30 years, and following the report of 1839 referred to above, in 1841 the Neath Canal Company asked for permission to build a railway down the Dulais valley to join the canal below Aberdulais. Permission was finally granted in 1846, but it was not developed.

The definitive project was begun in 1861 and was authorised in 1862 by the Dulas [sic] Valley Mineral Railway Act. In the following year authorisation was obtained for extending this line over the route of the BFT and on to Brecon. This was when the BFT ceased operations. It survived longer than most early

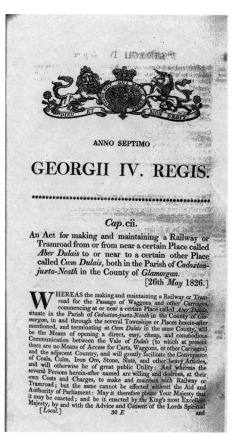

Title page for the 1826 Aber Dulais Railway or Tramroad Act.
National Archives

The seal of the Dulas [sic] Valley Mineral Railway Company. *Tudor Watkins Collection*

With the coming of the railway, Colbren Junction became an oasis in the desolate moorland scene. Engine No. 8751 has just arrived from Neath.

John Davies

The only activity in this scene is centred directly on the railway; strange to relate, there are four trains in this picture at Colbren Junction looking north. No date.

Hugh Davies

tramroads mainly because railways came late both to the north and to the south of it. This was not for a total lack of interest. As Starling Benson of Swansea told a House of Commons Committee in 1864, 'The history has been simply this, that Wales was left very much behind at first and that those local lines have gradually been developed into what are now becoming through lines.'

As early as 1845 the Welsh Midland Railway had been projected from Swansea to Brecon and then on to Hereford and Worcester. Its route from the Swansea valley skirted the northern side of Mynydd y Drum in its search for a more gently graded track, before joining the route of the BFT near the Drum Colliery and Capel Coelbren. Thereafter it followed the route across the mountains and down to the Usk at Sennybridge. The project failed in Parliament.

In 1853 and 1854 the Newport, Abergavenny & Hereford Railway (NAH), with backing from the LNWR, sought powers to construct a line up the Tawe valley from Swansea which would have turned eastward at Capel Coelbren, and crossed the upper Neath river valley and that of the Mellte. It was to join end-on the NAH Aberdare Extension. This project failed twice, in successive years. Something like it was raised later in 1866 in the form of the Aberdare and Central Wales Junction Railway to link the Taff Vale at Aberdare with Colbren Junction, but although this obtained parliamentary approval it made no headway.

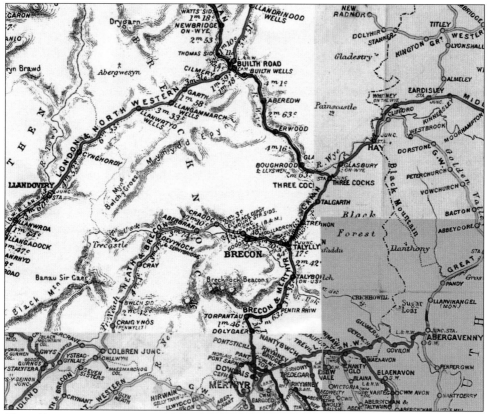

The railways around Brecon as they eventually materialised.   *Railway Clearing House*

In 1858 an attempt was made to promote what was called the Hereford & Brecon & Swansea Railway. One of the promoters was William Lawrence Banks, a Brecon solicitor who will reappear in the next chapter. Although the project found appeal in Brecon, there was not enough interest in it in Swansea to enable it to proceed in that form, and so it became the HH & B of which Banks became Secretary.

By the time in 1862 when powers were sought to construct a railway line over the top at Bwlch Bryn-rhudd and down to Brecon, the principal railways in Wales had been opened. Brecon on the other hand was still fairly isolated. It had the canal connection to Abergavenny, and for some 40 years the Hay Railway had been operating horse-drawn wagons into Herefordshire over what was in reality a tramroad from a Brecon yard beside the canal at Watton. By 1863 this was in the process of being converted into a proper railway as a result of an agreement with the B & M, the HH & B, and the Mid Wales Railway (MWR). These three shared the approximate route of the tramroad into Brecon from a point east of the town called Talyllyn Junction.

The MWR ran roughly north to south from the eventual cross-country Shrewsbury and Aberystwyth line to Brecon and arrived in 1864, and in that year the HH & B also arrived from Hereford sharing the Mid Wales route from Three Cocks Junction. The B & M had been the first railway to reach Brecon, arriving in early 1863 with its single-track line across the Usk at Tal-y-bont, thence to Talyllyn Junction where it was joined by the other two. Its line southward over the Brecon Beacons reached at that stage as far as Pant, above Dowlais. To move on from there towards Merthyr and Newport, the B & M was going to be involved in lengthy and complicated negotiations and frequent parliamentary bills over the next four years. In the same area of high ground, in 1862, the Merthyr, Tredegar & Abergavenny (MTA) had reached Bryn-mawr up the Clydach valley from Abergavenny. Now owned by the LNWR, it became entangled in four years of tough and complex haggling with the B & M over access to Dowlais and Merthyr.

Further south, in 1858 the NAH had moved westward across the valleys and had reached the Taff valley at Quakers Yard. In 1864 this line linked end-on with the broad gauge VoN from Neath to Aberdare. This railway had been an early starter and had reached Aberdare in 1851. Neath itself had been connected to Cardiff and to Swansea by the broad gauge South Wales Railway (SWR) since 1850, while the oldest railway in the area, the Taff Vale, had been opened as early as 1841 from Merthyr down to Cardiff.

Further to the east the lines linking Shrewsbury to Newport through Hereford and Abergavenny had been completed in 1854. To the north the Central Wales line had reached Knighton from Craven Arms in 1861 and was slowly pushing on to Llandrindod. To the west the Swansea Vale had reached Ystalyfera in 1861.

The route westward from Brecon still lay open.

Chapter 2

SWANSEA OR BUST 1861–66

1862 Dulas Valley Mineral Railway Act Vict. 25, 26 cap. cxciii
1863 Neath & Brecon Railway Act Vict. 26, 27 cap. cxxx
1864 Neath & Brecon Railway Extension Act Vict. 27, 28 cap. cccxvi
1864 Swansea Vale and Neath & Brecon Junction Railway Act Vict. 27, 28 cap. ccxciii
1865 Swansea Vale and Neath & Brecon Junction Railway Act Vict. 28, 29 cap. cxxxix
1866 Swansea Vale and Neath & Brecon Junction Railway Act Vict. 29,3 0 cap. cxii

CHAIRMEN OF THE NEATH & BRECON RAILWAY COMPANY
1862 Richard Hanbury Miers, landowner, of Gloucestershire
1865 William Lawrence Banks, solicitor, of Brecon.
1868 Thomas Cave, of Richmond, Surrey, MP for Barnstaple, and Sheriff of London and
    Middlesex
1870 J. Woolley, stockbroker
1870 W. Montagu Baillie
1871 Alexander Young
1889 Sir Edward Watkin MP, chairman of the Manchester, Sheffield & Lincolnshire
    Railway (MS & LR)
1900 Col. R.P. Laurie CB, MP
1905 T. Holland
1906 W.B. Partridge
1909 John G. Griffiths

Other *Dramatis Personae*

Joshua Williams, general manager Vale of Neath Railway; John Dickson, contractor;
    Benjamin Piercy, engineer; J.G. McKenzie, engineer; Capt. C. Miller Layton, director
    B & M; R. Green-Price, MP for Radnor, director Central Wales Railway; Henry
    Robertson, entrepreneur; J.N. Williamson, barrister; G.B. Strick, solicitor, director
    Swansea Vale Railway; Starling Benson, chairman Swansea Vale Railway; T. Glascodine,
    secretary Llanelly Railway; J. Palmer Budd, owner Ystalyfera tinplate works; T. Morley,
    secretary N & B, later traffic manager also; Hans St. George Caulfield, N & B engineer,
    later general manager; T.B. Forwood, financier; J. Allport, general manager Midland
    Railway; William Pollitt, general manager MS & LR; J. Morris, asst. superintendant
    GWR; Charles Talbot, general manager N & B; Joseph Cobb, solicitor to B & M

FIRST STEPS

The plans of a railway over a similar route to that of the Aberdulais Railway were
drawn up in November 1861. In spite of efforts with scissors and glue to correct the
spelling on the original plans and sections submitted to Parliament, it was called the

The track-bed of the railway north of Craig-y-nos, emphasised by the low winter sunshine, with Fan Gyhirych on the skyline, c.1997.   *DD*

Dulas [*sic*] Valley Mineral Railway. As noted in the previous chapter, this followed decades of discussion about the desirability of constructing a railway up the Dulais valley. On 7 January 1862 a meeting was held in the Castle Hotel at Neath to consider these plans. The record does not relate how many attended but those named included a powerful figure in Swansea, Dillwyn Llewelyn, William Price, chairman of the NAH, and later chairman of the Midland, Joshua Williams, general manager of the VoN who had been asked to attend by the board, William Lawrence Banks, a solicitor from Brecon who was an enthusiast for railway investment and Company Secretary of the HH & B, the Rector of Neath and the Vicar of Cadoxton.

They were presented with the drawings and plans for a mixed-gauge railway up the Dulais valley from a junction with the VoN at Cadoxton to the Drum Colliery at Onllwyn. These Plans and Sections had been submitted to Parliament in the previous November by engineer James Samuel who estimated the cost at £60,000. The bill was said to be promoted by the VoN, and the preamble to the eventual authorising Act of July 1862, the Dulas [*sic*] Valley Mineral Railway Act, states that it was expedient that the powers created by the Act were granted to the VoN Company. This is odd because the VoN board minutes, while reporting that the project was drawn to the attention of the board, give no suggestion that anyone connected with the VoN had had anything whatsoever to do with promoting it. It is possible that there was internal disagreement within the VoN management and that Joshua Williams was more enthusiastic than his chairman. It is also possible that

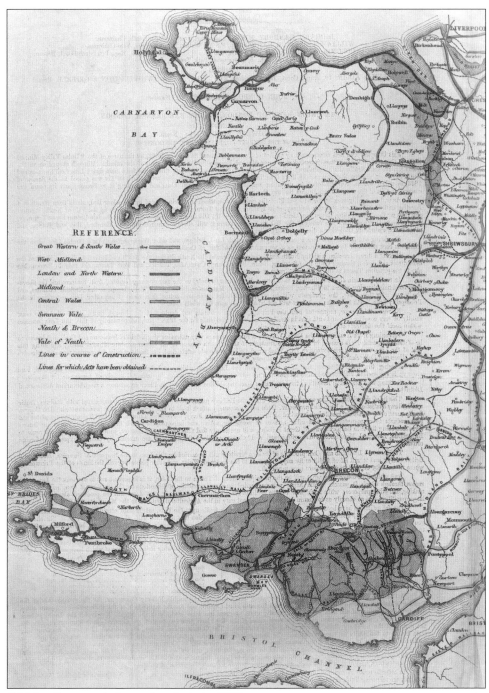

Welsh railways existing and projected *c*.1864.   *National Archives. RAIL 1014/2*

Pannier tank engine No. 9716 makes its own contribution to an attractive winter scene in January 1969 as it hauls its freight train past Cadaxton towards Onllwyn.   *John Davies*

Another pannier, No. 8732, near Cilfrew, wends its way through the verdant shades of an attractive Dulais valley with a rather mundane load of pit-props for a colliery up the line. 1963.

John Davies

the plans were submitted in a rush. Because of the volume of railway bills at that time, there was a deadline then in place which required that plans which were to be considered in the current session of Parliament were to be in Westminster by the end of November. At first sight it looks even more odd that the VoN appealed against the bill on 20 February 1862. This was, however, a device for obtaining some concessions during the Committee stage. They were particularly concerned about the nature of the junction in Neath which was originally planned to take place on a gradient of 1:80 which was felt to be too steep.

Joshua Williams.

Only a week earlier, at a meeting in Neath on 13 February 1862, it was Joshua Williams of the VoN who played a leading role in forming a subscription list to establish a company to be called the Dulas [*sic*] Valley Mineral Railway. He told a House of Commons Committee in 1864 that John Dickson was a promoter. Dickson had been involved in some way with the S & N and so may well have been in the background. Williams went on to say in recognisably Welsh style, 'Originally I believe I almost assisted the Dulas Valley in actually starting into existence because at the first meeting of the promoters I think there was such a want of accord amongst them that without I think saying too much I probably put the thing in train to start it into existence.' At a VoN Wharncliffe Meeting of Shareholders on 13 June the Dulas [*sic*] Valley Bill was unanimously approved. Bruce, the VoN chairman told the meeting that the Dulais valley project had been brought to Parliament by an independent company. This was strictly true, though some in Parliament may have been led to believe that the VoN was in fact the ultimate promoter. He added, 'I hope it may do much good, and it can do us no harm.'

Local solicitors were appointed, directors were elected and preparations were made to make formal application to Parliament for the plans, which had already been submitted, to be legally authorised and receive the Royal Assent. Two personalities immediately emerged who were shortly to be working together on the Anglesey Central Railway. They were Richard Hanbury Miers, from Dean Hall in Gloucestershire, a landowner in the Dulais valley, who became the first chairman, and William Lawrence Banks the solicitor from Brecon. Capel Miers, another landowner and nephew of Richard, George Knox, a former associate of Dickson, and Captain J.A. Cox from London completed the board. Benjamin Piercy, the widely experienced railway engineer, was appointed engineer. The bill received the Royal Assent on 29 July 1862.

The first board meeting was held in Neath in the offices of the solicitors Cuthbertson and Kempthorne on 6 September 1862. Thereafter until 1900, when two meetings a year were held in Brecon, every board meeting took place in London, for some years in Westminster Chambers and later at 17 Tokenhouse Yard in the City. At that first meeting a letter dated 3 September from John Dickson was read. At the time his address was Bank House, Wellington, in Shropshire but by now he had an office in London as a contractor. He offered to construct a single track, standard-gauge railway line from Neath to Onllwyn for £75,000. This was to cover the cost of land acquisition, bridges, stations, track, sidings and one year's maintenance. Provision was to be made for eventual doubling of the track. The contractor would find the capital and was to have the right to determine the purchase price of land. Any land acquired surplus to railway requirements was to be sold by the company for the benefit of the contractor. Piercy had been in close contact with Dickson and wrote simultaneously from the Hotel Louvre in Paris recommending acceptance of this offer. The board agreed.

In his letter Dickson recommended a further application to Parliament in order to achieve improvements at the Neath end. These would entail a direct link to the S & N without reversal to allow main line passenger trains to be operated. He also wanted to extend the line at the northern end to a junction with another line which was being discussed. This was to run from Brecon to an end-on junction with the Swansea Vale Railway (SV) down in the Swansea valley. Right from the outset it must have been apparent to Dickson that the Dulais valley project offered the prospect of rather more than just a local mineral railway to carry coal to Neath. He was more interested in Swansea than Neath and for him this was a means of reviving the old idea of the Welsh Midland.

A present-day view of the Dulais valley and the track of the Neath & Brecon Railway at Cilfrew; beyond the ridge lies the Vale of Neath. 2004.   *DD*

A short train climbs up the valley, near Cilfrew.   *John Davies*

Simultaneous with the submission to Parliament of the Dulais valley project in November 1861, the same engineer produced an estimate for another railway project, this time promoted by the VoN and the HH & B of which Banks was secretary. This, the Swansea & Neath & Brecon Junction Railway was estimated to cost £250,000 and was for a line from Glyn Neath, on the VoN, up the Mellte valley through Ystradfellte and then up the Llia valley to a pass and across the open mountain to Glyn Tarell, and so to Brecon. Instead of going through the town it was to pass it to the north, terminating at an end-on junction with the already authorised HH & B. A branch was to leave the VoN west of Hirwaun and head for a junction with the projected new line just to the south of Ystradfellte. No mention of this was made in the board minutes of the VoN and the projected line was never authorised. Presumably Banks as secretary of the HH & B was involved, but the HH & B was short of funds. Something similar was projected a year later in the Aberdare Northern Railway Bill which described a line from the same point of departure at Hirwaun on the VoN through the Llia pass but then in a north-westerly direction to Devynock. This the N & B opposed. It was equally unsuccessful. A similar project, namely the Aberdare & Central Wales Junction Railway (of which more later), was approved in 1866 but was not progressed.

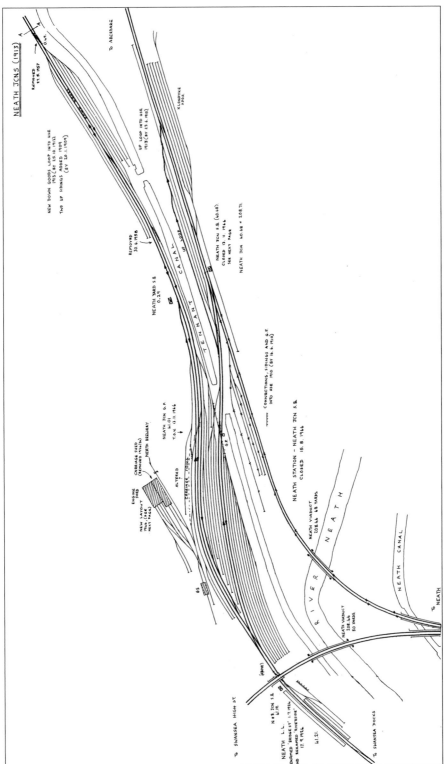

Courtesy R.A. Cooke

The railway system at Neath (1913). The line to Brecon features in the upper right corner

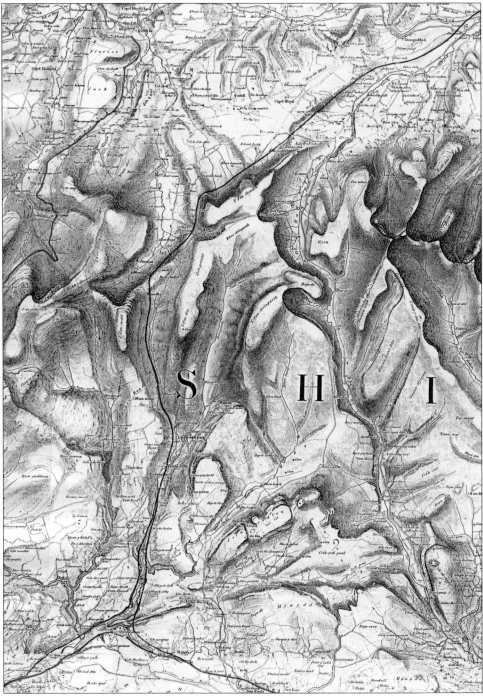

The route of the 1861 Swansea & Neath & Brecon Junction Railway. The line (in black) is shown leaving the VoN (in yellow) by junctions near Blaen-gwrach and Hirwaun (*bottom left*) and terminating just north of Brecon (*top right*). Part of the route of the BFT is marked in red (*top left*).

House of Lords Record Office

The direct rail contact between Swansea and the Midlands and the north of England was the topic of much discussion. There were in principle two possible routes: one, the eventual Midland route, was through Brecon and then to Hereford and Worcester; the other, the eventual LNWR route, by-passed Brecon some 20 miles to the north and made for Shrewsbury and Crewe. A third, a sort of hybrid, linked the two between Devynock and Llangammarch.

At the end of 1862 the state of railway development in the direction of Swansea was as follows. To the west, the Vale of Towy had opened from Llandeilo, at the northern extremity of the Llanelly Railway, as far as Llandovery. It was leased to the Llanelly Railway. This company which connected Llanelly and Llandeilo was now working on two new lines, one to Swansea from Pontarddulais, and one to Carmarthen from Llandeilo. By way of a hedging bet it had plans to build a branch from Llandovery to Brecon. From the north the Central Wales Railway (CWR), with discreet backing from the LNWR, was on the march from Knighton towards Llandrindod and Llandovery, avoiding Brecon altogether. It was not destined to reach Llandovery until 1868. Brecon would, however, be on the route of the HH & B from Hereford up the Wye, and of the MWR from Moat Lane Junction on the Shrewsbury to Aberystwyth line and down the Wye. These two met at Three Cocks Junction and then, as already noted, followed the approximate route of the Hay Railway into Brecon. At this time it looked probable that there would also be a line from Brecon down the Usk valley to Abergavenny.

From Brecon to Swansea there were at least three possible routes. Besides that through Ystradfellte, followed by the old turnpike road and by the abortive railway project of 1861, there were two other routes both using the mountain pass occupied by the BFT known as Bwlch Bryn-rhudd. One then ran down to the Swansea valley at Ynysygeinon (the path of the future Junction Line) and the other took the Dulais valley, through Neath and then proceeded along the coast. At the northern end both these routes assumed access to Brecon down the north bank of the Usk from Devynock.

Banks was determined that one way or another Brecon should be on the route from Swansea to the Midlands and the north of England. Twice Mayor of Brecon, in 1859 and 1861, he attempted to manipulate the railway developments in the town, becoming chairman simultaneously of the three leading players, the HH & B, the B & M, and the N & B. He was clearly a man of vision and an enthusiast, but his financial judgment was poor and he steadily lost money until, in the early 1870s, he had to move to north Wales. He emerges from this

William Lawrence Banks.
By kind permission of the Hergest Trust

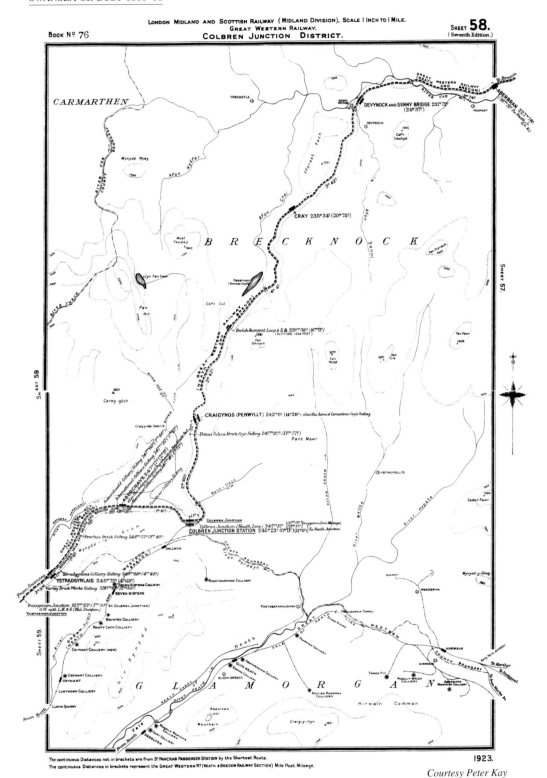

LONDON MIDLAND AND SCOTTISH RAILWAY (MIDLAND DIVISION), SCALE 1 INCH TO 1 MILE.
GREAT WESTERN RAILWAY.
COLBREN JUNCTION DISTRICT.

Book No. 76

SHEET **58.**
(Seventh Edition.)

The continuous Distances not in brackets are from St. PANCRAS PASSENGER STATION by the Shortest Route.
The continuous Distances in brackets represent the GREAT WESTERN RY. (NEATH & BRECON RAILWAY SECTION) Mile Post Mileage.

1923.

Courtesy Peter Kay

story as a muddler; amusing, good company, a raconteur and an artist, but not an efficient business man.

It appears that both he and Conybeare, the engineer of the B & M, saw, at least by the end of 1862, the desirability of all lines in the neighbourhood of Brecon being served by one station in the middle of the town. This must have become obvious to all parties but there were rivalries to contend with. The B & M were suspicious of the intentions of the N & B and accordingly sought to extend beyond Brecon to Llandovery. The N & B saw a potential ally in the Vale of Crickhowell, approaching from Abergavenny and linking Brecon. The MWR board were ambitious to reach Llandovery and ultimately Milford Haven and saw Brecon as a possible route.

Ever since the days of the BFT it had been apparent that the greatest potential for the route over Bwlch Bryn-rhudd through Devynock to Brecon lay with traffic to and from Swansea rather than Neath. On 30 September 1862 Banks and Knox convened a meeting in Brecon between the HH & B of which he was then company secretary, the B & M, and the SV to discuss the options. The VoN were noteably absent. The B & M were included as they were promoting the route westward from Brecon through Devynock to Llandovery (Brecon Junction Railway Bill). It was agreed that two routes would be pursued: first the BFT route from Devynock to Colbren and down to the SV (later known as the Junction Line), and second as above but from Colbren down the Dulais valley and over the S & N along the coast to Swansea. Since the distances were similar either over the Junction Line or via Neath it was agreed that proceeds should be shared according to the mileage. The meeting concluded that the Dulais valley route should be the main line. No mention is recorded of the Ystradfellte project. It is likely that the existence of the BFT was seen as a way of gaining a lower cost project, for that through Ystradfellte lay over totally unprepared ground and involved at least two 300 yard long tunnels along the Mellte valley.

From the point of view of the N & B board and Dickson, in particular, resolving the position at Swansea was critical and over the following four years Dickson explored every avenue to gain a strong position there. This was not entirely without justification as, at the end of 1862, the railway and dock system at Swansea was still underdeveloped. The Swansea Harbour Trust, of which Starling Benson was a trustee, was keen to develop the docks but so far there was only a North Dock and an emerging South Dock, both on the west bank of the river Tawe. The Trust was developing a network of link lines in the dock area. The broad-gauge connection with Carmarthen, Neath and Cardiff over the SWR lay north of the city centre, with a branch from Landore to a terminus on the west side of the river. This company was the largest shareholder in the VoN, also broad gauge, which diverged from it at Neath towards Aberdare, with a branch to Merthyr. However, the VoN was building the S & N, a direct mixed-gauge line from Neath to Swansea along the coast, by-passing the SWR. The third player was the SV with an independent standard gauge line up the east side of the Tawe as far as Ystalyfera which had been reached by passenger trains in 1861. This was near the point from which a short line (the

Junction Line) would eventually be built to join the N & B at Colbren Junction. On the west side of Swansea the Oystermouth Railway ran from the dock area along the coast to Oystermouth. It had operated horse-drawn trams since 1804 and was thus the first passenger railway in the world.

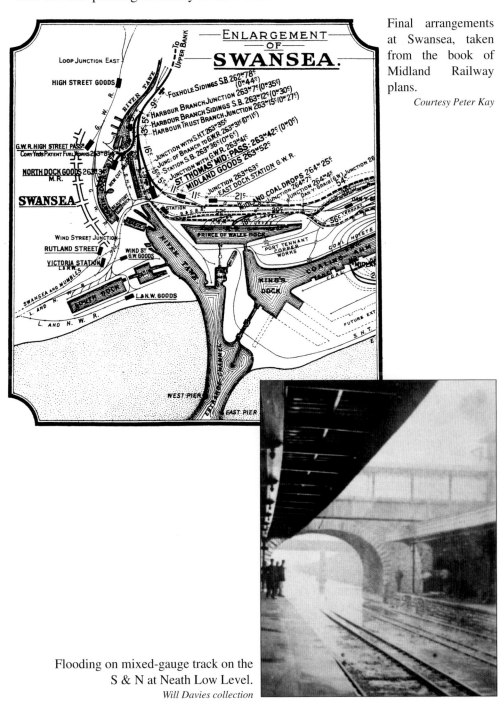

Final arrangements at Swansea, taken from the book of Midland Railway plans.

Courtesy Peter Kay

Flooding on mixed-gauge track on the
S & N at Neath Low Level.
Will Davies collection

The N & B had a delicate balancing act to perform. On the one hand, the VoN had to be kept on good terms as they were currently the only path to the outside world, and the eventual station landlord at Neath. On the other hand, the VoN was proving an obstacle to progress in the direction of Swansea. The VoN itself needed access to Swansea Docks because the closer outlet at Neath – Briton Ferry Dock – was inadequate, but the SWR line to Swansea suffered from a serious incline against loaded west-bound trains. The VoN, therefore, had an incentive to gain access to Swansea along the flat land near the sea. Relations between the SWR and the VoN had become vexed because the latter was beginning to realise that its future lay in accommodating standard gauge as well as broad gauge trains. This was being pressed by the West Midland, inheritor in 1860 of the NAH, which was seeking an end-on junction at Middle Duffryn, just to the east of Aberdare with a view to establishing a standard-gauge route from Hereford via Pontypool Road to Swansea. Matters came to a head with the passing of the Swansea & Neath Railway Act of 1861 which laid down that the S & N was to be a broad-gauge railway but, if the VoN became mixed, it was to do likewise. In the event it was laid with mixed-gauge track and opened in July 1863 and as the VoN took it over they gained access across the flat land directly into the Swansea dock area. This held out the prospect of just what the N & B needed, a standard-gauge line from its junction right through to the heart of the Swansea Docks. However, the VoN initially refused to handle through traffic to and from Swansea for the N & B. It was concerned at the threat of competition down the Swansea valley.

JOHN DICKSON

At this point it is worth pausing to look more closely at the man who was effectively running the N & B. John Dickson was born in Berwick-on-Tweed in 1819. As a young man he went to Ireland and found work as a railway contractor. He learned about railway construction by contributing to the building of part of the main line of the Great Southern & Western Railway between Dublin and Cork. In 1847 he returned to England and settled in Wellington in Shropshire. There is some reason to believe his family came from there as he obtained a family vault in the local churchyard for his eventual burial. He carried out some railway contracting in the

Portrait of John Dickson.
Courtesy of Paul Reynolds

West Midlands though without any great success and, having been sacked by Brunel from a job on the South Wales Mineral Railway, it was only bankruptcy in 1857 which saved him from a claim for negligence from the Swansea Harbour Trustees when a retaining wall he had built collapsed. This was his first bankruptcy, followed at roughly ten year intervals by two more.

St Andrew's Presbyterian Church, Swansea.   *Courtesy of Paul Reynolds*

It was this contract which introduced him to Swansea. In the early 1860s he moved to Swansea and was approached by a local group of Scottish Presbyterians who wanted to build their own church. Dickson became chairman of the Building Committee and became the contractor for the construction of what became St. Andrew's Presbyterian Church. He claimed that he was owed £3,000 at the end of the contract but his obituary in *The Cambrian* described it as his share of the expenditure. In Swansea he became enthused with the prospect of improving the rail connections with industrial England and in building a new coal exporting port at Mumbles. He was a man of tremendous energy and simultaneously worked on a railway in Anglesey. The flaw in his make-up was his excessive optimism and a tendency to cut corners when money was tight. But he must have been a charmer and appears to have had many friends, some of whom were even prepared to back him.

After his second bankruptcy in 1867 he moved away from Swansea for a time and was next involved as contractor for the Whitby, Redcar & Middlesbrough Union Railway. He was dismissed for delays and faulty workmanship and once again only avoided being pursued in the courts for negligence by being declared bankrupt. He was simultaneously working on a tunnel under the Mersey but did not succeed in completing it.

He returned to Swansea and became involved again in the Oystermouth Railway. His residual rights to the railway were revived with the help of his friends and he ran steam trains on the railway until 1885. He then turned his hand to property development but achieved nothing material. He died in 1892. *The Cambrian* in his obituary referred to the loss of a 'kind heart and a great keenness and capacity'.

This was the man to whom the directors of the N & B consigned the fortunes of their shareholders' company.

In the absence of further evidence it is hard to judge how the relationship between Dickson and the N & B directors came about. Was he just an available contractor known to Piercy who originally recommended him, whom the local enthusiasts were content to employ, or was it he who had the vision and hunted out the potential developers? Evidence of his energy and his resilience, and his ability to set things alight in different parts of the country points to the latter, but we will probably never know for sure.

OFF TO BRECON

In order to handle applications to Parliament, it had been decided to locate the N & B Head Office in London, initially in the premises of the London solicitors Green and Allin at 27 Duke Street. The second application to Parliament adopted Dickson's recommendations, and took the railway a long way beyond the original concept of a local mineral line by adding an extension all the way to Brecon. The original draft of the bill was entitled the Swansea and Neath and Brecon Railway Bill and included a line to the SV from Colbren Junction. This stretch of line was removed from the bill at an early stage at the insistence of the VoN, though with the qualification recorded in the N & B board minutes, 'at all events for the present'. When Swansea was accordingly dropped from the title of the bill, permission was sought to change the name of the company to the Neath and Brecon Railway. The bill included the right to purchase the BFT. Stations at Brecon and Neath were not included in the deal with Dickson, and the Act when passed stated that at Brecon the line was 'to terminate by a junction with the B & M at the authorised terminus thereof'. The N & B was authorised to agree with the B & M arrangements for a joint station at Brecon (see Chapter 5).

At Neath the Act allowed the N & B use of the new VoN Low Level station which was to be on 'terms very liberal'. This wording Joshua Williams told a House of Commons Committee was derived from a similar agreement with the B & M over access at cost to the VoN's station at Merthyr. The timing of the arrangements at Neath was perfect for the N & B, especially as the S & N was being laid with mixed-gauge track. Although the bill provided that the N & B be laid with mixed-gauge track as far as Onllwyn, it is not clear whether this was actually done. It is quite likely that since the S & N was being built to the mixed gauge the advantage was taken of saving the cost of a line of rail. The N & B directors then agreed with Dickson that he would effectively take over the railway, taking all the share capital and becoming responsible for all payments. Although this was common practice at

A view of Neath dating from around the turn of the century showing the Neath & Brecon
Railway (foreground), whilst beyond the Vale of Neath line occupies an embankment.

DD Coll.

the time, it was to prove in this instance a disastrous course, made worse by inability
or unwillingness to keep a proper eye on what Dickson got up to.

Capel Miers and Hanbury Miers were sufficiently concerned about the
competitive threat from the Swansea valley route reducing the value of their land in
the Dulais valley that they sought and obtained a guarantee that the Dulais valley
route would be the main line. Green, the N & B's London solicitor confessed he
had been in favour of the main line following the route to Swansea by way of the
SV, but he recorded that he was now convinced that the route down the Dulais
valley should be the main line. He presumably expected the VoN objections to be
overcome one day. By 1864, out of concern for what Dickson was up to, the VoN
was prepared to allow the N & B the right to fix its own terms for moving coal to
Swansea over the S & N provided they did not undercut the VoN. Later, when the
GWR had taken over the VoN, running powers were in fact granted to the N & B
through to Swansea, but the GWR proved an unreliable partner and goods routed
from Swansea over the N & B would often find their way to their destination over
the GWR, irrespective of the routeing instructions and the mileage. So the N & B
preferred to rely on the SV. Much later, the position was reversed and the N & B
even hauled coal up from the eventual Junction Line for movement over its own
line to Neath and then on to Swansea.

Opposition to the bill from the VoN was partly justified by the fact that the
Junction Line was planned at a continuous 1:50 for its five miles which was felt
unworkable. Opposition also came from the SWR, but more as a way of extracting
a benefit. In order to minimise the cost of debate in Parliament, on 18 April 1863, a
deal was done with the SWR by which the N & B undertook to put pressure on the

Railway activity at Neath looking north, with pannier tanks Nos 8732 and 2706 shunting on the Vale of Neath line. The foreground tracks form the link line with the N & B at Riverside, which is behind the camera. March 1962.

John Davies

Another view of the link line between the Vale of Neath and Neath & Brecon at Neath. The N & B has already started to climb past the signal-box on the embankment, on the left. The link line crosses the picture to join with the line to Aberdare on the right-hand side. 1960.

G.H. Platt

A view taken from the Aberdare train at Neath Junction, as it makes for Neath General station, showing clearly the link line to Riverside diverging to the right. 1960.

G.H. Platt

VoN to ensure traffic flowed from the new line to the SWR. How this was to be done was not spelt out at the time, though shortly after, Dickson put up a scheme for laying a third rail along the SWR main line. This was an interesting acknowledgement from the temple of broad-gauge orthodoxy that supping with the devil was permissable on terms.

To neutralise further opposition, it was agreed on 13 January 1863 to offer running powers between Brecon and Devynock to the Brecon Junction Railway then promoting a line from Brecon to a junction with the Vale of Towy Railway at Llandovery. This project was fostered by the B & M, the HH & B, and the MWR and was one of several unsuccessful attempts to link Brecon and Llandovery. It was partly intended to prevent the N & B having an independent entry into Brecon. The engineer was Benjamin Piercy and with an estimated cost of construction of £210,000, it was authorised in July 1863. The first attempt to bridge the gap between Llandovery and Brecon had been in an Act of the Llanelly Railway in 1861. It was subsequently withdrawn but the drawings, plans and sections were similar to those used by the N & B in due course for its route from Devynock to Brecon. In November 1863 plans were drawn up by the B & M engineer Conybeare for a third project, under the name Brecon & Llandovery Railway. This assumed a crossing of the Honddu in Brecon by a single arched bridge where the N & B later built a viaduct with seven arches, and the Act specified that a junction was to be made with the B & M 'in a field east of and adjoining Free Street'. In 1864 a fourth attempt was made under the name of the Brecon & Llandovery Junction Railway of which Banks was a director. It was similar to the Brecon Junction but followed a slightly different course west of Devynock and joined the Vale of Towy south of Llandovery, by-passing the town altogether. This project was authorised in 1865 but also failed. A fifth attempt was made in the following year when Parliament authorised the Brecon & Llandovery Junction Act 1866. The chairman of this last attempt was Edward Parker, deputy chairman of the MWR and a director of the Llanelly. It was prevented from proceeding by an agreement between the N & B and B & M to make a joint station in Brecon, thus blocking out the others. In any case, the Llangammarch Branch at this time appeared to be a feasible prospect which would by-pass the MWR, whose position was thus looking distinctly uncomfortable. For the record, a final attempt to link Brecon and Llandovery was made in 1883 by the Usk and Towy Railway. This too failed.

On 13 July 1863 the Neath & Brecon Railway Act was duly authorised. That July, Piercy resigned as engineer to the N & B, possibly because he was heavily engaged with the constituents of the

Neath & Brecon Railway Company common seal.
NRM

A present-day view of Onllwyn showing, to the right, a coal-washing facility and to the left the track-bed of the original route to Brecon, passing beneath an accommodation bridge. 2004.   *GBJ*

Cambrian Railways and with the MWR. It would enrich the story if evidence could be found of his suspicion of Dickson's methods, but nothing has come to light. He was replaced by J.G. McKenzie an engineer and former associate of Dickson. By November the new man had fallen out with Dickson who threatened to terminate his contract. However, McKenzie apologised and stayed on. From the evidence of House of Commons Committee proceedings in both 1864 and 1869, McKenzie appears to have been a somewhat naive individual, content to work for no agreed fee, professing no knowledge of the financial arrangements of the company, and evasive on the subject of project costs. It is possible to infer that he may have been somewhat in awe of Dickson.

By this time work on the line was almost complete as far as Onllwyn, though it was nearly a year before it was ready for the first train on 2 October 1864. Land acquisition was proceeding well and had progressed as far as one last area at Brecon. At about this time, Banks became vice-chairman of the N & B. On 5 April 1864 he was to become chairman of the HH & B and on 22 April 1865, chairman of the N & B.

In a prospectus issued Autumn 1863, when the Junction Line project was being revived, the N & B pointed out the mileage advantages of their potential route from Swansea to the Midlands and the north of England. Three routes were compared:

Miles	N & B	S. Wales	VoN
Swansea to Brecon	40	-	56
Birkenhead	166	205	192
Birmingham	148	187	174

The assumed N & B route was by way of Neath and Colbren Junction, Brecon, then for Birkenhead by way of the MWR and LNWR, and for Birmingham by way of Hereford and Worcester. Presumably in order to avoid alerting the VoN, no mention was made of the alternative Junction Line route. For the SWR the route was presumably over the GWR. The VoN route to Brecon lay in the future as the opening of the end-on junction at Middle Duffryn with the West Midland, recently taken over by the GWR, was authorised as part of that Act and did not occur until 1864. From there to Brecon would require a link to the B & M at Merthyr which was not yet in place. For Birkenhead and Birmingham, it would appear that the route lay by way of Pontypool Road over the LNWR.

To encourage investors some comparative earnings were shown:

Receipts in pounds per mile per week	
Taff Vale	£101-18-0
Caledonian	£72-17-0
Vale of Neath	£54- 8- 0
Swansea Vale	£29- 0- 0

It was pointed out that should the N & B achieve even a modest £36 per mile per week, a yield of 5% would be achieved. No attempt was made to show an estimated Operating Ratio, the basic yardstick then in use for comparing railway profitability, i.e. the percentage which operating costs represented of the receipts. At the time, other Welsh railways were achieving figures in the area of 50%. The N & B never quite reached this level.

A FLIRTATION WITH THE LNWR

In December 1863 the N & B board made a remarkable and unexpected move and approved a third application to Parliament (the N & B Extension Bill). This was to obtain authority to build short extensions to Banwen and Maesmarchog collieries in the Onllwyn area, but these minor coal sidings were overshadowed by a major and surprising new venture in the form of a 12 mile extension northward from Devynock, across the Usk and then over high and sparsely populated ground, to Llangammarch on the Central Wales Extension Railway (CWE) which was then being built from Llandrindod to Llandovery. This proposal was authorised by Parliament on 29 July 1864. It was a surprising move as it sought to by-pass Brecon, but it can best be understood in the context of LNWR strategy.

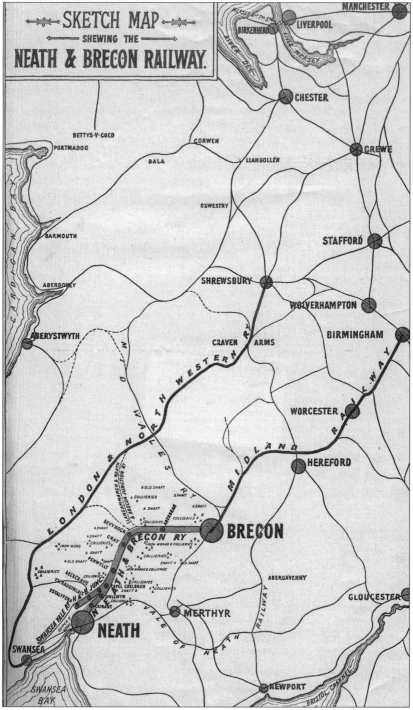

An undated map, showing the position of the Llangammarch Branch. The junction with the N & B is facing the wrong way and a connection never made between Devynock and Llandovery, is indicated by a dotted line.

National Archives RAIL 1014/2

The LNWR-backed line from Craven Arms through Knighton to Llandrindod was not yet complete to Llandovery and it was not yet clear whether the LNWR would be able to reach Swansea over the Vale of Towy and the Llanelly. This was mainly because the latter was making very heavy weather of the construction of its new line from Pontarddulais to Swansea. There was also uncertainty over the future of the lease of the Vale of Towy to the Llanelly which was due to expire at the end of March 1868. The N & B offered an attractive part of alternative routes from Swansea to Craven Arms (between Hereford and Shrewsbury) thus, in miles:

GWR	112
Swansea Vale, Colbren, Brecon, Hereford	109
Swansea Vale, Colbren, Brecon, Builth	105
Swansea Vale, Brynamman, Llandovery	103
Swansea Victoria, Pontarddulais, Llandovery	95
Swansea Vale, Colbren, Llangammarch	90

Because the LNWR was bound by an agreement with the GWR and West Midland not to make any arrangements with third parties without their consent, the CWE was put in to bat on their behalf in the negotiations for the new line from Llangammarch to Devynock. In July 1864 a draft agreement was prepared along the lines of those made by the LNWR with the Knighton and the CWR but substituting the CWE for the LNWR. The CWE would exchange traffic with the N & B and share profits in perpetuity 'on a perfectly friendly footing'.

The route of the projected Llangammarch branch today, with use restricted mainly to the military and farmers.

GBJ

At this time, on receipt of the Royal Assent, a contract, again with Dickson, was agreed for the construction of the extension to Llangammarch. In June 1864 questions were already being asked in Commons Committee as to whether the Brecon line from Devynock was now going to be completed, even though it was a term of the Llangammarch Act that the Brecon line was to be opened at least six months before the Llangammarch branch. There was apparently no obligation to complete the Brecon line by a certain date but the works were reported to be set out, masons were building the bridge over the Usk, property in Brecon had been purchased and houses on the route were being pulled down.

In September 1864 preliminary work on the Llangammarch branch began and it was now agreed that the CWR/CWE would work the N & B. In February 1865, £51,000 was authorised to be spent on materials for this extension and work eventually began in the following September. Land was expected to be relatively cheap, especially on the high ground where it was simply open grazing. Throughout 1865 the alliance between the N & B and the CWR acting for the LNWR was nurtured. In November 1865, Richard Green-Price, MP for Radnor, a promoter of both the CWR and CWE became a director of the N & B. In March 1866 it was expected that the track would be completed from Devynock to Llangammarch by August 1866.

The Vital Link

While these negotiations were proceeding, it was obvious that a line was still needed to form a connection between the SV and the N & B at Colbren Junction. Because this had been withdrawn from the earlier N & B bill under pressure from the VoN, an independent bill was promoted in 1864 to effect construction of this so-called Junction Line. It was sponsored by Banks, Captain Miller Layton, a friend of Banks and a co-director on the B & M, now a director of the N & B, J.W. Williamson of Lincolns Inn, also a director, G.B. Strick a Swansea solicitor, director of the SV and managing partner of the Amman Ironworks, and T. Maskelyne, a local landowner. This group could scarely conceal the identity of the real promoters and from the Commons Committee proceedings it was obvious that no one was deceived.

The case for the line was well argued by the spokesman for the Onllwyn Ironworks who told the committee how he was having to supply his product to the Ynysgedwyn Ironworks in the Swansea valley by tramroad (Claypon's Extension) involving a 'steep, difficult and dangerous' incline and transshipment to the canal. He and other supporters of the line foresaw the movement of tinplate and anthracite northward to Liverpool and Birkenhead for an export trade with Canada. This was preferred to using Swansea as by that route the anthracite would apparently be badly broken in transshipment. They also wanted to bring high quality iron ore from north Wales, limestone from Penwyllt and agricultural products from Brecon to feed the large population in the Swansea valley.

One of the petitioners against the bill was the SV itself. This may seem odd and it put Starling Benson in some difficulty. In the Commons Committee hearing in 1864, he professed to knowing nothing about the petition:

> 'You do not know the petition's allegations?'
>
> 'No. No doubt it included everything . . . We look to ourselves and that is the reason we petitioned against it . . . I know nothing about how it is prepared in the office.'
>
> 'You have some arrangement with the promoters of the scheme?'
>
> 'Yes.'
>
> 'Were you party to those arrangements?'
>
> 'I know them.'
>
> 'Were they made with Dickson?'
>
> 'No with Edward Strick, solicitor.'
>
> 'Who are the directors?'
>
> 'I do not know who they were. I believe [crossed out in the record] Mr Lawrence Banks and Mr George Strick I think . . . We petitioned to get some arrangements till we knew what was going to be done . . . An arrangement has been made between the two companies.'

This 'arrangement' was to prove the undoing of the N & B's independence in the form of a schedule permitting the N & B running powers to Swansea and the SV running powers to Brecon. Access to Swansea over the SV was imperative in the absence of progress on Dickson's other schemes (see below), and at the time it seemed no doubt a small price to pay to grant the SV reciprocal rights in return. At the time, the alliance with the LNWR group was flourishing and the probability

Starling Benson, chairman of the Swansea Vale.
Courtesy of D.I.L. Bayliff and J.N. Harding

The information submitted to the Commons Committee in support of the Junction Line.
House of Lords Records Office

of the N & B taking a lease of the SV seemed more likely than the Midland appearing on the scene.

Much of the discussion in the Commons Committee was about the gradients and the mileage advantage achievable. A calculation was provided to the Commons Committee to support the case. Glascodine, secretary to the Llanelly Railway countered by arguing that there was no advantage compared with the route from Ystalyfera over the pass at Brynamman and then up the Vale of Towy. On the contrary, it was pointed out, this entailed bad curves and worse gradients. The new line was a significant improvement on that which had been planned the year before and withdrawn. It left the SV line three miles further south and although it was thus longer, it had only short stretches at 1:50 and no tunnels. It also by-passed Ystalyfera which was to cause trouble with the owner of the works, J. Palmer

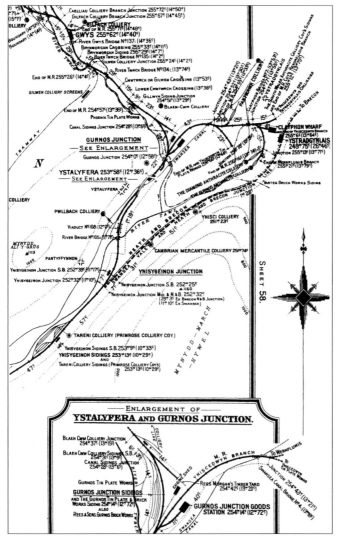

A further extract from the book of MR Plans.

Courtesy of Peter Kay

Budd. It was now estimated to cost twice as much. Against £60,000 of the previous year it was now £120,000. The authorised capital being sought was this amount plus £60,000 in mortgages. McKenzie was distinctly evasive when cross-examined in committee on the size of this increase. One reason he said was the increased length and connections to adjacent works, but he steadfastly avoided saying what the other reason might have been. Dickson was no doubt marking every word he uttered for when he was asked to identify for whom he was working and how much he was paid, he said a number of engineers were involved, that he did not know for whom he was working, and that it was common practice for an engineer to spend money on plans 'he gets up' without knowing how he would be eventually remunerated.

The bill was also attacked on somewhat unusual grounds. Readers of *The Origins of the LMS in South Wales* will be familiar with the unattractive personality of J. Palmer Budd who had for some 20 years been running the Ystalyfera Ironworks which he inherited from his father. He was undoubtedly astute and had built what was, by this time, the largest tinplate works in the world. But he was an extraordinarily combative and cantankerous man. When he was a director of the SV he had made much difficulty over the route of the railway past his house and had resorted to less than honourable behaviour. He had been on a six months winter holiday in Italy when the notices were published in connection with this latest railway bill and had given instructions for a petition against the bill to be issued as a matter of principle. His solicitor had misunderstood these instructions and so Budd had missed the opportunity to appear before the House of Commons Committee. However, the House of Lords Committee was persuaded to hear him in July 1864 and he made the most of the opportunity. Firstly, he objected to the proximity of the line to his house.

J. Palmer Budd.   *DD Coll.*

This was in spite of the fact that the line was in a 30-35ft deep cutting for 286 yards along the side of the mountain, 506 yards away from his house and shielded by a belt of trees. He complained that 'his ladies', as he termed them, would be disturbed by onlookers from the trains while they were playing croquet on the lawn outside his house. He further considered the new line worse than that of the previous year because it failed to pass close by his works, thus necessitating a short siding. Furthermore, the previous line was to have passed his house in a tunnel. It was pointed out by counsel for the promoters that Budd had himself been a promoter of the Welsh Midland in 1845 which had been planned to run a much shorter distance from his house and that he had accepted the route of the SV only 50 yards away behind his house.

The bill received the royal signature shortly afterwards in 1864. Work on the line began on 1 February 1865 under yet another contract with John Dickson. At a price of £160,000, this was generous for a mere seven or so miles of straightforward single track, though with provision for doubling. Work was soon delayed due to another dispute with J. Palmer Budd. In 1865 another Act introduced a small mineral branch at Abercrave which was never built, in spite of local coal interests raising it again in 1873. In April 1865 Banks became chairman of the N & B and persuaded the board to take a 999 year lease of the Junction Line. This was approved by Parliament in a third Junction Line Act in 1866. Once the Llangammarch branch was complete there would be a second route for the LNWR to Swansea.

THE LNWR HANGS ON

In 1866 a new draft agreement was prepared by the CWE to take account of the new route potentially opened up by the lease of the Junction Line. By this agreement the CWE was to work the N & B for 99 years, running its own locomotives over both the N & B and the Junction Line. The proposed rates were stated as follows:

General tolls and receipts on CWE and N & B to Fund A	80% to N & B
Local traffic to Fund B	50% pass. to N & B
Earnings from traffic on other railways	60% goods to N & B

This is not immediately intelligible, but it probably meant that Fund A was for all traffic starting or finishing outside the CWE/N & B. 80% of the receipts on the mileage proportion over the N & B and over the CWE would be put into an account called Fund A. 20% of total receipts in this category would go to the CWE as operator. On purely local traffic the N & B would receive 50% of passenger receipts and 60% of goods. Similar percentages would be received by the N & B on that proportion of traffic derived from or destined to the N & B over lines other than the CWE. It is not, however, clear how the two accounts, Funds A and B, were to be allocated between the parties.

This was approved by an Extraordinary General Meeting of the N & B on 12 June 1866. An attempt was made to rescind the decision at a Special General Meeting on 19 June. It was however confirmed, though only on a vote and after concerns were expressed, especially by the Imperial Mercantile Credit Co., a major shareholder, at the small size and minor stature of the CWE and fears that the N & B would be subject to decisions made elsewhere on the routing of traffic, i.e. by the LNWR.

A get-out clause in the event of traffic being diverted was insisted upon. By the summer of 1866 the parties were optimistic and were considering leasing the SV. In fact, they opened discussions with Starling Benson. Henry Robertson took the lead. He was active behind the scenes in facilitating the LNWR's progress towards Swansea, but it is hard to understand their true motivation.

By early 1866 the Llanelly Railway had managed at last to reach Swansea from Pontarddulais, the place on its line from Llanelly to Llandeilo whence the Swansea line had been authorised in 1861. Furthermore, by the summer of 1866, a joint lease of the Vale of Towy was looking likely, with the CWR and Llanelly in partnership as co-lessees. This would mean that as soon as the last link between Shrewsbury and Swansea was completed, the LNWR could have a reasonably direct route under its control. In 1866 the tunnel under the Sugar Loaf Mountain was causing problems, but, although the delay was expensive, it was not going to prevent completion of the railway which was finally achieved in June 1868. The financial difficulties of the Llanelly were well publicised and Robertson, Green Price and others had been talking to the Llanelly about links with the LNWR since 1860. If the Llangammarch link to the N & B was an alternative main line, it looks an expensive duplication for the sake of just a five mile saving in distance to the Midlands and the north. It looks more likely that it was seen by the LNWR as a hedge and a spur to the Llanelly to be co-operative.

Perhaps it should also be seen as a part of a bid by the LNWR to gain alternative access to Cardiff as well as Swansea for in 1866 the Aberdare & Central Wales Junction Railway was authorised. Its board was nominally independent though firmly in the LNWR camp with Richard Green Price and Sir Charles Rouse Boughton, chairman of the CWR, among the directors. It was to link the N & B at Colbren with the Taff Vale at Aberdare. This interesting idea came to nothing though it was authorised by Parliament.

SCHEMES IN SWANSEA

Between 1863 and 1867 Dickson produced a number of schemes to secure access to Swansea and thence to Mumbles. He displayed tremendous energy, persistence and resource but in the process created a number of enemies among his competitors and potential partners. Four attempts were made to put different schemes to Parliament but none was successful.

In November 1863, as part of the Llangammarch Bill, an attempt was made to overcome the VoN's refusal to grant running powers to Swansea by obtaining rights to lay a third rail over the SWR and its short-lived pawn the Swansea Valley. (This seems a far-fetched scheme as the Swansea Valley had been promoted in the previous decade to enable the broad gauge to take over the SV and was already a dead duck.) Not surprisingly this was rejected on standing orders.

Simultaneously, new plans were submitted for connecting lines in Swansea in what was called the Neath & Brecon New Lines Bill 1864. This was intended to get the N & B into the heart of Swansea to a site between the North and South Docks.

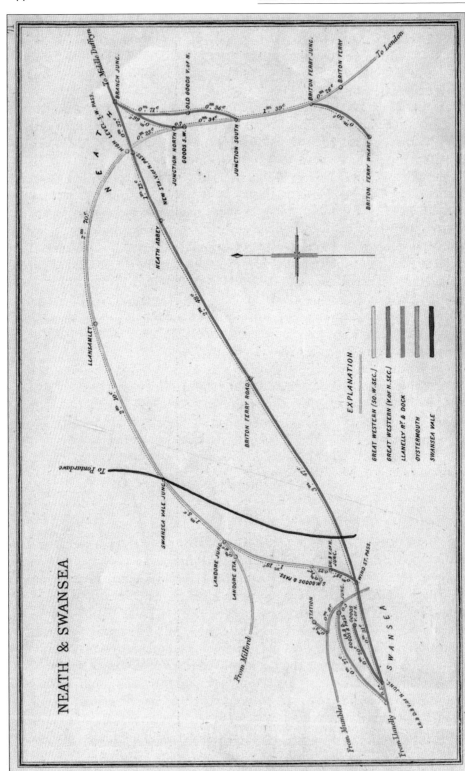

NEATH & SWANSEA

National Archives RAIL 1082/3

This Railway Clearing House map of 1868 reveals that the N & B was not yet part of the recognised railway fraternity. It also shows the state of development in Swansea.

Here land was to be taken for what was to be a joint station to be shared with the GW, S & N, Swansea Harbour Trust and the Llanelly. Line 1 was a 59 chain connection between a point on the N & B 88 yards from its junction with the S &N and the SWR at a place called Blaenhonddan. Line 2 was to be a 43 chain mixed-gauge link between the SWR and the SV at Llansamlet where the existing lines crossed. Line 3 was a mixed-gauge 35 chain link from a junction with the SV at Llansamlet across the Tawe to a junction with the SWR on the west bank. The new crossing of the Tawe was to be over an 11 arch viaduct with a drawbridge over the river. In addition, new rails were to be laid on broad-gauge track to enable the N & B to get anywhere round Swansea over the track of the SWR, SV, and the Swansea Harbour Trustees. This bill was not progressed to authorisation. It had clearly caused much opposition and dislike. Joshua Williams referred to this scheme in House of Commons Committee in 1864, saying Dickson had intended to find another way of getting to Swansea over the SWR and 'by using a bit of almost everybody's line'. Glascodine of the Llanelly Railway told the Commons Committee in 1864 that Dickson had proposed taking over all the stations in

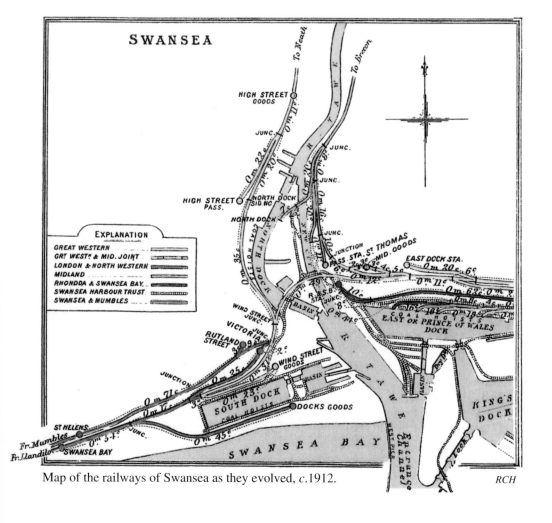

Map of the railways of Swansea as they evolved, c.1912.   RCH

Swansea. The Llanelly were particularly aggrieved as they had just paid £50,000 for the site of Victoria.

In 1865 the idea of a joint station was revived by other parties though almost certainly with Dickson's connivance. The need for a central station was becoming apparent with St Thomas and Wind Street already in operation and Victoria on the horizon, but there was insufficient space. Indeed, Wind Street was to move in 1873 for that very reason, aggravated by the increasing number of coal trains proceeding to the growing docks. The proposal failed partly because it assumed that streets would be blocked off. This was opposed by both the Corporation of Swansea and the Board of Health.

In 1864 Dickson turned his attention to Mumbles and established a relationship with George Grant Francis, a local business man who was interested in developing Mumbles as a coal port for ocean-going ships. In the summer of 1864 Francis acted as intermediary in enabling Dickson to purchase land on the foreshore between Swansea and Oystermouth from the Duke of Beaufort. Dickson then set about acquiring the Oystermouth Railway but found himself in competition with the Llanelly Railway who were building their line from Pontarddulais to Swansea to what was later the LNWR terminus at Victoria. Dickson with the help of his friends was able to prevail and made an agreement to become the owner of the residual interest in the mortgaged railway.

Armed with land and the railway, Dickson then set about preparing a bill to authorise construction of a new railway and a pier 400 yards long at Mumbles. With McKenzie as engineer a project was prepared and a nominally separate set of subscribers was formed. They were all associates of Dickson: Francis, Banks, Miers, Layton and a new name Bulgin.

The resulting Mumbles Railway and Pier Co. Bill appeared before Parliament in the summer of 1865. Simultaneously, the Llanelly produced a similar bill to extend from Blackpill (the point on the coast of Swansea Bay where their line from Pontarddulais emerged) to Mumbles. Parliament favoured the Llanelly project whereupon Dickson took the matter to court. In the end he had to concede defeat and the Llanelly got its Act in 1866.

Meanwhile Dickson had still been working on access to Swansea. In October 1864 a new N & B board member was appointed in place of Colonel St. Barbe Browne of Rugby who had been appointed in March 1862 on the death of George Knox. His early departure is not explained but he was succeeded by a man who was a colleague of Banks on the board of the B & M. The new man, Captain C. Miller Layton, soon made his presence felt as, with Banks now in a strong position as chairman, together they set about acquiring a lease of the Swansea Canal. This was seen as a means of obtaining independent access to Swansea such that the N & B would be able to control its own line from Llangammarch right through to Mumbles. Initially, the board approved either a 10 year lease of the canal at £5,330 a year or an outright purchase for £75,000. Banks and Layton went to negotiate. They came away believing they had a deal and reported back enthusiastically. When the Canal Company chairman heard, he expressed surprise and denied that there had

been anything more than a discussion of terms. Banks and Layton had clearly been over enthusiastic. In their haste to recover their position they agreed on their own account to a 999 year lease at £9,000 a year, subject to parliamentary approval. Happily
for them this was endorsed by the board. The agreement contained the right for the N & B to construct a railway over the route of the canal from Morriston to Swansea. Two bills to authorise the transfer of the canal to the N & B failed in successive years, once through failure to secure the support of the Canal Co. General Meeting. In parallel with this initiative, in November 1864, the N & B submitted revised plans in their first Swansea Extension Bill which included the construction of a new line up the west bank of the Tawe from the harbour, past High Street station, through Morriston and as far as a farm at Ynystawe. It included rights over existing mixed-gauge track in the harbour area and the right to lay a third rail where there was no mixed track. Access at the northern end was to be over the SV. In several locations it overlapped the simultaneous Canal Bill. It failed on standing orders due to defective levels. (Was Dickson really so careless or was he doing too much?)

In November 1865 Dickson tried again with a second Swansea Extension Bill which failed due to unacceptable terms required by some of the canal traders. This led to the cancellation of the agreement with the Canal Company.

At that time Dickson had nine bills before Parliament:

1. Swansea Canal Transfer
2. N & B Swansea Extension
3. Swansea General Railway Station & Hotel
4. Aberdare & Central Wales Junction Railway
5. Avan Valley Railway
6. Swansea Vale & N & B Junction Railway
7. Anglesey Central Railway
8. Avan Valley Railway Capital
9. N & B Capital

Having failed so far, Dickson had one more attempt to gain access to Swansea. The nominally independent Swansea Vale & Harbour Junction Railway was promoted by N & B directors Banks, Cox, Layton, Capel Miers, Williamson and Montague Baillie. It foresaw a line from the SV near Glais to Swansea with running powers over the Swansea Harbour Trust lines. Parliament preferred a similar project of the SV to increase capacity by the construction of a loop line from Glais to Morriston.

By this time Dickson was becoming uneasy and his final throw was the N & B Additional Powers Bill which was passed in 1867. This was a move to unload some of his assets onto the N & B. It authorised the sale to the railway of his land on the foreshore, his interest in the Oystermouth Railway, his powers to work the railway, and the BFT. The Act failed to prevent Dickson's second bankruptcy and was repealed two years later as part of the eventual restructuring of the N & B.

TROUBLE AHEAD?

At the end of 1864, after lengthy negotiations, the acquisition of part of the BFT had been completed by Dickson for the modest sum of £8,000. (The Hay Railway, a similar enterprise, had been sold to the HH & B for £11,000.) He then managed to sell it on to the N & B for a massive sum of £85,000. Montague Baillie, a financial adviser associated with the BFT, joined the board. As a result of the negotiations Dickson acquired some land in excess of the needs of the N & B. In March 1865, J. Woolley, a London stockbroker and friend of Dickson, joined the board, but was replaced by Henry Gartside from Saddleworth near Manchester when in August he succeeded Dickson as the company's contractor. Dickson obtained the approval of the board to assign his contract to John Woolley in order 'to complete his financial arrangements'. In the light of subsequent events, this sounds ominous but as we have seen he had a lot on his plate in 1865.

In October 1865 the board minutes record a strange little problem when two un-named directors were sued by the company's bankers who were refusing to honour a cheque signed by them. The board expressed surprise at the conduct of the bank and the matter appears to have been dropped. In the absence of more information this can only provide a hint of a company whose affairs were not being conducted in an impeccable manner.

Later that year, in November 1865, Henry Robertson was appointed engineer in succession to McKenzie. At the same time, as noted previously, Richard Green-Price MP joined the board in place of Hanbury Miers. Both Robertson and Green-Price were closely involved with the LNWR's discreet progress across Central Wales. But money was getting tight and, in November, Woolley asked for £100,000 to be advanced; this was agreed. Shares to that value were issued to the Imperial Mercantile Credit Co. In April 1866 he needed a further £90,000.

In March 1866 the external position was still looking positive. The line from Neath to Brecon was due to be opened in May with over 22 miles of track already laid. The permanent way on the Llangammarch branch was expected to be complete by the end of August. Discussion was progressing well with the CWE and once the lease of the Junction Line was approved, there would be routes to Swansea over the N & B, with and without Brecon.

An end to the general feeling of optimism was signalled when Dickson wrote to the company on 30 June 1866 requesting a 20% increase in his contract price.

Chapter 3

BUST 1866–69

1866 Neath & Brecon Railway Capital Act cap. xv Vict. 29, 30
1867 Neath & Brecon Additional Powers Act cap. cxxii Vict. 30, 31
1869 Neath & Brecon Amalgamation and Amendment Act cap.cxiv Vict. 32, 33

TO THE EDGE

The dark clouds that began to gather in the summer of 1866 were ushered in by a further authorisation of capital in May by the Neath & Brecon Capital Act 1866. This permitted a further £200,000 to be spent on what was already an expensive railway. As the bill was unopposed there was no discussion in committee and the Act itself merely acknowledged that there were insufficient funds to complete what Parliament had previously authorised. Woolley was having further difficulty in obtaining advances to enable him to continue the work on completing the line to Brecon. £20,000 of Lloyds Bonds were required to be issued to him, funded either by what available authorised capital remained or out of the new capital just being released. In July a further £100,000 was issued in preference shares to cover his increased costs. He was now asking for a further £25,000 to be advanced against 3 or 5 year debentures. By September he needed a further £50,000. This was against a background of the collapse of bankers Overend Gurney that summer. This led to a period of generally dear money and tight credit.

Yet, in spite of this, Henry Robertson was still at work on the strategic plan and busy negotiating with the SV a lease by the N & B and the CWE. On behalf of the LNWR he was also exploring a wider alliance in the form of an amalgamation of the Knighton, the CWR, the CWE, the Llanelly and the N & B. This may have been stimulated by the financial crisis which became national after the collapse of Overend Gurney. One of the consequences of this was widespread bankruptcy, including that of the Cambrian, the Potteries, the Wrexham, Mold & Connah's Quay, the Bishops Castle and the B & M. In response to this, a number of worried investors were seeking to form a union of as many as 19 independent Welsh railways with a view to improving their ability to compete against the GWR and LNWR but also with a view to enabling the less profitable lines in the north to ride on the backs of the more profitable coal carriers in the south. The N & B was still firmly in the LNWR camp and stood apart.

However, its financial position was becoming precarious. The decision to withdraw from the proposed lease of the Swansea Canal incurred a penalty of £2,000 which the company could not afford to pay. Taylor of the company's solicitors together with Bell, the parliamentary agent, had to pay it on the company's behalf. In spite of this, on 29 September 1866 when the board met for the first time in Brecon at Banks' home, Watton House, they were persuaded by Dickson to take an assignment of land he had leased in Swansea from the Duke of Beaufort for £30,000 or £3,000 a year. Dickson also persuaded them to apply to Parliament for authority to take over his assets in the Additional Powers Bill described earlier.

No doubt they were encouraged by the Royal Assent to the Junction Line lease (SV and N & B Junction Railway Act 1866) and the fact that goods traffic had started to run to Brecon on 13 September. In order to celebrate the event a special passenger train was run. It was

Watton House, Banks' residence in Brecon.

DD

free of charge as there was, as yet, no authorisation from the Board of Trade to operate passenger trains for revenue. A locomotive was borrowed from the VoN and an enormous crowd of 700 people were given a free ride over the mountains from Neath for the celebrations. The board minutes did not include details of the discomfort to which these pioneer travellers over the N & B were exposed. According to *The Cambrian* a late start led to slow running, and the return from Brecon scheduled for 8.30 p.m. did not leave until 10.30 p.m. It rained heavily, the train was seriously overcrowded and there were no refreshments. They got back to Neath at 6.00 a.m. the following morning. The completion of the line to Brecon was an achievement which, as it was reported to the board, was 'mainly attributable to the energy and determination of the Contractor Mr John Dickson in carrying on the works so uninterruptedly during the late financial crisis'. In fact, the financial crisis had not yet reached its peak.

CRISIS 1866-67

At the start of the new year, on 21 February 1867, the board was notified of an application by their bankers to the Court of Chancery for the appointment of a receiver. T. Morley, the company secretary was appointed. At the same time he was appointed traffic manager. It was agreed that the locomotives and rolling stock would be bought from Dickson, and in order to generate cash, all surplus land would be conveyed immediately to Dickson as originally agreed. But meanwhile the Additional Powers Bill was in Parliament and, as we have seen, received the Royal Assent in 1867.

Meanwhile, in November 1866, Dickson had taken over the job of contractor again from Woolley, and Hans St. George Caulfield, who had been assistant engineer from the very beginning, was promoted to become engineer. McKenzie was also back, in the role of consultant. A significant move was made when Henry Robertson was no longer required by the LNWR to attend the board. This would suggest that the LNWR by that time was already beginning to lose enthusiasm for the flirtation with the N & B. Work on the Llangammarch branch was faltering and by this time access to Swansea by way of Llandovery was beginning to look more likely.

Although as we have seen there was no great enthusiasm in the N & B board for the wider type of amalgamation being floated at that time, it was agreed that a lease of the SV should be pursued and that cooperation was desirable with the B & M, MWR, Llanelly and Vale of Towy. However, a bill to authorise a lease of the SV was withdrawn in March pending, it was said, completion of the CWE agreement. This left the SV available to the Midland and relied on an assumption about the outcome of the CWE negotiations which were already looking doubtful. Indeed, already in March 1867 there were further signs that the CWE party were getting cold feet. Special General Meetings to approve the CWE proposals had to be adjourned seven times between February and May for want of concrete proposals. In March these negotiations were felt by the ever optimistic N & B board to be so far advanced that a satisfactory conclusion was 'scarcely a matter of doubt'. Two months later the CWE declined to continue negotiations. In House of Lords Committee on 28 May, Dickson was challenged that work had ceased on the Llangammarch branch and it was suggested to him that the project had been abandoned. He denied this and said it was 50% complete. Work had, in fact, stopped towards the end of 1866 due to a lack of cash and was never resumed. There is no evidence that the cash shortage was in any way connected with the LNWR's coolness and Robertson's withdrawal, but the LNWR showed no inclination to provide assistance at this time.

Nevertheless, the idea took a long time to die and on 13 November 1871, there was a meeting with the LNWR at which it was decided to seek a prolongation of time for the completion of the branch, to seek running powers for the N & B to Hereford, and to grant authority for the LNWR, GWR or Midland to purchase or make working arrangements with the N & B. These discussions must have been overtaken by the action of the Midland in taking over the SV. On 9 May 1872 Lord Redesdale refused permission for a further extension of time, and agreed that £75,000 of the £150,000 set aside for the completion of the branch could be used on other essential works.

That appeared to put an end to the matter, but in 1882 the idea was revived by

Col. Laurie and others, who managed to get the Llangammarch & Neath & Brecon Junction Railway authorised by Parliament. It was authorised to generate capital of £130,000 and to borrow up to £43,300. The company itself or any companies working it were to have running powers or the power to work:

1. The CWE, the CWR, and Knighton Railway between Llangammarch and Craven Arms (odd, since they were now part of the LNWR).
2. The N & B.
3. The SV, now part of the Midland.
4. The B & M from Brecon as far as Talybont.
5. The GWR from Neath to Swansea.

After three Acts to extend the time allowed, abandonment was finally authorised in 1890. It is remarkable that this idea took so long to die. Even in 2004 the accompanying document turned up in a Cardiff sale.

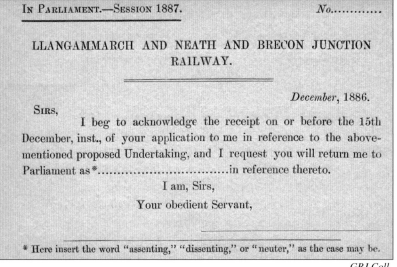

In Parliament.—Session 1887.   No..............

LLANGAMMARCH AND NEATH AND BRECON JUNCTION RAILWAY.

December, 1886.

Sirs,
        I beg to acknowledge the receipt on or before the 15th December, inst., of your application to me in reference to the above-mentioned proposed Undertaking, and I request you will return me to Parliament as *.............................in reference thereto.

I am, Sirs,

Your obedient Servant,

_____

* Here insert the word "assenting," "dissenting," or "neuter," as the case may be.

GBJ Coll.

The idea of the N & B being part of the LNWR system was diminishing as early as November 1866, and already in April 1867 Dickson was talking to the Midland about traffic. Without the Llangammarch branch, the Midland was the N & B's only potential saviour. Both companies could see this but it did not make the eventual terms of agreement any more palatable to the N & B.

This opening of discussion with the Midland preceded the opening on 3 June 1867 of N & B passenger trains to Brecon, providing a route to the north of England which although longer than through Llangammarch was still attractive. The 1865 contract with the CWR allowing LNWR running powers over the N & B was still thought to be in existence though the LNWR had taken over this company as authorised by an Act of 1868 and the contract was to be referred to Parliament by either party if it was required to be implemented. It never was.

The Financial Mess

Underlying all these events was the financial position of the company which had been deteriorating. At the end of 1863 the position had looked healthy. Progress was being made and there was capital authorised and forthcoming. The position was recorded in a simple Funds Flow Statement and showed the following, in pounds:

EXPENDITURE		PAYMENTS	
PARL. EXP. 1862	£4,000	LLOYDS BONDS	£4,000
PARL. EXP. 1863	£15,000	SHARE CERTS	£26,000
BFT	£85,000	DEBENTURES	£20,000
LEGAL	£5,500	SHARE CERTS	£24,000
LAND	£7,000	,,	£38,000
MATERIALS	£142,500	,,	£27,000
		,,	£120,000
	£259,000		£259,000

This statement is odd as it shows the acquisition cost of the BFT as an outgoing when authority for it to be transferred from Dickson was only given in 1867. Lloyds Bonds were commonly in use at the time, particularly for railway projects. They were named after a barrister and not the bank or the coffee house. They were usually at a relatively high interest rate and had the merit of being easily transferred.

The capital account was also shown, in pounds:

AUTHORISED	DULAIS VALLEY ACT 1862	£60,000
,,	N & B 1863	£405,000
		£465,000
LESS EXPENDITURE		£259,000
UNEXPENDED CAPITAL AVAILABLE		£206,000
DEBENTURES TO BE ISSUED		£135,000
TOTAL AVAILABLE		£341,000

There was no indication, at that stage, of the problems which later emerged though it was already an expensive railway. However, if the line to Brecon could have been completed within that sum of £341,000, all might have been well. It is also noteworthy, especially in the light of how Dickson went about raising cash, that at this stage no recourse to bonds was envisaged until all the shares had been sold.

However, this was soon to change and by the end of 1867 the company had issued shares and bonds a long way in excess of its real cash expenditure. The table opposite showing a balance sheet for year end 1866 is one of the few financial statements to survive, but it is tantalising in what it leaves unsaid and without further figures, in particular to show the real cost of building the railway and the actual price realised for shares and bonds, it is only part of the picture. This statement falls short of the standards of reporting required today and its odd assortment of balances have the slender merit of providing cosmetic comfort to the casual observer. The fact that the sums are incorrect to the tune of £700 in line 18 was only discovered by an accountant in 2003, and appears to have eluded Whittington, the auditor at the time. It does, however, reveal the astonishingly high cost attributed to investing in the railway. It seems incredible now that Parliament should in the first place have authorised so much capital for so little. A glance at some comparisons reveals the enormity.

AMOUNT AUTHORISED BY PARLIAMENT IN SHARES AND BONDS			
	ROUTE MILES	CAPITAL	£/MILE
Neath-Onllwyn	10	£80,000	8,000
Onllwyn-Brecon	20	£540,000	27,000
Devynock-Llangammarch	12	£280,000	23,000
Ynisygeinon-Colbren	7	£160,000	23,000
Hereford-Brecon	40	£280,000	7,000
Pembroke-Tenby	11	£106,000	9,500
Bala-Ffestiniog	22	£190,000	9,000
Brecon-Llandovery	21	£210,000	10,000

On top of this there was the further £200,000 authorised by the Neath & Brecon Capital Act in 1866. All the above lines were single track and there would have been variations in land values, earthworks and structures, yet on all these counts the N & B should have been at the low end of the range. According to Engineer Caulfield's evidence in 1869 the N & B actually cost 'about £12,000 a mile in money – in cash'. There is evidence that some were aware of the large sums being estimated. In 1864, in Commons Committee, Joshua Williams of the VoN was asked if he could explain the increase in the cost of the N & B between 1862 and 1863 from £60,000 to £480,000. He simply put it down to the extension through to Brecon. Similarly, when Engineer McKenzie was cross-examined in the same committee, he was notably evasive on the subject of the doubling in cost of the Junction Line from one year to the next. McKenzie knew more than he was prepared to admit with Dickson breathing down his neck and was quite firm and deliberate in the way he avoided the question. Anyway, the subject was not pursued. It seems that if sums were forecast by engineers and judged by promoters to be capable of being raised, Parliament was not going to intervene. This is borne

NEATH AND BRECON RAILWAY COMPANY.

1, WESTMINSTER CHAMBERS, VICTORIA STREET, WESTMINSTER, S.W.

97.

CAPITAL ACCOUNT.

						£ s. d.	£ s. d.
SHARES:—6,000 Original Shares of £10 each authorised by original Act of 1862						60,000 0 0	
40,500 Shares of £10 each		"	"	Act of 1863		405,000 0 0	
21,000	"	£10 each	"	"	Act of 1864	210,000 0 0	
15,000	"	£10 each	"	"	Act of 1866	150,000 0 0	825,000 0 0
LOANS :—			Authorised by original Act of 1862			20,000 0 0	
			"	Act of 1863		135,000 0 0	
			"	Act of 1864		70,000 0 0	
			"	Act of 1866		50,000 0 0	
							275,000 0 0
Total amount authorised by Shares and Loans							1,100,000 0 0

BALANCE SHEET TO 31ST. DECEMBER, 1866.

RECEIPTS.

	£ s. d.	£ s. d.	£ s. d.
To Capital:—			
67,500 Ordinary Shares £10 each	... ...	675,000 0 0	
15,000 Preference " "	... ...	150,000 0 0	
Debentures	... ...	275,000 0 0	
		1,100,000 0 0	
Issued:—			
61,595 Ordinary Shares	615,950 0 0		
10,000 Preference	100,000 0 0		
Debentures	268,700 0 0	984,650 0 0	984,650 0 0
Unissued:—			
5,905 Ordinary Shares	59,050 0 0		
5,000 Preference	50,000 0 0		
Debentures	6,300 0 0	115,350 0 0	
		1,100,000 0 0	
To J. Dickson's Contract Account:—			
By Contracts	... ...	1,072,100 0 0	
Less retained against unfinished work	70,950 7 2		
Retained under Contracts against completion	15,000 0 0	85,950 7 2	
		986,849 12 10	
To Ordinary Shares	615,950 0 0		
" Preference "	78,000 0 0		
" Debenture "	268,700 0 0	962,650 0 0	
			24,199 12 10
			1,008,849 12 10

PAYMENTS.

	£ s. d.	£ s. d.	£ s. d.
By Property &c.:—			
Works and Materials	... ...	852,049 12 10	
Lands and Buildings	... ...	92,000 0 0	
Parliamentary and Legal Expenses...	... ...	36,500 0 0	
Current Expenses	... ...	6,300 0 0	
		986,849 12 10	
By Preference Shares deposited on trust	... ...	... ...	22,000 0 0
			1,008,849 12 10

W. L. BANKS, Chairman.

W. WHITTINGTON, Auditor.

Financial Capital statement for 1866.

out by the Neath & Brecon Railway Capital Act of May 1866 which acknowledged the cost increase without comment and sought no reasons for it.

What further exacerbated the position was the extent to which the company was trading at a loss. This was in spite of opening goods services from Neath to Brecon in September 1866. There is evidence to suggest the loss was at some 40% of revenue and matters came to a head early in 1868. By that time the company was virtually insolvent, the infrastructure was in bad shape, the Junction Line was still incomplete, and the shareholders were desperate to find ways of recovering at least some of their money.

A principal source of the financial problem lay with the arrangement made with Dickson. This was recorded in two agreements signed in 1863. The first, dated 16 July, included provision for payment to be made to the contractor on delivery of certificates from the engineer confirming the value of work done. This was normal practice. A clever means of avoiding the company finding, near the end of the contract, that there were insufficient funds left to complete was provided by a requirement that as the works were drawing to completion, the engineer's certificates, instead of recording the value of work done, were to record the value of work remaining to be done. Any payment at this stage was to be limited to the balance between the total contract sum and the sum of work done and work remaining to be done.

The company was to pay nine tenths of each certified valuation up to £20,000 as a surety against completion, a retention as it is termed today. £10,000 of this was to be paid on certified completion and the remaining £10,000 was to be paid after one year's operation of the railway, as a surety against proper maintenance. Payment was to be in shares at par and debentures, and these were to be with three or five years to run at the contractor's option and bearing interest at four or five percent. The first instalment was to be £55,000 in shares and £4,000 in Lloyds Bonds. The balance was to be paid as follows: £400,000 in shares and £155,000 in debentures. An unusual concession was made to the contractor in allowing him the right to request shares in advance of his entitlement in respect of works done in cases where he saw advantage in the share market so to do. These additional shares were to be deposited at the company's bank, the proceeds from their sale being deposited in a joint account in the name of three directors as trustees and the contractor.

On 11 November 1863 the agreement was modified, 'the Company being desirous of enabling the Contractor more effectually to carry out the terms of the said contract'. On signature, the contractor was to be paid £35,000 in Lloyds Bonds with three years to run at five percent. As regard further payments of Lloyds Bonds, the company was to retain shares to the value of twice the value of the Lloyds Bonds issued as a security against failure by the contractor to meet his obligations. On satisfactory fulfilment of his obligations, the contractor was to receive shares at twice the value of the Lloyds Bonds. The whole capital authorised in the 1862 and 1863 Acts was thus put in the contractor's hands and he was, in return, to cover all expenditure. Debentures were issued to him at a 25% discount and Lloyds Bonds at as much as 50% discount. The total capital was, in summary:

Shares issued.	£416,170
Loans N & B	£274,900
Loans SV & NBJ	£24,970
Lloyds Bonds N & B	£334,500
Lloyds Bonds SV & NBJ	£5,500
Total	£1,056,040

Of the Lloyds Bonds issued, £213,650 were issued to Dickson between September 1862 and November 1864.

In detail this all amounted to:

1862	Shares	£60,000
	Loans	£20,000
	Total	£80,000

By 1869, out of the 6,000 shares at £10 each, only 495 had been sold and the balance of 5,505 was still in the hands of the company.

1863	Shares	£405,000
	Loans	£135,000
	Total	£540,000

By 1869, only 1,710 of these 40,500 shares had been placed, leaving a balance of 38,790 still in the company's hands. But the whole of the borrowing powers had been exercised. This was contrary to law and the terms of these Acts as these required that borrowing powers may only be exercised when all the shares are subscribed and 50% paid up.

This was subsequently increased to cover the cost of the Llangammarch line and the two short mineral branches:

1864	Shares	£210,000
	Loans	£70,000
	Total	£280,000

The sale of these shares had been more successful and by 1869 only 670 were left in the company's hands.

1866	Shares	£150,000 (N & B Capital Act)
	Loans	£50,000
	Total	£200,000

Of these 15,000 shares, 12,280 had been taken up and only 2,720 remained with the company. Only £100 remained of the loans permitted under this and the previous Act.

1867	Shares	£75,000 (Neath & Brecon Additional Powers Act subsequently repealed)
	Loans	£25,000
	Total	£100,000
	Grand total	£1,200,000

The 1869 Act repealed this last Act so the total capital authorised became £1,100,000. Of this, £623,050 had been subscribed and paid. But £175,000 had been subscribed as debentures illegally. Thus the amount legitimately raised amounted to £448,050. Nevertheless, if the £334,500 raised by way of Lloyds Bonds is taken into account and the illegality is ignored, the company actually raised £957,550 for 30 miles of track.

There was, in addition, the capital of the Junction Line Company:

1864	Shares	£120,000 (Swansea Vale & Neath & Brecon Junction Railway Act [SV & NBJ Act])
	Loans	£40,000
1865	Shares	£15,000 (SV &NBJ Act) Abercrave Branch
	Loans	£5,000
	Total	£180,000

Of the total 13,500 £10 shares issued by the Junction Line Company, only 6,802 had been taken up. Of the 6,698 remaining under the company's control, 688 had been deposited as security for £5,500 worth of Lloyds Bonds. Of the £45,000 of loan capital authorised under these two Acts, £24,790 had been raised. Thus, of the £180,000 total for the Junction Company, shares and loans had produced £92,990, Lloyds Bonds £5,500, making a total of £98,490. All for seven miles of uncompleted single track.

Thus the total authorised capital of the N & B and SV & NBJ together amounted to £1,380,000 and the total paid up was £1,056,040.

With the whole capital at his disposal and a group of directors who were either his friends, idle landowners not really interested or, as in the case of Banks, incompetent enthusiasts, Dickson proceeded to cash Lloyds Bonds under the company's name. These, he argued, were easier instruments for raising money as they took the form of high interest tradable securities which had a more ready market than shares. When he received Lloyds Bonds, he was due to hand back to the company a percentage of the shares he had received in order to enable the company to cover its liabilities under the Lloyds Bonds issued in its name and bearing the company seal. Although it was the company which issued the bonds, it was Dickson who would ultimately have to indemnify the company over and above the liability covered by the shares handed back. This whole arrangement was dependent on Dickson remaining solvent.

It later emerged that real expenditure in cash on building the line had amounted, by 1869, to some £330,000 on the main line and £10,000 on the Junction Line, compared with paper costs of over £1 million. It is not clear from the available evidence how exactly Dickson managed to incur this major discrepancy but in addition to receiving the debentures at a discounted price, many of the shares were also transferred to him at a discount. In 1869, Cave admitted to the House of Commons Committee that Dickson was authorised to sell shares at a 50% discount and debentures at 75%. Thus, for say £10,000 worth of works, he might have received that value in shares discounted by 50% which would have been charged to the company's books at par i.e. £20,000.

Another area where Dickson seems to have taken advantage of the railway was in connection with land. By the agreement between the company and Dickson, any property acquired by the contractor not permanently required for future use was to be disposed of by the company for the benefit of the contractor. Dickson completed his contract in June 1867 but owing to his financial difficulties he did not pay all his creditors and he had failed to complete either the Llangammarch branch or the Junction Line. He had acquired a considerable quantity of land beyond what was required for the railway and, indeed, beyond what he was bound to acquire under the terms of his contract. In February 1867 he raised the subject of the surplus land with the company and asked them to convey it to him. This would have had the advantage of saving cost and would have avoided the risk of seizure by creditors. This the board agreed to do, subject to the pre-emptive rights of adjoining landowners, as they wanted to help Dickson. However, the company's solicitors felt it unwise to convey the land until Dickson had satisfied all his liabilities under the contract, unless his claims upon the company were more than sufficient to balance his contractual liabilities. In spite of this advice, the company went ahead and an absolute conveyance was made on 17 July 1867. Thus, the value of the surplus land, which we cannot determine but we know was considerable, became a cost to the company.

In September 1867 Dickson became bankrupt, largely indebted to the company, which was now liable for large sums against which they held his indemnity. His liabilities were to a considerable extent due on the surplus lands for which he had not paid. However, in April 1868 his bankruptcy was annulled and the estate passed into the hands of inspectors under the Inspectorship Clauses of the Bankruptcy Acts.

On 4 July Alexander Young, acting as inspector of Dickson's estate, agreed with Cave, the new N & B chairman:

1. The estate now had no significant surplus assets;
2. Dickson was to abandon any claims for rent charges;
3. The company was to have peaceful possession of all land needed for its role;
4. Cancellation was to be made of the rolling stock deal and all rolling stock delivered already to the company was to be forfeited to the company.

Armed with the conveyance of the surplus lands, Dickson proceeded to raise money on them. One such case was in Brecon where he obtained £5,000 from the Rev. Wilts on the security of some land in the town. Before the conveyance, he had also executed to a Mr Tippetts an equitable mortgage on other land in Brecon which he had acquired for the company as security for certain advances and interest. Large arrears of interest were due to these gentlemen. Dickson also executed in favour of a Mr Collett Saunders an instrument whereby he charged (*inter alia*) all his Brecon Forest Tramroad Estate and also several pieces of land comprised in a deed of 28 February 1867 as security for an advance of £3,000. This mortgage was subsequently invested in Mr Tippetts who held £5,000 of shares and debentures under it, in addition to the property. The problem was that this land was needed for the necessary expansion of Mount Street station.

A view at Colbren Junction as No. 9746 took water on its journey to Brecon on 5 November 1960.   *E.T. Gill/Courtesy Reverend Brian Arman*

There were other instances where Dickson's transactions represented dubious practice. In May 1866 the company was notified that Dickson's son James had assigned his interest in the entire fleet of engines and rolling stock to a Mr T.B. Forwood. Dickson had no right to assign them to his son as they had already been leased to the company. Nevertheless, the name-plates were changed in favour of people nominated by the Dicksons. There were also cases where Dickson had assigned land to his son prior to the conveyance to the company. A report of 1869 judged, 'His conduct was undoubtedly reprehensible but it was also a fact that the directors had allowed themselves to be bamboozled by his sharp practice.' There was also a suspicion of collusion between Dickson and those directors he had recommended to the board. He was clearly a gambler at heart as he became bankrupt twice again, in 1874 and in 1880.

RECONSTRUCTION

On 28 February 1868 a special meeting of the board was called at the instigation of the bankers to consider a reconstruction of the board. Banks' chum Miller Layton offered to retire if the board would relieve him of the burden of a surety which he, together with Banks and Hanbury Williams, had offered a financier called Forman in respect of advances he made to Dickson. Forman was now pressing and threatening not only to put in force judgments he had obtained but also 'to resort to other extreme measures to recover his money'. Banks sympathised with Layton and said he too would gladly resign on those terms. Not altogether surprisingly the rest of the board did not agree. It was initially agreed to resolve the matter by the deposit of preference shares in the names of Banks and Layton, but this was abruptly rescinded and the Union Bank were to be told that these shares were the property of the company.

On 30 March there was a board meeting in the morning attended by Banks, Layton and Williamson. They agreed to adjourn and meet again at 1.00 p.m. However, this was the time at which a Shareholders General Meeting had been called. Williamson, a London barrister, was the only director present at this meeting so he took the chair. The shareholders present in person were:

Williamson..	35 shares
Whittington (N & B auditor)...........	346
Morgan (N & B secretary)................	10
Bell (solicitor)..................................	10
Hughes......................................	10
Dickson (contractor).........................	35,000
Ball and A. Young (administrator)......	unquantified due to liquidation Imperial Mercantile Credit Assoc. another major shareholder
In addition holders of proxys	14

Whittington and Ball proposed that in the place of Layton and Capel Miers, the two directors who were retiring by rotation, two new directors should be appointed, Thomas Cave MP and W. McAndrew. This was agreed. Banks was not present and although he ceased to be involved and was, in fact, consistently ignored, he remained a director. In 1869 Cave, his successor, said rather vaguely in Parliamentary Committee that he never actually retired: 'I am not quite sure that he is not still on the list.' He had clearly ceased to matter. He is last recorded as attending a board meeting on 24 February 1870.

The meeting was then adjourned until 30 April as the accounts were not yet ready. At a board meeting on 2 April 1868 only two directors were present, Cave and Williamson, so the meeting was adjourned to the following day. On this occasion Banks, in an effort to keep his chums on the board, suggested in writing that, rather than have Cave and McAndrew replace two retiring directors, they be voted on as extras, but this was rejected. The board elected Cave as chairman and Williamson as vice-chairman. A committee was set up to devise a Scheme of Rearrangement of the company, its members being the chairman, the vice-chairman, Baillie and McAndrew. Banks and Layton now protested at the legality of the General Meeting, arguing that there was not a legally constituted quorum. The decision of the meeting was subsequently upheld by counsel.

At a further meeting of the board on 6 April the secretary was asked to produce statements of assets and liabilities, rents, and rent charges, and a list of employees with their terms of service and salaries. The engineer, Caulfield, was asked to produce a schedule of urgent work needed to restore the track to a suitable condition. A General Purposes Committee was appointed, consisting of the chairman, vice-chairman and McAndrew. It is hardly a surprise that Banks was dropped as managing director.

SURVIVAL 1868–77

From available records it is hard to draw firm conclusions about the role of individuals in this sad tale. John Dickson was almost certainly brighter than all of them and had taken the initiative from before that first board meeting in September 1862. It was also notable that as contractor he assiduously attended nearly every board meeting. He was therefore privy to everything and clearly much relied upon. He it was who urged, from an early date, making for Brecon in order to capture the route from Swansea northward. He no doubt persuaded Banks and Layton of the need to gain a position of strength in the heart of Swansea dockland and was an enthusiastic ferret, good at digging up deals, particularly where he saw the chance of personal profit on the way. He was also a tough and resilient gambler, impervious to the strains of impatient creditors and bankruptcy.

Banks was clearly a muddler when it came to management and the closer work of implementing strategy. He made a mess of the B & M lease of the HH & B, some would say a monumental error considering his legal background. He and Layton between them made a complete shambles of the negotiations with the Swansea Canal, only escaping heavy personal losses by a combination of luck and a still optimistic climate. He signally failed to sort out the relations between the companies on whose boards he sat, even when chairman of three of them. And he allowed a quite absurd situation to exist in Brecon not only between these companies but also between a few key landowners, other members of his profession, and Dickson. He showed poor financial judgement in a number of other railway projects in which he was involved, and although an apparently engaging personality, he must have been a commercial liability.

The result of a grasping contractor with an instinct for a gamble and under little restraint, indeed backed by much charm and enthusiasm, was a company with liabilities too great for its earning capacity. There may have been justification for a railway from Swansea to the Midlands through Brecon and Hereford and the original concept of a mineral line from Neath to Onllwyn was quite definitely sound. Its survival in 2005 supports its case. But in 1868, with creditors battering on every door, a new team had to find ways of deriving value from the available assets and reallocating the burden of debt.

The task fell on the capable shoulders of Thomas Cave, Liberal MP for Barnstaple, a resident of Richmond in Surrey, and a sheriff of London and Middlesex. We know little about him except for his dislike of income tax and his ability as a liquidator. He was brought in by the liquidator of the Imperial Mercantile Bank who owned £300,000 of the company in Lloyds Bonds, and on behalf of others who owned some £200,000. He was to be paid a commission 'if any good above a certain amount results to them'. We have no record of what he actually earned, but the recovery was a slow process so whatever it was it would have taken time to materialise. When questioned in committee as to his general occupation he admitted he had none, but he went on to say he had no leisure either and with a fine choice of words refuted the suggestion that he was unoccupied.

For most of 1868 Cave devoted a high proportion of his time to the company's affairs, handling complaints and requests for payment of debts, as well as managing the ordinary business of a railway company, and by his own testimony spent two months in the area. On 4 April there was an accident at Howel Siding near Neath which led to the death of an engine driver, one John Dixon. (Presumably no relation of James Dickson, son of John, whose interest in these engines was more financial than practical.) A report to the Board of Trade was required. On 4 June the Metropolitan Carriage Company threatened to seize the rolling stock they had supplied. Cave negotiated the hire of replacements from B.H. Harris & Co. These consisted of two composite carriages, four third class, two brake vans, five vans, and 10 seven ton wagons.

On 14 July Cave was viewing the Aberdare & Central Wales Junction Railway which had recently been authorised by Parliament and would require running powers over the N & B. Since this company was part of the LNWR's Llangammarch strategy, there cannot have been a lot to talk about.

On 4 September Cave was at a meeting with Joshua Williams formerly of the VoN and now the GWR's area superintendent. It was agreed that the N & B would pay rent for part use of the former Swansea & Neath Low Level station at Neath and the track between that station and the N & B junction, the GW to provide

Neath Riverside, looking south at No. 3706 on a Neath to Brecon service. The high level of 'clutter' around the site at this time reflects its use as a maintenance yard. April 1962.

John Davies

The close proximity of the South Wales main line, crossing the N & B at Riverside, illustrates the logic of creating an interchange point here.

John Davies

labour, all for £300 a year. In response to a request from Banks, he agreed to attend a meeting in Gloucester with James Allport of the Midland, together with representatives of other railways. The discussions came to an abrupt end when the MWR announced that they were to operate the HH & B with effect from 1 October. The SV were still interested in friendly relations with the N & B but had no spare capital with which to assist the cash-strapped company.

On 14 September a special train was run in connection with Neath Fair. What was described as a 'diabolical attempt' was made to derail the train by placing timber and stones on the track. No one was injured.

On 9 October it was agreed that A. Giles, a civil engineer, should be appointed arbitrator in settling arrangements between the company and the Dickson estate.

Cave was writing many letters at this time to creditors, especially those who had sold land to the railway, recommending patience, drawing their attention to the involvement of the Court of Chancery, and alluding to possible future legislation and eventual additional capital. To this end he had undertaken to produce for the board a plan for restructuring the company. This eventually bore fruit on 26 July 1869 as the Neath & Brecon Amalgamation and Arrangement Act. This stands as a monument to Cave's achievement, reflecting months of negotiation while searching for a solution which would provide some hope of satisfaction for the company's creditors and a credible basis of operating profitably. It therefore tackled both the financial structure and the generation of traffic.

FINANCIAL

Under the Neath & Brecon Amalgamation and Arrangement Act, all existing legal proceedings in which the company was involved were to be suspended. All powers to raise funds under any previous Acts were 'cancelled, extinguished and determined'. The Act converted mortgage and other debt into debentures and created a five year moratorium. The debentures created were expressly not to be used in connection with surplus land:

A	Debs	225,000
B	,,	299,870
C	,,	460,000
D	,,	120,000
Pref. shares		122,800
Ord. shares		256,230
		1,483,900

The A Debentures bore interest at up to 6% per annum and had priority over all existing mortgages and were redeemable at a premium of up to 10%. The Act listed the priorities to which A Debenture stock was to be applied:

First, the costs associated with the Act itself, including the weeks of expensive professional time taken in debate before the parliamentary committees.

Second, the works on land taken by the company to build the railway.

Third, purchase cost of land acquired.

Fourth, the costs of Cruikshank, the principal petitioner.

Fifth, to complete the authorised works except the Llangammarch line. Any residue of the A Debenture stock was to be available for completing the Llangammarch line, but, if it was not proceeded with, the power to issue A Debentures would be reduced to £150,000.

Sixth, rolling stock and plant.

Seventh, interest on A Debentures.

Eighth, costs incurred by the companies since 31 March 1868.

Ninth, payment of net cash disbursements by solicitors, engineers, secretaries prior to 31 March 1868.

B Debenture stock bore interest at 5% and ranked after A Debentures. It was divided into four classes:

1. Up to £150,000 for holders of debentures issued under the 1862 and 1863 Acts;
2. Up to £25,000 for holders of 1864 'Junction Line' debentures;
3. Up to £75,000 for holders of debentures under the Llangammarch Line Act of 1864;
4. Up to £50,000 for holders of 1866 Act debentures.

C Debentures bore interest at 5% and could be issued to substitute the following:

a. Lloyds Bonds;
b. general debts not already provided for in the Act;
c. shares in the Junction Company which had been issued.

D Debentures at 5% were for the substitution of interest on debentures and Lloyds Bonds issued by the companies.

On leaving Riverside station, a Brecon-bound train heads straight across the N & B junction (centre foreground). The lines to the right connect with the Vale of Neath line.

G.H. Platt

A saddle-tank, some four-wheel coaches and N & B lettered wagons help to date this view of the engine shed at Riverside before the Grouping.
P. Korrinson Coll.

Any income from railway operations was to be allocated first to working expenses and proper maintenance, then to rents and tithes, and then to interest payments on the debentures. It was specifically stated that if the company failed in any one year to meet in full or in part any of these obligations, only interest to A Debenture holders could be carried forward to a subsequent year. Tough.

The total capital of the company in shares and loans before the Act was £1,380,000. The Act of 1867 was repealed. This reduced the authorised capital base by £100,000 to £1,280,000. But an additional £140,000 was to be authorised to permit certain necessary investments to secure the future of the line. This consisted of the following:

	£'000s
To complete the Junction Line	40
rolling stock	30
repairs	15
payment of debts incurred by 1867 Act	55

The £15,000 repairs needed were listed by Caulfield and recorded by the clerk to the Lords Committee as shown below. The largest items were new facilities at Ely Place in Brecon. This was a coal yard and locomotive facility west of Mount Street. Major repairs were needed to the top of the Brecon viaduct. This was because a timber top had been installed as a temporary measure to save money and accelerate completion.

The bill was opposed and was therefore debated before committees of both Houses of Parliament during May 1869. The opposition was mainly from those who resented others' interests being awarded priority, but since further investment was needed in order to put the company on a sounder footing, there was also much discussion of the financial prospects.

Caulfield's list of repairs required, as recorded for the Parliamentary Committee.
House of Lords Record Office

To achieve the proposed solution required a prioritising of claims and Cave emerges from the record as a fair man and a good negotiator. By early 1869 he had won support from most of the creditors with only 3% dissenting. The principal thorn in the flesh was J. Palmer Budd of the Ystalyfera Ironworks. In addition to his earlier objections he had a claim for trespass against Dickson which he alleged was unpaid. He had then threatened an 'extraordinary series of litigations', and now objected to the bill on the grounds that the company was 'hopelessly insolvent' and that works begun on his land had not been completed. Cave complained about his conduct to the Committee of the Lords: 'He was in a very irate state of mind, altogether against the whole thing unless I would alter my whole plan and everything else to suit his convenience.'

A more sympathetic victim was McKenzie, the engineer, who had been replaced by Robertson. He claimed £17,000 unpaid for professional services and £1,000 due to be paid for his resignation. McKenzie expected Woolley to pay him but Woolley was insolvent. He had been warned by the company's London solicitor Green to be careful and to be quite clear as to the nature of his relationship with both the company and the contractor. The only payments he had received were to pay his staff. McKenzie had had a dust-up with Dickson as early as 1863 and ended up having to apologise to him. As may be deduced from the Commons Committee evidence of 1864 he appears to have been a conscientious engineer but out of his depth when it came to keeping up with Dickson's manoeuvres.

GENERATION OF TRAFFIC

There were understandable fears about embarking on further investment to complete the Junction Line. Cave said only some £10,000 had been spent in cash hitherto on the line and that the further £43,000 was going to produce a considerably lower total cost than the £160,000 allowed to Dickson by his predecessors. The company had paid in paper some three times the true costs incurred.

It was critical to the proposed solution that there should be a reasonable prospect of being able to run a profitable railway. To this end, in the first instance the generation of a sound basis of traffic was sought by merging the Junction Line in the N & B. The resulting short route from Swansea to Birmingham, which had been in so many plans hitherto, was seen as the source of financial salvation. Merger of the two companies would save costs.

The profits for the second half of 1868 had been enough to keep the rest of the railway under repair and indeed to make some small improvements. Before that, it was said that the company had been running at a 40% loss. Gradual improvement over the 15 months to June 1869 had enabled the company to pay its employees and open two new stations (Crynant and Aberbran). Now with the line to Swansea in place, it was reasonable to expect to be able to pay off capital by attracting purchase 'by one of the main lines of the kingdom' (such as the Midland). Indeed, Cave told the Committee of the Lords that the Midland had told him they wanted him to go ahead with the scheme. Prospects were good for moving anthracite to south Staffordshire and timber and agricultural products to Swansea.

Morley, the traffic manager, produced a statement of revenue from the start of passenger operations to Brecon in 1867. The figures were available through to April 1869 although they were only produced in early May. It is odd that nothing was produced for the first section of line up to Onllwyn although that had been in operation since October 1864. It points to a fairly chaotic management before Cave

Neath and Brecon Railway

Traffic Receipts

Months	Passengers				Merchandise				Receipts									Total Receipts		
	1st Cl	2nd Cl	3rd Cl	Total	Carted	Not Carted	Tons Cs	Total weight	Passenger			Parcels &c			Merchandise					
1867																				
April					16	99	943	1050							65	7	10	65	7	10
May					80	487	6424	6999							389	4	9	389	4	9
June	175	495	3589	4259	73	606	6804	7483	315	14	9	.	5	2	369	17	11	685	17	10
	175	495	3589	4259	177	1192	14171	15540	315	14	9	"	5	2	824	10	6	1140	10	5
July	211	530	7553	8294	90	686	7449	8233	498	0	7	10	12	4	363	19	2	872	12	1
August	271	491	11069	11831	103	654	7920	8677	718	9	1	10	10	3	351	15	9	1080	15	1
September	220	302	6545	7067	70	776	6971	7817	414	11	4	8	8	9	492	11	1	915	11	2
October	132	309	4570	5011	75	989	6967	8031	270	6	10	9	5	7	464	7	6	743	19	11
November	130	276	5580	5986	81	829	7407	8317	295	8	3	38	0	1	445	10	9	779	7	1
December	136	261	4032	4429	90	1018	6733	7841	237	12	10	38	2	7	372	12	3	648	7	8
	1100	2169	39369	42638	517	4952	43447	48916	2434	8	11	115	7	7	2190	16	6	5040	13	0
1868																				
January	97	184	3533	3814	72	1304	7641	9017	191	7	7	34	1	9	459	1	7	684	10	11
February	82	204	3593	3879	37	1127	6926	8090	183	3	2	34	10	8	406	18	4	625	0	2
March	95	240	4154	4489	75	1021	4837	5933	235	5	10	50	4	10	396	6	6	681	17	2
April	120	274	4310	4704	96	1363	6803	8262	242	14	11	36	0	10	495	8	11	774	4	8
May	123	393	7060	7576	97	1026	6451	7574	353	15	5	41	17	6	420	18	9	824	11	8
June	196	317	6738	7251	87	1197	8490	9774	383	11	0	32	10	1	454	11	10	871	0	11
	713	1612	29388	31715	464	7038	41148	48650	1589	17	11	230	1	8	2641	5	11	4461	5	6
July	162	507	7224	7893	85	703	8086	8874	445	5	6	40	7	9	414	17	10	900	11	1
August	195	363	5917	6475	99	588	4043	5530	374	8	11	44	1	11	290	9	7	709	0	5
September	198	306	7466	7970	116	1067	5359	6542	419	13	0	63	18	5	4 442	0 4	2 9	929	16	4
October	153	343	5961	6457	156	1165	6801	8122	299	17	2	52	14	9	490	17	9	843	9	8
November	103	254	7016	7373	147	1133	4813	6093	316	4	7	43	0	0	446	17	8	806	2	3
December	89	204	5379	5672	147	791	5424	6362	230	14	7	12	19	4	371	12	6	10 596	10 15	10 7
	900	1977	38963	41840	750	5447	35376	41523	2086	3	9	257	2	2	2461	0	3	4804	6	2
1869																				
January	114	271	4871	5256	116	921	4857	5894	223	15	5	37	0	0	361	6	11	622	2	4
February	43	253	4219	4515	151	665	4736	100 5452	185	16	2	40	13	6	368	13	10	595	3	6
March	101	276	5599	5976	190	1181	5126	100 6405	252	13	1	37	0	0	471	7	2	761	0	3
April	100	404	5569	6073	196	849	6219	7264	282	9	2	41	0	0	495	13	2	819	2	4
	358	1204	20258	21820	661	3616	20938	25215	944	13	10	155	13	6	1697	1	1	2797	8	5
Abstract																				
	175	495	3589	4259	177	1192	14171	15540	315	14	9	.	5	2	824	10	6	1140	10	5
	1100	2169	39369	42638	517	4952	43447	48916	2434	8	11	115	7	7	2490	16	6	5040	13	0
	713	1612	29388	31713	464	7038	41148	48650	1589	17	11	230	1	8	2641	5	11	4461	5	6
	900	1977	38963	41840	750	5447	35326	41523	2086	3	9	257	2	2	2461	0	3	4804	6	2
	358	1204	20258	21820	661	3616	20938	25215	944	13	10	155	13	6	1697	1	1	2797	8	5
	3246	7457	131567	142270	2369	22245	155030	179844	7370	19	2	758	10	1	10114	14	3	18244	3	6

Morley's statement of Traffic Receipts from April 1867 until April 1869.

House of Lords Record Office

started to get a grip. Cave predicted that the current rate of profit of £2,000 to
£3,000 p.a., based on revenue of some £8,000, should rise to £5,000 now that a
new ironworks had opened at Onllwyn. That has to be put in the context of the
investment. If the line had really cost in cash about £300,000, a minimum profit of
£15,000 was needed to yield even 5% return. In fact, of course, it had cost more.
Morley predicted that, once the Junction Line was open, revenue would rise to
£43,500 p.a. (not in fact achieved until 1900). He drew encouragement from the
recent strong performance of the VoN. The N & B was already sending coal from a
recently opened colliery at Hearthyell (*sic*) as far as Dowlais, Welshpool and
Montgomery and foresaw sending 7,000 tons of copper and 17,000 tons of tinplate
annually from the Swansea valley.

The approach to
Ystradgynlais
station, looking
towards Ynisy-
geinon Junction,
1956.
J.J. Davies

Further progress
towards the
junction; the
Swansea Vale
line from
Ystalyfera trails
in on the right,
1956.
H.C. Casserley

A view down
the junction
line, below
Abercrave.
1956.
H.C. Casserley

Ynisygeinon
Junction signal-
box, looking
north; the
junction line
curves away to
the right. 1956.
H.C. Casserley

Some concern was felt about the prospects of the Neath arm once the Junction Line was opened. Strick in evidence before the House of Commons Committee let slip that it should never have been built. However, he then corrected himself and mentioned the new collieries being built. He did, however, go on to say that, without the Junction Line, to continue with the line to Brecon would be useless. Francis Mortimer, general manager of the SV believed that without the Junction Line the N & B would be unable to cover its expenses. The SV with a 20 mile line in the intense industrial area of the Swansea valley was earning only £25 per mile per week and paying an average of 3% a year on all its capital. This meant that the ordinary shareholders got nothing and only the 5% preference holders were remunerated.

In defending the ability of the company to remunerate the additional £150,000 authorised in 1866 to complete the works and buy new rolling stock, Cave argued that this would only require an incremental £9 per mile per week or additional net profit of £1,040. He hoped the £33,000 for new rolling stock would be insufficient but he had to admit that he feared that it would in the event be enough. Extension of time for completion of the Llangammarch branch was allowed in the Act though it would only proceed with the agreement of three quarters of the debenture owners and it was clear that no one believed in it. Cave had to concede to the Committee of the House of Commons that the position was changed by the LNWR now having access to Swansea, though he could not refrain from adding that it was 'rather a bad one'.

But the railway was saved. The Junction Line was going to be completed and now all depended on the generation of traffic. Caulfield, Morgan and Morley were left to get on with it. Caulfield took over as general manager on 27 October 1870, a position he held until he left in August 1879 to take up a job as manager of the Mauritius Government Railway. He was succeeded by F. Kirtley as general manager and E. Medley as engineer. Morley was shortly dismissed over delays in handling paperwork. This looks a hard judgement on a man who had shouldered much of the legal, financial and operating burden, but perhaps he was exhausted. Cave went back to London. John Dickson went off to pursue his career elsewhere and, as noted earlier, he survived another bankruptcy in the north of England before returning to Swansea for good.

N & B poster.

National Archives RAIL 1014/2

Chapter 4

DERBY TO THE RESCUE 1869–90

As mentioned above, as early as April 1867, Dickson had been talking to the Midland about traffic. Cave had met Allport, the Midland's general manager, at Gloucester in September 1868 and by November a draft of working arrangements was being considered. The Midland lease of the HH & B in 1868 must have set tongues wagging all along the route to Swansea, but although the Midland appears already to have been seen by Cave as a way out of the troubles, on 12 November 1869 a board minute records that 'no guarantee was forthcoming'. In July 1870 the N & B hired a locomotive from the Midland for which they were charged £498-4-0. The N & B thought this too much and Morley, the traffic manager, was sent to Derby to negotiate a reduction. This he managed to do, coming back with a price of only £201. In March 1870 Cave resigned as chairman. Woolley succeeded him for a few weeks from 3 March to 17 March when Baillie took over. On 19 January 1871 he was succeeded by Alexander Young who had been the administrator of the Dickson estate. He had what was felt to be an important advantage at the time of being based in London.

On 8 September 1870 Allport attended a board meeting and undertook to provide copies of the Midland agreements with the HH & B, B & M and SV. Meanwhile, the N & B Amalgamation and Arrangement Act of 1869 vested the Junction Line in the N & B. It was important that this seven mile line be completed and brought into use. In September 1869 a contractor called Rummens offered to complete it but his bid was considered too high and, after an inexplicable delay, Dickson was brought back in June 1870 when he offered to do the work for £40,500. The Union Bank, who stood surety for the payment of this sum, wrote, 'I am most anxious there should be no further delay in completing this short line, affording as it does the only prospect of their or anyone else getting a penny return for their money.'

Nevertheless, the line took a long time to complete and even then, when inspected on 4 September 1873, was judged by the Board of Trade Inspector unsuitable for passenger traffic. It was a single track railway though built on land and overbridges suitable for doubling later, but the works were incomplete. The turntable at Swansea was not large enough to accommodate an engine and tender and it would take six months to build one.

At some £50,000, this line cost less than a third of its original authorised amount of £160,000. And it was Dickson who had the gall to do it for this price. The line opened on 1 October 1873 and the N & B began operating four trains a day through from Swansea to Brecon, though the official clearance from the inspector was not given until 29 November. The SV began operations through to Brecon with goods trains from 1 February 1874, but by 1 September the Midland had obtained authority from Parliament to lease the SV.

The N & B was still struggling as the following extracts from profit and loss statements show:

		INCOME	EXPENDITURE
1st half	1869	£4,581	£5,077
1st half	1870	£5,397	£5,549
1st half	1871	£4,989	£4,946
1st half	1872	£6,890	£6,471
1st half	1873	£8,277	£7,718
1st half	1874	£10,267	£10,514

However, in the second half of 1874 there was a loss of some £16,000 due to the need for major repairs to the track. In 1875, 119,720 passengers were carried, mainly third class. In the first half income was £13,940 but expenditure was now slightly less at £12,951 but at this level was insufficient to cover the interest on the debentures. Further track repairs caused a loss of some £5,000 in the first half of 1876

Under a Chancery Court order of 1874, Alexander Young, by then chairman of the N & B, was to receive on behalf of the debenture holders all the company's revenues and to spend up to £50,000 restoring the infrastructure. The Midland were in discussion with the N & B on rates for the use of their track. Under the 1874 Act, by which the Midland obtained the right to lease the SV, the Midland was authorised to take running powers over the N & B and to fix the rate. The N & B

The archetypal view of Devynock, with a Midland passenger train *en route* to Swansea.

GBJ Coll.

A Midland train from Swansea at Brecon, facing the camera. On the right, an elegant
Cambrian 4-4-0 awaits to depart for Moat Lane Junction.   *GBJ Coll.*

were not happy with this and on 10 November 1875 the board rejected a Midland
proposal to use the line for a mileage proportion of the through rates. Failing to
reach agreement, the N & B referred the matter to the Railway Commissioners.
Their consideration of the problem was quite thorough and raised some interesting
points. They noted the severity of the gradients, particularly in the northbound
direction, and that it was in this direction the majority of the traffic was moving. As
a result of the 1,070ft altitude gain over only 10 miles in the north-bound direction
and a 790ft rise over 7 miles south-bound they noted that the average length of
train was half the normal. They therefore laid down a rate of 40% of gross receipts
less terminal charges. This was to be reviewed after one year. In fact it lasted until
1877. In 1876 the Midland began operating through goods trains from Swansea to
Brecon, taking advantage of the SV running rights, and eventually on 29 June 1877
an agreement was made between the N & B and the Midland:

- possession of the whole line from B & M Junction in Brecon to Ynisygeinon
  Junction was handed over to the Midland. This was now termed the 'worked line';
- facilities at Colbren Junction were to be shared, the allocation of costs being
  determined by arbitration;
- a total of £20,500 was to be paid to the Midland for necessary works on the line by
  them against monthly Midland engineer's certificates;
- Midland to work both local and through traffic on the 'worked line'. Local was
  defined as that originating and terminating on the 'worked line';
- Midland to pay taxes and subsequent maintenance on the 'worked line';
- N & B responsible for capital liabilities on the 'worked line', the Midland being
  under no obligation to make any contribution to capital expenditure;
- N & B to account monthly to the Midland for all receipts from third parties in
  respect of the 'worked line';

- Midland to fix fares and charges for through traffic. Both to fix rates for local traffic;
- Midland to keep the records of:
    1. receipts from local traffic less costs of cartage on 'worked line';
    2. mileage proportion due to the 'worked line' of receipts from through traffic less terminal costs as determined by the Railway Clearing House formula;
    3. station to station terminal charges on the 'worked line';
- accounts to be settled monthly, 30% of net earnings to the N & B;
- N & B not to exercise its running powers over the SV.

This agreement was to run for five years from 5 July 1877. Income was to be applied with the following order of priority:

1. Working expenses and maintenance other than that to be born by the Midland under the May agreement;
2. Rates, tithes, and rent charges;
3. Interest and dividends.

The position about issuing passenger tickets was not recorded but the N & B continued to issue tickets even at stations on the 'worked line' and to stations beyond Brecon. It would therefore appear that passenger stations other than Brecon Free Street continued to be manned by N & B staff. Tickets illustrated below demonstrate the point.

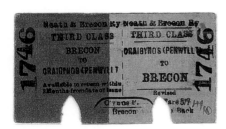 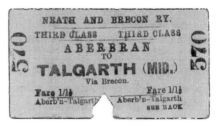

Courtesy of Roy F. Burrows, Midland Collection Trust

Other N & B obligations, for example debts in respect of land purchase and work done, were dealt with by what was called a Scheme of Arrangement, dated 2 August 1877. Under this the financing arrangement of the 1869 Act was modified. The interest on debentures and preference shares was reduced in 1878 to 1½%. In 1879 an additional 115,000 first debentures were created at up to 4% on the first 85,000 issued, and the A Debentures were increased to 300,000 or a maximum value of £235,000. Interest on B and C Debentures was to be 3% and on D Debentures 1½%. The total capital became £1,673,900. In 1892 there was a further restructuring which led to the total capital being reduced to £1,362,902.

These arrangements then continued in force though not without difficulty. A problem of the type to be expected where ownership of the track is in different hands from those running the trains arose over a station at Abercrave on the

Junction Line. The local inhabitants' campaign for a station to be built came to a peak in 1889. The N & B were responsible for capital investment but there was no point in building a station if trains were not going to stop there. The Midland refused to promise to do so. They would be influenced by the potential and realised traffic. In fact, the station was built and some trains did stop there.

An evocative view of Colbren Junction sometime during the earlier part of the twentieth century, showing an 'up' N & B coal train on the left, with two Midland Railway Swansea–Hereford passenger services crossing in the centre of the picture.   *TW Coll.*

Midland and N & B locomotives at Colbren Junction; the N & B engine is 2-4-0 No. 6.
Perkins/Tudor Watkins Coll.

An example of how the agreement worked in practice is a contract dated 30 September 1885 between the Midland Railway's land agent and a London company called Kershaw and Pole over the construction of a siding at Penwyllt. This was expressed on a standard Midland Railway contract document by which the Midland undertook to construct the siding and to maintain it and its associated signalling at the expense of the contractor. The only reference to the N & B is a statement that the new siding would connect with an existing siding owned by them. In accordance with the Scheme of Arrangement, the Midland would presumably have conveyed the siding on completion to the N & B.

The main agreement of 1877 between the two companies, extended in 1882, 1883 and 1888, was due to expire on 30 June 1889. On 1 July 1889 the Midland ceased to operate the 'worked line'. This sudden action was precipitated by a demand for improved terms from the N & B's new chairman Sir Edward Watkin. He was chairman of the Manchester, Sheffield & Lincolnshire Railway (MS & LR) and was a man of great vision and boundless ambition. His vision of a new railway from the north of England to London, linking with a route to a Channel Tunnel was his principal interest at the time but he also saw the prospect of linking the diverse and varied Welsh independent railways. He believed that they would be better able to compete with the GWR and LNWR if they were able to quote single rates rather than rates based on a series of independent calculations. One of his co-directors, J.W. Maclure, was also a director of the Cambrian and through him he engineered the support of the Cambrian. This got him as far as Brecon by way of the MWR. The N & B held a key position from there to the Bristol Channel, handicapped only by the presence of the Midland. Accordingly, in August 1888, in the company of

Although Price's Hotel at Coelbren rather dominates this composition, additional interest is created by the station sign inviting passengers using the Midland platform to change trains for Neath.   *Will Davies Collection*

The N & B sign on their platform was not as helpful.   *Martin Connop Price Collection*

Maclure and the general manager of the MS & LR he visited the N & B. Colonel Laurie, the deputy chairman of the N & B, reported at the next N & B half-yearly meeting in September: 'The agreement with the Midland terminated on the 30 June last but for the convenience of both parties it had been decided that it should continue until the 31 December. The directors were carefully considering their future policy and they did not intend to renew the agreement on anything like the existing terms. For the use of 29 miles of the company's main line . . . the Midland paid them only £4,200 a year and after deducting their portion of the general expenses the net result to the company was only £3,200. Their line was essential to the Midland Company who, if they desired its exclusive use, would have to deal with them more liberally in the future than they had in the past.' Watkin had evidently emboldened him and on 27 February 1889 himself became chairman.

The agreement with the Midland had been further extended until 30 June 1889. In that first half-year period the N & B income from a share of Midland sales revenue was £7,798 against which £5,458 had to be paid to the Midland in expenses. Negotiations over yet another extension had been in hand when they were suddenly broken off on 21 June. This was because Watkin had proposed that the Midland should be satisfied with 50% of the gross receipts for working the line instead of the 70% as hitherto. (In fact, it was 30% of net earnings not gross receipts that had been agreed in 1877.) John Noble, general manager of the Midland wrote to Watkin stating that his company would give up working the line at the end of the month. He did, however, offer a temporary agreement to avoid inconveniencing the public. Watkin made no reply. On 26 June Noble wrote again, this time to the secretary of the N & B, but again there was no reply.

On 1 July the Midland started withdrawing its vehicles onto the SV line and discontinued trains from Swansea to Brecon. For a week the intermediate stations between Ynisygeinon and Brecon were without trains which meant, among other things, no post. This had to be taken by road. Swansea was still in contact with Brecon by way of the B & M and Merthyr but it was a longer journey. For long distance freight to the Midlands and the north of England the Midland was dependent on the GWR handing over their traffic at Gloucester.

After the first week, on 6 July, the N & B started a through passenger service from Neath to Brecon using carriages borrowed from the MS & LR. Goods and mineral traffic resumed between Swansea and Brecon but the N & B took over the traffic from Ynisygeinon. Passengers from Swansea to Brecon had to change at Neath. However, by this time, the dispute had become of wider interest and on 8 July the MP for Swansea raised it in the House of Commons. The President of the Board of Trade replying said he had no authority in the matter but reported the partial resumption of services from 6 July. The parties then resumed negotiations and normal service was reinstated on 22 July. Watkin had proved the ability of the N & B to act independently of the Midland and this was particularly important just at that time as his bill, the Welsh Railways Through Traffic Bill, was being taken through Parliament. When it became an Act it authorised the MS & LR and others to quote through rates for certain traffic and to set up a managing committee to run the scheme. In practice it came to nothing.

That the Midland felt able suddenly to cease operations without risking a serious undermining of their customer relations appears surprising. However, they did have a fall-back position. This dated from negotiations with the GWR as far back as 1863 when the GWR was obliged, as a condition of Midland acquiescence in the take-over of the West Midland, to grant running powers from Worcester to Swansea by way of Hereford, Pontypool Road, Aberdare and Neath. Whether they actually exercised this right in July 1889 is unclear. The image of a Midland tank engine hauling a train of red carriages over the Crumlin viaduct probably never materialised, but there may have been some Midland goods traffic hauled that way. In any case this alternative was expensive, both for the Midland and indeed for the N & B. They needed one another.

As to the N & B, when the Midland cancelled their operating agreement, they were faced with no income from the 'worked line' as they were ill-equipped to run at short notice such an increased activity themselves. We know from an accident report the type of assistance provided by the MS & LR. The accident in question occurred on 13 July, some 22 miles north of Neath to a north-bound train on its descent from the pass. The train consisted of N & B engine number 2, an 0-6-0T, and four MS & LR carriages, a third class, a composite, another third class and a brake van. The train was running at about 22 m.p.h. and when the left-side leading locomotive wheel rode up on the track it was possible to stop within 150 yards. No one was injured and although two carriages were pulled off the line they remained intact and standing. The Midland, whose permanent way staff were still employed, provided assistance in getting the train back on the track. It was thought the engine manufacturers, Avonside, had failed during a maintenance check to identify a crack in the wheel. The Midland, on the other hand, were considered to have failed adequately to maintain the track.

There is evidence that the N & B and the MS & LR between them made a good job of managing without the Midland. At least one customer wrote to the N & B to praise the railway for coping so well during a difficult time, and actually moving more of his coal than usual because he had had an unforeseen surge in demand.

When the Midland resumed operations, instructions were given to N & B staff not to credit them at the previously agreed rates until new rates had been established by William Pollitt, the MS & LR general manager. The Midland were also presented with a claim for £20,000 worth of extra maintenance to restore the track to its 1877 condition. In a report dated 2 August 1889 Mr I. Russell broke this down as follows:

	£s
bridges	697-6-7
stations	157-2-0
fencing	4,808-16-8
gates	58-0-0
perm. way immediate	3,435-0-0
perm. way future	8,554-0-0
	17,710-5-3

In addition, he commented specifically on the state of Mount Street station. Although not used by passengers, this was still being used by the N & B for goods traffic and was said to be in 'exceedingly bad condition'. In particular, the timber platforms needed replacement. There was generally a lot of rotten wooden fencing along the railway. This had been noted as early as the time of the first Board of Trade inspection in 1866 and was clearly a major problem in a damp climate in a countryside well stocked with sheep. The Midland took the claim to arbitration and Sir Alexander Miller QC found that £6,077 was justified.

By agreement on 26 November 1889 between Noble and Hodges of the Midland and Pollitt, working expenses allowed to the Midland on traffic carried by them over the N & B were to be:

– Midland through traffic ....Pass. 33⅓%..............Goods 37%
– N & B local traffic.....................................15%...........................15%
– Cambrian and lines beyond Brecon...........20%...........................20%
– N & B to pay rent for N & B traffic demanded by B & M
– working expenses were defined as based on the net mileage proportion of the N & B after deduction of 'terminals, paid-ons and other normal allowances'.

What this esoteric railway jargon meant in the language of ordinary people is that whereas from 1877 the N & B had only received 30% of the proportion of net receipts derived from all traffic carried over the 'worked line', wherever it originated and whatever its ultimate destination, from 1889 the N & B received the balance after the Midland had deducted varying percentages of receipts to cover their expenses. Thus, on a Midland passenger ticket from Swansea to Worcester, the proportion over the 'worked line' would be calculated, and the resulting proportion of receipts would be reduced by one third for the Midland's operating costs and the balance passed to the N & B. On local traffic, i.e. that starting and finishing on N & B track whether worked by the Midland or the N & B, the allowance to the Midland on that proportion over the 'worked line' was only 15%. This would be important for the burgeoning mineral traffic from Ynisygeinon up to Colbren and down to Neath. For traffic starting or finishing on that part of the N & B operated by them, and moving onto other lines beyond Brecon, the Midland would receive 20% on that proportion of the total mileage covered which was represented by the 'worked line'. Thus the receipts from a passenger ticket from Neath to say Llanidloes on the MWR would be split in such a way that the N & B received 100% of the proportion of the journey represented by the distance from Neath to Colbren Junction, 80% between Colbren Junction and Brecon, and whatever the Clearing House rate was from Brecon to Llanidloes.

Pollitt considered this was a reasonable outcome. As he said later, the N & B would barely break-even if they had to operate the trains themselves.

This arrangement continued until, in 1911 the N & B proposed a revision. This was felt to be justified by the fact that as a result of a pooling arrangement between the LNWR and the Midland, the N & B had noted a drop in gross receipts thus:

	1909	1910
carted tons	8,660	5,644
not carted tons	63,621	37,052
mineral tons	23,987	11,947
cereal tons	67,653	40,478
N & B proportion gross receipts	£11,948	£7,403
Midland Railway working exp.	£4,299	£2,610
net receipts	£7,649	£4,793

The N & B argued that, as a result, over the 29 miles of 'worked line' they were being paid £255 a mile, whereas the Midland had agreed in 1874 to pay the HH & B £768 plus the cost of working and maintaining the line. They were paying the MWR over 8 miles at a rate of £750 and paid the SV £900 plus repairs. The N & B reckoned it was costing them at least £400 a mile, but the weakness of their position was that the Midland could do it cheaper than they could do it themselves.

From 1 January 1912 until 31 December 1914 the rates were simply:

– all Pass.. 27½%

– all Goods.. 27½%

Thereafter at three months notice they would revert to the previous arrangements.

INTO THE PROMISED LAND 1890-1922

RECEIPTS AND EXPENDITURE IN £s			
YEAR	RECEIPTS	EXPENDITURE	NET REVENUE
1870	10,875	12,001	Nil.
1880	21,818	16,243	5,575
1890	31,469	18,053	13,416
1900	46,450	32,683	13,767
1905	59,481	41,548	17,933
1907	73,469	44,689	28,780
1910	79,443	44,355	35,088
1913	92,089	52,088	40,001
1919	122,197	88,122	39,075
1921	162,641	123,299	39,342

After the excitement of the row with the Midland, things settled down, though the railway was still being run on a shoestring, and its methods were open to criticism. Board of Trade Reports continued to find faults and in 1899 the N & B board decided to invite a senior officer from the GWR to inspect the line, and report on possible economies and 'all matters of expenditure as well'. The assistant superintendent, J. Morris, was appointed to the task and he made a most detailed report which reveals some interesting characteristics of business management at the time and some of the peculiarities featured on the N & B. He was invited back in 1901.

He recommended shortening the railway opening hours from 24 to 18. This required altering the times of trains. On the three days he examined the effect of this, there were five engine failures on a total of 18 trains. By adding an additional passenger train he had caused the passenger revenue to rise threefold, but the locomotives were old. Four goods saddle tanks numbers 1, 2, 3 and 4 were built in 1872 or 1874 and one of the two passenger bogie tanks number 5 was from 1871. In the previous six months there had been 19 failures. When he returned in 1901 there were two new engines numbers 7 and 8 but there had now been 29 failures in the previous six month period. Morris recommended discontinuing operating the company's own workshop and using contractors instead. He felt the same principle should apply to station maintenance.

On staff, he recommended that the board should approve staff numbers on a regular basis. There was some difficulty in retaining staff once trained. He advised against losing a man for the sake of a shilling a week. He was concerned at the practice of paying certain staff during absence and felt this should only occur with the consent of the board. He also thought all staff aged over 60 should have eyesight tests.

Morris saw the need for a water column at Colbren Junction. The Midland were particularly suffering for want of one and Morris was concerned to ensure that they had no grounds for complaint that might cause them to discontinue moving coal up

The water column at Colbren Junction was still in place in 1959 although by that time
passenger trains were confined to the Neath line. 1959.

G.H. Platt

to Colbren. This they were doing rather than down their own line to Swansea, to
the great advantage of the N & B who would be unable to make this movement of
coal as cheaply. This is a particularly interesting observation since only two years
later, in 1903, the N & B took over the running of these trains. The investment in
the water column was expected to be £1,751 and would yield estimated savings of
£35 a year, a 2% return. The investment was made and the savings proved to be
exactly as predicted. The rate of return is hardly exciting but was presumably
considered reasonable in 1901.

One of the matters which had caused concern to the Board of Trade was the
running of mixed trains for colliers with carriages without brakes. This practice
was stopped. The state of the line was also poor. The main line was not too bad but
the Neath branch lacked numbers of sleepers and adequate ballast. The drainage
was poor with much of the line covered in water, and the fencing was broken. By
1901 things had improved but as many as 79 sheep had been killed on the line in
the previous six months. He noticed that the Midland had put up their own trespass
notices. These should be replaced with N & B signs. And there were no public
lavatories at Seven Sisters, Cilfrew or Crynant.

On operational matters he thought the signal-box at Brecon operating the end of
the double-track section at Mount Street could be closed if the B & M could take
over the operation from their box. This was the very box required by the Board of
Trade Inspector in 1871, the absence of which caused the delay in the N & B
gaining access to Free Street. He foresaw the need for extra staff at Cray station
during the building of the reservoir. The rental to the GWR for the use of Free
Street and Neath Low Level stations he considered reasonable at £200 each.

Colbren contrasts. A 1930s excursion emerging from the Junction Line.

R. M. Butterfield/R.C. Riley Coll.

An enthusiasts special, again on the Junction Line, 14 July 1956.

H.C. Casserley.

Freight activity on the Junction Line *c.*1960 with 0-6-0PT 7799.

Millbrook House Ltd.

Finally, he wanted to see a comparison made in regular reports to the board between expenditure on each item compared with the previous year.

The financial results were adequate if not exciting for the half years ending December:

	1897	1898
GROSS RECEIPTS £s	22,073	24,331
WORKING EXPENSES	13,554	14,442
PROFIT	8,519	9,888
OPERATING RATIO %	61	59

The Operating Result or Ratio was annual expenditure expressed as a percentage of total receipts.

The 1898 cost figures include £2,696 allowance to the Midland in respect of expenses. Behind these figures were some startling improvements in the number of passengers originating on the N & B, upset only by the strike of 1921:

YEAR	1ST	2ND	3RD	TOTAL
1896	2,074	543	197,421	200,038
1900	2,890	1,306	325,089	329,285
1905	2,869	3,198	545,538	551,605
1907	2,352	3,346	761,111	766,809
1910	2,305	2,001	956,037	960,343
1913	2,966	-	1,160,994	1,163,960
1921	1,728	-	718,661	720,389

Coal traffic (in tons) also grew:

1881	144,112	1905	599,413	1913	1,322,576
1890	243,827	1907	861,356	1921	611,851
1900	500,692	1910	1,045,883		

Between 1903 and 1912 the N & B made a unique improvement in its operating result while its neighbours were working hard to stand still. Admittedly there had been a deterioration since 1898 but the following table makes the point:

	1903 %	1912 %
Barry	51.54	58.81
Cambrian	63.15	62.02
Rhymney	58.76	59.70
Taff Vale	56.69	56.96
Brecon & Merthyr	63.63	63.93
GWR	61.49	63.92
Neath & Brecon	70.20	54.25

This improvement seems to be due to a large increase in goods train miles. These rose by 58.7% between 1903 and 1912 whereas every other railway in Wales, except the Rhymney, saw a reduction. There was a slight drop in percentage receipts per train mile whereas most other railways were improving these figures by increasing the size of trains. On the N & B, no doubt, there was little scope for much increase in train loads due to the length of sidings and the gradients. It would therefore seem as though it was purely increased traffic, particularly as it coincides with the N & B taking over the movement of coal on the Junction Line with effect from 1903.

As seen in the earlier table, the whole year results deteriorated after the war but were healthy by comparison with other railways. Since 1910 the business had doubled in volume and in 1919, for instance, it was achieving an operating ratio of 68.

The Railways Act 1921 created the Grouping of the railways. On 1 January 1922 the N & B was absorbed into the Great Western. The GWR formally took possession on 24 June that year. It acquired some 40 route miles of railway, 15 locomotives, 44 carriages, 120 goods vehicles, 12 service vehicles, some 280 staff, and a horse. The final issued capital was £1,334,744. An inspection was made by GWR divisional officers for the area accompanied by Henry Denby who had succeeded Charles Talbot as general manager of the N & B in 1921. Thereafter the profitability of the line is not identifiable. It was run as a small part of a large system under a style of management which may be likened to benign neglect.

A short train
leaves Colbren
for Onllwyn
during the early
1960s.
DD Coll.

Chapter 5

REAL ESTATE

The infrastructure of the N & B had little of particular merit. Neither of its terminal stations was its own. Its intermediate stations were very basic, and its greatest feat, its track over the mountains, was nearly all single, and, apart from altitude, had to overcome few major obstacles. An iron bridge over the Usk at Sennybridge and a brick and stone viaduct over the Honddu at Brecon were the only significant structures. It had no tunnels.

Not much is known about the first station at Neath and it is almost certainly inaccurate to refer to a station at all. There were no passenger trains before the opening to Brecon in June 1867 and no evidence of Board of Trade approval of the line. The only references to trains are about goods trains. There may have been some movement of miners up the line but this seems to have been informal and no station appears to have been provided for them.

Neath Low Level had been opened on the mixed gauge S & N line to Swansea East Dock on 1 August 1863. By the Neath & Brecon Act of 1863 the N & B was allowed to use 'Low Level' as it was called but according to a GWR record this opportunity was not taken up until 3 June 1867. By 8 August 1868 over a year later, the GWR at board level was getting impatient for the agreement to be confirmed. Accordingly, Cave met Joshua Williams and agreed to pay £300 a year, though this was soon to be reduced as the GWR realised that the N & B had no money.

The first passenger trains served stations at Neath, Crynant, Onllwyn, Penwyllt, Devynock and Brecon and in the first year, from June 1867 to the end of June 1868, ticket sales were as follows:

Single			Return		
1st	2nd	3rd	1st	2nd	3rd
907	1,453	16,840	338	817	8,243

Between about 1865 and 1877 the main line GW station at Neath, known as High Level, was located above the Low Level station, partly on the bridge over the S & N line. Although more convenient for changing trains, this proved to be a cramped site and the GW later moved to a new site near its original site closer to the centre of the town. There it remains to this day.

The economics of the station operations at Neath were spelt out in a GWR memorandum of 23 May 1868. This covered both the Low and High Level.

JOINT USE OF NEATH STATIONS		
	COST £	AMOUNT TO BE DIVIDED £ p.a.
buildings etc	12,188 at 5%	609-8-0
maintenance		195-0-0
perm. way	127-10-0	47-16-3
salaries/wages	990-4-0	373-0-9
gas/water	140-0-0	
rates/taxes	30-0-0	
		1,395-5-0

Victorian accounting methods are not always immediately comprehensible but it seems that investment in the buildings was depreciated at 5% per annum. The permanent way costs were split between 102 passenger trains and 170 goods a week on both the Low and High Level lines. Out of these totals, the number of passenger trains of each company were GWR 64 a week, N & B 38. The total salaries figure included staff at High Level. High Level was handling 40,606 passengers per annum while Low Level was handling 42,674. It would seem that the N & B had a good deal at £300.

According to the timetables and a GWR record, after 2 August 1878 N & B trains ceased using Low Level and started using a station in their goods yard publicised as 'Neath Cadoxton'. This was presumably a consequence of trains from Neath no longer going any further than Colbren Junction and the need to save money. Cadoxton was the name of the place where the goods yard was located and the name by which it was widely known. The waiting-room and booking-office were located in two covered vans placed on the ground between two running lines in the goods yard. It must have been of a fairly rudimentary nature because in October 1883 a director of the Penwyllt Dinas Fire-Brick and Silica Cement Company wrote to the President of the Board of Trade to complain about the arrangements for passengers on the N & B: 'The station at Neath, the terminus, is a novel arrangement of a dirty old wagon divided in two parts; one the head office we believe, the other the waiting room. To gain the station is not unattended with a certain amount of excitement as it is placed between rails.' The N & B management made a spirited defence. The station was described as being a booking-office and waiting-room constructed from two covered vans 'kept as clean as paint can make them'. The head office was described as a 'good house'. The complaint was blamed on the fact that the complainant owned a locomotive repair business in Neath which the company had recently ceased using.

This was not the only expression of disapproval. *The Cambrian* of 26 July 1878 described the facilities as a 'comfortless, dirty, and inconvenient structure.'

In 1878 the LNWR requested that the N & B consider providing them with stables for three horses at Neath. Presumably they had a local parcels service. Caulfield felt that the investment of £75 was hardly justified but the board decided to go ahead.

From 1 August 1889 the N & B, under the influence of their new chairman, reverted to using the Low Level station in Neath. They were informed of the rental of £200 by letter from the MS & LR whose chairman Sir Edward Watkin had become chairman of the N & B. Watkin told the GWR they should have accepted his earlier offer of £150 but was magnanimously prepared to make a deal at the higher figure. Low Level continued to be used by N & B line trains until closure to passengers on 15 June 1964. It was renamed Bridge Street on 1 July 1924 and Riverside on 17 September 1926.

In 1879 *The Swansea Boy*, a local satirical rag wrote, 'It is currently reported but very generally discredited that the Neath & Brecon company intend building a splendid terminal station at Neath. We have no space for architectural details; all we can say however is, that if business is meant, the new station will rival even St Pancras station.'

In 1895 the N & B built an office and booking-hall at street level above the Low Level station. This rather handsome building survived until the end. It had the appearance of a small country house. Its unique feature was two pagoda-like towers containing lifts from the platform level, joined by what looked like a suspended conservatory but which was, in fact, a footbridge. The two platforms were never busy and it is remarkable that it lasted as long as it did. In 1954 the footbridge was taken down and one of the platforms was closed. After 1964 it was dismantled altogether. One platform survives in 2004.

Neath Riverside station building in 1961.   *R.M. Casserley*

Neath Riverside, the 'up' platform, showing the elaborate over-bridge and one of the lift towers.

DD Coll.

The 'down' platform at Riverside in 1947, before removal of the canopy and over-bridge.
G.A. Hookham

Neath Riverside 'down' platform in 1959, after removal of the canopies, over-bridge and lift towers.
G.H. Platt

The following description of the route over to Brecon is derived in part from a journey made in 1960 by John Davies at a time when the railways to Brecon from all directions were under threat of closure and some documentation of their character was commendably felt to be needed.

An elevated view of the engine shed at Riverside. The presence of pannier tanks, GW coaches and an attractive Western Welsh bus confirm the date of this view, *c.*1936.

W.A. Camwell/R.S. Carpenter

The yard and the final engine shed at Riverside, built in 1946, features in this rather gloomy view. On shed that day were 3650, 4653, 577S, 7799, 8732 and 9734.

Tudor Watkins Coll.

No. 5223 occupies centre-stage in this view of the final shed taken shortly before closure.

John Davies

Nearby Cadoxton Terrace Halt provides a classic example of a delapidated wayside halt; the long grasses on the platform, the glass-less windows in the paint-starved shelter, a broken platform light and an almost illegible running-board. At this time (1959) it was served by half a dozen services daily.

R.M. Casserley

Cadoxton Terrace Halt appears in an altogether more favourable light in this 1962 view of a pannier-hauled single-coach train on a 'down' service.

Alan Jarvis

This attractive low-level viewpoint makes the most of the of minimal facilities at Penscynor Halt. 1962.

John Davies

Neath Riverside was by 1960 one of the quietest stations in the country. Although still located on a through line to the Swansea Docks, the former S & N, passenger trains from Swansea East Dock station had ceased in 1936, and so this was, as far as passenger trains were concerned, a terminus. And by this date only one train a day ran to and from Brecon, so it was rarely congested.

On leaving the station the train forked left at N & B Junction away from the VoN line to Aberdare. To the left was the N & B shed which had been newly built in 1946; it replaced a succession of adaptations of a shed believed to have been first built when the line opened in 1864. To left and right were the sidings of Cadoxton Yard. The single line token was obtained at Neath Yard Box and the single line section began half a mile further on at what was by 1960 the disused Cadoxton Box. Already the climb had begun at a gradient of some 1:64 past two halts, Cadoxton Terrace and Penscynor, only half a mile apart, built in GWR days in an attempt to stimulate custom.

The bridge over the main road from Neath to Glyn Neath caused the company some legal problems in 1893. At this point the railway was already on an appreciable incline and in periods of heavy rain the water flowed down to the bridge and dripped onto the road through gaps between the sleepers. As a result the road became pitted and waterlogged. The company was prosecuted at the Glamorgan assizes for committing a nuisance. The defence was that the bridge was authorised by Parliament and so, since no specification was included in the Act, it was legal. Nevertheless, the question was whether it was reasonable to build a bridge in such a way that it caused a nuisance. Defence counsel tried to threaten the jurymen by reminding them that many people had houses adjacent to the road which doubtless dripped water from their roofs onto the road; notwithstanding the company was found guilty and had to insert iron sheeting under the track to stop the drips.

The current girder bridge slewed across the road from Neath to Glynneath, photographed in March 2004.
DD

At a distance of two miles the train reached Cilfrew where there was a passing loop. It had been decided in 1884 to improve the siding arrangements at Cilfrew and at Seven Sisters so that the goods vehicles could be hauled up the line behind the engine instead of being propelled. The improvement was to take the form of doubling the running line in the stations and providing a loop from which the sidings were led back downward. This work appears not to have been put in hand as there was trouble with the Board of Trade a few years later. Cilfrew station had begun life in about 1889 as a crude platform where trains stopped occasionally. It came to the attention of the Board of Trade in 1892 who were not happy. It was dangerous as the platform was rotten, the line here was on a gradient, and there was no passing loop. The economics of upgrading were however shakey:

Current receipts......................	£200
Expenses after upgrade..............	£100
Gross profit...........................	£100
Less interest 4% on £500............	£20
Contribution...........................	£80

The signal-box and loop at Cilfrew, on a wet and dark January day in 1962, viewed looking down the line towards the station.

Tudor Watkins Coll.

Sunshine at Cilfrew, looking south, as a signalman cycles along the grassy platform, possibly on his way to the box, a quarter of a mile or so up the line. 29 April 1961.

R.M. Casserley

The company did not want to lose the contribution but it was clearly uneconomic to make the upgrade required by the Board of Trade. In the end the board agreed to do without the loop on condition that, in the siding, trains would always have the locomotive at the Neath end of the train, i.e. the downhill end. The company spent £300 on a waiting-room which was completed in October 1895.

After Cilfrew the line entered thickly wooded country on a rising gradient of 1:60, winding its way through the trees with distant mountains appearing above them. Here it crossed the river Dulais. Suddenly, all changed as the train rounded a corner and reached the blackened area surrounding the Cefn Coed Colliery, with slag heaps and empty sidings built in expectation of massive quantities of coal which never materialised. The halt which was derelict by 1960 had been built in 1929 when the colliery opened, a venture with high hopes and major disappointments. At the time of writing, winding gear and a few buildings survive as a museum.

From here the line continued to climb along the side of the mountain to Crynant. This was approximately half way to Onllwyn and was one of the first stations. It was

In 1956 the little platform at Cefn Coed Colliery Halt shows evidence of regular usage by the miners.

DD Coll.

This later view, towards Neath, shows part of Cefn Coed Colliery.

DD Coll.

located on the side of the hill with a fine view across the valley to the high ridge to the west. The attractive little station was built in 1889 in a style unique to the southern section of the N & B. The station building was single storey and made of wood with a curved roof like a railway carriage or a gipsy caravan. Similar structures appeared at Ystradgynlais, Colbren, Onllwyn and originally at Seven Sisters. At Crynant there was a passing loop with a 'down' platform. At the far end of the 'up' platform there was a water tower where most freight trains stopped on their way up the line. To the right could be seen the now disused Crynant sidings and remains of a tramroad from the former colliery. The gradient then increased to 1:57 and the countryside opened out. A little further on the line ran beneath some of the buildings at Dillwyn Colliery and into a cutting, then round a bend and into the Ynisdawley Crossing Loop. This was just below Seven Sisters where the station was located in what has become a small town, named after the local colliery which was in turn named by the owner's son who had seven sisters. The brick station building, which replaced the earlier one, stood by the single platform on the side of the hill with a narrow road bridge crossing at the platform end.

The first of two views at Crynant, looking up the line, featuring the characteristic gable-end of N & B station buildings. A wagon-loading facility at Crynant Colliery is visible in the middle distance. June 1962.

H.B. Priestley/
Tudor Watkins Coll.

A view from the signal-box showing a double-headed 'down' train hauled by Nos 3706 and 9796. July 1962.

John Davies

Looking in the opposite direction, this general view of Crynant is full of interest, not least being the signalman on the board-crossing with the token for the 'up' train.

DD Coll.

On this occasion the signalman balances somewhat precariously on part of the cross-over, to receive the token from the driver of a Brecon-bound train, headed by No. 3768, at 4.32 p.m. on 28 April 1962.

E.T. Gill/GBJ Coll.

The earlier station at Seven Sisters, with an expectant group of travellers anticipating an exciting time at Neath Fair.

Tudor Watkins Coll.

Just beyond the station was the Seven Sisters Colliery and then the gradient eased to 1:75. Here was located the stop board for descending freight trains. A short distance further on was another halt, built by the GWR, at Pantyffordd, and after a mile or so over increasingly open moorland country the train reached Onllwyn. To the right were the sidings and the short colliery branch to Banwen. The station at Onllwyn had two platforms with a signal-box on the downside. From the first opening in 1864, this became an important coal centre and the blackened and torn countryside still testifies to 150 years of coal extraction and treatment.

From here the line curved left past the coal washery, rising at 1:70 to Colbren Junction. In 1902 improvements were made to the passenger facilities and a loop was installed on the Neath side. The platforms were also lengthened. There was a distinctive line of fir trees which still shelter the site when all other vestiges of the railway have disappeared. Shelter was desirable at this windy spot out on the open moorland where the Junction Line from the Swansea valley came in on the left.

A pre-Grouping view of the new station building at Seven Sisters.
Tudor Watkins Coll.

The platform here lay on a gradient which contributed to a problem of levels for the builder of the later brick-built station building. Matters were not helped visually by the introduction of decorative courses of lighter-coloured bricks. This was the only station so treated.
GBJ Coll.

The train featured previously was photographed further into its journey, at Seven Sisters at 4.40 p.m. on 28 April 1962.

E.T. Gill/Revd Brian Arman Coll.

A single-coach train left Seven Sisters for Neath on 6 October 1962. Access to the colliery was beneath the rather substantial footbridge.

Alan Jarvis

Pantyffordd Halt, at the 9½ mile post on 30 May 1954. By 1959, the meagre platform building had been replaced by a rudimentary corrugated iron shelter and the dilapidated platform edge rebuilt.

R.H. Marrows Coll: ref. 733

A view looking
south from the
road bridge at
Onllwyn with
the signal-box
(lower left) and
the characteristic
waiting-room on
the right.
30 May 1954.
DD Coll.

Two panniers,
Nos 3634 and
8732 lurk
beneath the
road bridge at
Onllwyn, on the
occasion of a
special working
up the line after
closure to
passengers.
John Davies

Colbren Junction; a
mecca for enthusiasts
and photographers
for many years. This
general view, looking
south, features the
NCB coal tips at
Onllwyn, in the
distance on the left
alongside the line to
Neath. To the right of
the box lay the
Junction Line to
Ynisygeinon.
July 1962.
John Davies

The box is prominent between the two lines in this view looking north, on 14 July 1956. The actual junction may be noticed in the distant curve.
H.C .Casserley

The rapidly diverging levels of the two lines are most noticeable in this view, emphasised by the relevant platforms. An enthusiasts special awaits its locomotive. 14 July 1956.
H.C. Casserley

Although these platforms had been closed to regular passengers since 1932, the Junction Line platforms looked remarkably neat in 1959.
G.H. Platt

This line branched away from the Midland's SV line at Ynisygeinon Junction and the first station was at Ystradgynlais. This had originally been called Ynysgedwyn after the nearby ironworks but there were few houses there and in 1873 Canon Walters, the rector of Ystradgynlais, wrote to Evan Griffith, the N & B manager in Neath, suggesting that it would be appropriate to follow the lead of the Post Office and alter the station name out of deference to the hundreds of people living in what was now a sizeable village. Nothing was done until Christmas Eve 1892 when Griffith wrote to Talbot in the N & B London office asking why the change had not been made in 1873 and expressing a belief that it would increase the traffic if the name were now changed. Talbot could find no explanation for the inaction but wanted to know why Griffith thought changing the name now would increase the traffic. He also thought Ynysgedwyn sounded 'decidedly pleasanter'. Griffith stuck to his guns and pointed out that the eponymous ironworks had now closed and that the original name was a serious misnomer. In 1889 the station building was described as 'a neat timber passage shed roofed with iron'. The name of the station was changed to Ystradgynlais on 1 May 1893.

Ystradgynlais station, looking north. No date.   *Tudor Watkins Coll.*

The next station up the line was Abercrave. This was built in response to a request from the local inhabitants. The N & B were inclined to agree but needed to know that if the station were built whether the Midland would stop trains there. It opened in 1882. Its site is still discernable even though it closed in 1932. Between there and Ystradgynlais lay the smaller settlement of Pen-rhos where the local inhabitants held a meeting with Evan Griffith in October 1894 in the hope of having their own station also. They currently had a two mile walk to the Midland station at Ystalyfera. Griffith's profitability assessment is interesting. He first took the receipts at the newly opened Abercrave. For the twelve month period to June 1895 these had been:

Foreign traffic	
booked from Abercrave	£41-16-10
booked to Abercrave	£33-1-2
Local traffic	
Abercrave to main line stations	£85-8-8
Abercrave to Neath branch stations	£128-5-9
Grand Total	£288-12-6

An undated view of Abercrave station, the condition of the buildings suggesting that the passenger service may still have been in use at the time.   *NMRW*

A desolate view of Abercrave, looking south, after closure.   *GBJ Coll.*

With 200 houses and an average household of six the population at 1,200 was 50% more than at Abercrave. Profitabilty was established as follows:

Working expenses	£100
Lighting and fuel	£10
Clothing	£7
Stationary/incidentals	£13
Total	£130
Receipts (50% more than Abercrave)	£500
Balance for train expenses	£370
Less 4% interest on £1,000 investment	£40
Balance	£330

The station was not built.

From Colbren Junction the gradient stiffened to 1:50 and the line climbed along the open side of the mountain high above the Tawe valley. Here, in 1907, a severe rainstorm washed away 50ft of embankment under the track, leaving it suspended in mid-air. The line was blocked with 6ft of debris. Fortunately, it happened on a Sunday and on the Monday passengers walked between trains halted at either side of the debris. Both the GWR and the Midland provided wagons to clear the debris and it was calculated that some 160-170 wagons must have been employed. By midnight Monday all had been cleared away and restored. The men who worked all night to get it done were generously rewarded by the company (see Chapter 8).

A general view, looking south, at Penwyllt station after it had changed its name to Craig-y-nos in 1907. Adelina Patti's private stone-built waiting-room is on the right; the wooden waiting-room opposite is in the style of the Midland.

GBJ Coll.

Looking north at Craig-y-nos; this later view shows some degree of modest railway activity. No date.

GBJ Coll.

Cray station in September 1951, showing the dilapidated state of the wooden buildings which were demolished shortly afterwards.

H.C. Casserley

This earlier view of Cray demonstrates that there was very little development here over the years, but that the company extended its meagre revenue by much advertising of various soap powders including Lifebuoy, Sunlight, Vim and Lux.

Tudor Watkins Coll.

At Penwyllt there was a handsome stone station building with two platforms and just beyond it a yard for the quarry. This station, which was one of the first on the line to be opened, in 1867, was extended for Dame Adelina Patti the opera singer (see Chapter 8). In 1907 it was re-named Craig-y-nos after her castle.

The railway continued along the flanks of Fforest Fawr through wild moorland. This is sheep country, where the harsh croak of the raven battles to be heard against the wind. Away to the left are the grassy slopes of Carmarthen Fan. Far below is the main road winding up the valley. In another mile the railway crossed it at the summit on a simple girder bridge through which the narrow road had to make a double turn. Just before the bridge, at Bwlch, was one of the loneliest signal-boxes in the country, built to manage a passing loop, where freight trains pounding up from one side or the other could pause, and wait. This box was closed in the 1930s when the passing loop was lifted.

The descent to Cray station was something of an anticlimax though still at a gradient of 1:51 with the large Crai reservoir on the left, built between 1898 and 1904. Beyond Cray the line continued its descent, through farming country. In 1898 Cray Parish Council were joined by the Swansea Town Council in pressuring the company to improve the waiting facilities at Cray, which were said to be in a 'deplorable state'. Local farmers also wanted a dock for cattle and sheep. The work was completed for £200 by December 1899.

Devynock station opened in 1867 with a substantial goods yard and the buildings bore echoes of a more important past when it was much used by the army and for agricultural produce. On the outskirts of the adjoining village of Sennybridge the line crossed the A40 road on a girder bridge. Immediately after this, a grassy embankment curving away to the left is the remains of what was to have been the Llangammarch branch.

A 1906 view of Devynock station, looking toward Neath.   *GBJ Coll.*

The picturesque nature of this location east of Sennybridge is well captured in this view by Alan Jarvis, looking down the Usk valley towards Brecon. The road is the A40.

Devynock station attracted considerable agricultural traffic to which was added a significant volume of military traffic in more recent years; a military vehicle may be seen in this photograph. 23 June 1962.

Alan Jarvis

Goods traffic is evident in the middle distance of this view of Devynock looking south towards Neath. 6 July 1958.

H.C. Casserley

Again at Devynock, this view out of the window of a Brecon-bound train shows, in the middle distance, the superstructure of the bridge over the A40. 1959.

G.H. Platt

Then the line made its way across the meadows on an embankment to a skewed crossing of the Usk on a lattice girder bridge, and so towards Aberbran. This is pastoral Wales. Occasionally the Brecon Beacons could be seen to the right, high above the trees in the distance. The sites of Abercamlais and Penpont halts are no longer detectable. They were built at the outset to serve two large houses nearby and each consisted of a 60ft long wooden platform with a 10ft sq. wooden cabin and survived until at least 1958. Here the company was asked, in 1894, to allow shooting rights across the line. This was turned down on grounds of safety.

The bridge over the Usk proved to be one of the few important structures on the railway; it crossed both a road bridge and the river on a skew. This view is of the western end.

Tudor Watkins Coll.

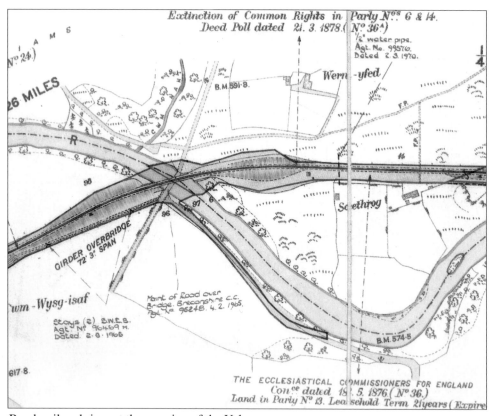

Road, rail and river at the crossing of the Usk.   *GWR Property Plan 1925/Tudor Watkins Coll.*

A family group, optimistically hoping for a train, at Penpont Halt, looking towards Neath.
No date.
Tudor Watkins Coll.

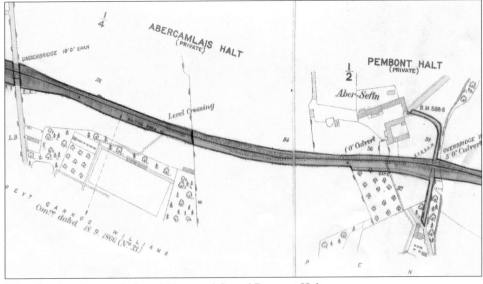

Map showing the proximity of Abercamlais and Penpont Halts.
GWR Property Plan 1925/Tudor Watkins Coll.

The spacious Aberbran station site, looking towards Neath, originally served by two loop lines and an island platform. The surviving platform featured here shows evidence of having been extended and raised. No date.

Tudor Watkins Coll.

A view from the road over-bridge looking down on the very neat single platform at Cradoc station. The approaching train, from Brecon, appears to be hauled by a Midland Railway 0-4-4T engine, *c*.1914.

Tudor Watkins Coll.

A later view, 18 June 1951, of Cradoc looking in the opposite direction, towards Neath.

GBJ Coll.

Like Aberbran, Cradoc station, the last before Brecon, served a small village. In 1889 both stations had an open-sided wooden shed as the sole protection for waiting passengers.

The approach to Brecon was high over the Honddu, a tributary of the Usk, on a masonry viaduct. Just before the viaduct, on the right, the remains of Ely Place goods depot, closed in 1955, could still be seen. The viaduct had been built on seven arches with iron girders at either end and with a capacity for two tracks, but this capability was never exercised. Financial constraints and the need for haste had necessitated it being finished off in wood. This quickly deteriorated and by 1870 it was necessary to replace it with stone. The 1869 Act allowed £2,500 for improvements but by 1872 Caulfield estimated the likely cost at £3,185-8-6. Double track was still felt unnecessary so all the timbers were replaced on the arches but only on one side on the girder portions. In the event the cost was close to Caulfield's estimate. The viaduct dominated that part of the town of which there were good views from the train.

Brecon: Ely Place goods yard entrance. 16 May 1965.
Tudor Watkins Coll.

The relationship between the railway and the goods yard entrance is just apparent in this view. Engine No. 3768, with a train from Neath. October 1962.

John Davies

Another passenger train from Neath, crossing the viaduct over the Afon Honddu. Engine No. 3652.
John Davies

This building is believed to have been used as Mount Street station.
DD

Brecon Free Street station photographed in September 1962. In the usual Neath platform stands No. 3768 with a Neath-bound train, whilst No. 46510, on the right, has brought a train from the direction of Three Cocks Junction. *John Davies*

Beyond the viaduct, on the left, is a row of houses, one of which was used as Mount Street station. This was in the middle of Brecon with the cattle market on the right, below a low embankment along which the railway ran into Free Street station. The handsome station building was across the track on the north side. Access to it was over a crossing, for there was no footbridge. Relatively few passenger trains have ever gone right through the station, and none without stopping, and the frequency of trains of all kinds in and out of Brecon was so low that it was not difficult for passengers making their way to and from the distant platforms to avoid them. It was only for just over an hour a week that Brecon was busy, even though it was the meeting point for trains from four directions. Between 5.30 p.m. and 6.30 p.m. on a Saturday there was a time when all four platforms were occupied. The train from Neath arrived at 5.00 p.m., followed at 5.25 p.m. by a train from Moat Lane, at 5.36 p.m. by a train from Newport, and at 5.56 p.m. by a train from Hereford. At 6.00 p.m. the tide began to ebb with a train to Hereford, presumably composed of carriages which had arrived earlier in the day.

THE BRECON SAGA 1863–72

The story of how the N & B eventually entered Brecon is complex. It may be thought odd that the provision of a single through station at a small town in the middle of the country could cause so much difficulty. The process which took nearly 10 years to be resolved involved five different companies, two of whom, the B & M and the N & B

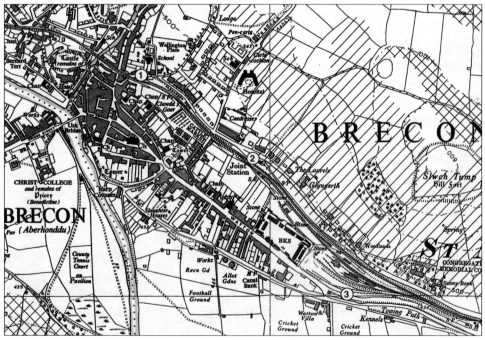

A plan of Brecon showing the path of the railway through the heart of the town and the stations at: 1 Mount Street; 2 Free Street; 3 Watton.

OS map, courtesy Brecon Museum

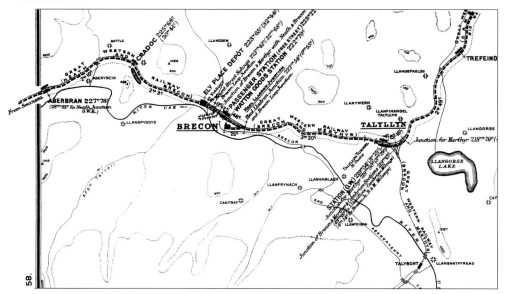

A further extract from the MR Book of Plans, showing the railway arrangements around
Brecon and Talyllyn Junction.

Courtesy Peter Kay

found it almost impossible to agree about anything, in spite of having the same
chairman. Perhaps it was Banks himself who could not prevent the muddle and
incompetence which bedevilled the process. He was not helped by the cantankerous
local solicitor to the B & M, Joseph Cobb, nor by the financial shenanigans of John
Dickson. Distrust within the B & M of the N & B intentions, the looming presence of
the Midland, and the financial problems of both the HH & B and the B & M
conspired to make a complicated situation worse. The MWR, as noted earlier, was for
a time looking for a way to Llandovery. To attempt to unravel the tangled and
incomplete evidence requires a gradual and step by step revelation of the facts, such
as they are, and some conjecture, but in the process the flavour of mid Victorian
railway practice is revealed.

Perhaps it will be forgivable at this stage to retrace some of the steps recorded
earlier in this tale. Brecon had benefitted from rail freight from a comparatively
early date, for the first rail-based operation was the tramroad known as the Hay
Railway which was completed from a canal wharf in Brecon as early as 1816. The
Brecon & Abergavenny Canal had itself been opened in 1800. However, the first
railway train into Brecon arrived nearly 50 years after the Hay Railway; this was a
B & M train which arrived from Pant, just above Dowlais, on 1 January 1863. After
climbing over the Brecon Beacons the line descended on a long incline to a
crossing of the Usk at Tal-y-bont. It then proceeded northward to Talyllyn Junction
where it joined the old Hay Railway. Here the line turned west again through an old
tunnel, originally built for the Hay Railway, and then towards the north bank of the
Usk in Brecon. It ended at a station near the canal at Watton where there was a
single platform.

The Hay Railway closed when it was taken over by 'proper' railways. Its route had been shared between three companies, the HH & B taking the eastern part as far as Three Cocks Junction, the MWR the central portion from there to Talyllyn Junction, and the B & M the western end from Talyllyn Junction into Brecon. Running powers into Brecon for the MWR and the HH & B were part of the deal. The next of the trio to get a train into Brecon was the MWR when they finally completed their line to Talyllyn Junction on 19 September 1864. The HH & B train followed within days.

As has already been mentioned, the HH & B had originally planned to terminate at a station to be located to the north of Brecon and just outside the town. It was to this station that the Swansea & Neath & Brecon Junction Railway had been projected in 1861. When at the end of 1862 the N & B decided to seek approval to extend their line to Brecon, Banks as a director of one and secretary of the other clearly saw the desirability of a through route going through the heart of Brecon rather than by-passing the town. Accordingly, the N & B plans for access to Brecon from the west provided for a line into the centre of the town, though the station arrangements were not very precisely specified. It was noted earlier that the concept of a joint station was authorised in the 1863 N & B Act and that by that Act the N & B was to terminate at an end-on junction with the B & M. The exact location of this was not prescribed. Conybeare, the engineer of the B & M, knew that Watton would not be able to serve all the railways expected at Brecon but recognised that it would be preferable to have a single station for all. He was therefore fearful of the possibility of a joint through station not including the B & M and set about identifying a site suitable for all the parties. Mount Street appeared the most obvious but it would be difficult to find adequate space there. Because of this Dickson, in November 1863, agreed to buy land on behalf of the N & B to provide sufficient space for a station at Mount Street. This site was close to the centre of the town and near the cattle market. The price of £7,000 was to be paid to the owner John Williams in £4,000 worth of debentures and the balance on completion. It is shown in red on the plan drawn up in 1867 (page 116).

The double-track link line between the N & B and the B & M, looking towards Mount Street station over what was N & B property. No date.
Tudor Watkins Coll.

Meanwhile, the B & M was engaged in some strategic action. In 1863 Parliament had authorised the Brecon Junction Railway from Brecon to Llandovery. This was put forward by the B & M as a means of keeping control of the western approaches to Brecon in the face of the N & B offensive. In 1864 the B & M put forward a bill to merge with the Brecon Junction and the HH & B. In spite of opposition from the N & B, Parliament approved the merger of two of the parties, the HH & B with the B & M, in 1865. Banks became chairman of the B & M in the process, having become chairman of the N & B on 22 February. The N & B was supportive of a bill of the Vale of Crickhowell Railway to approach Brecon up the Usk from the east and this authorising Act contained, as we shall see shortly, confirmation of the B & M's authority to build a line to a junction with the N & B.

This carefully constructed house of cards suddenly collapsed when, early in 1866, Thomas Savin the railway speculator and contractor who had been managing both the HH & B and the B & M suffered a financial collapse. Like Dickson, he had relied on cheap finance. The B & M nearly collapsed too and for the next three years had continuous trouble with creditors. On top of this, in 1868, the deal with the HH & B had to be unwound as preference shareholders had not been consulted. The deal was held to be invalid. Banks' enthusiasm to get things done had again let him down.

Against this background the N & B was slowly gaining physical access to Brecon, and as early as April 1865 the B & M wrote to the N & B suggesting joint use of a station at Brecon. During 1866 the N & B line was completed, including the building of a stone viaduct over the river Honddu. A temporary station with a wooden platform was built at a house in Mount Street, between the viaduct and Free Street. On the far side of the bridge over Free Street there was to be an end-on junction with the B & M. On 7 August 1866 the first notification was made to the Board of Trade that the line from Neath to Brecon would be ready for inspection within the space of 2-3 weeks. On 8 January 1867 the N & B notified the board that all the necessary drawings, required before ten days notice to open was given, had been sent to them. On 29 March the board were told that the N & B were ready to open.

Nothing appears to have happened for a month. Then, on 1 May Captain Tyler reported on his inspection. There was a long list of inadequate features:

- rails needed straightening;
- fencing needed strengthening;
- there were 47 bridges under and five over, and the girder bridges needed strengthening, including possibly that over Free Street though no specific reference was made;
- the junction at Neath needed improvement; (Reference to a new station suggests that it was already planned to switch to the Low Level from the makeshift arrangement at Cadoxton Yard.)
- cuttings required better draining and the banks were to be made good;
- at Penpont, where there was to be a private station, signals were needed and telegraphic communication with the next stations;

This plan of part of Brecon was drawn up in 1867, in connection with a legal dispute. It shows, from left to right, the site of Mount Street station, the double-track connection between the N & B and the B & M, and the boundary between the two. The smudged pencil square on the bottom right corner of the plan is Watton station. The site of the future Free Street station is just above the words 'Tydfil Junction Railway'. The pink area, bottom left, shows where John Dickson had purchased land and the critical location of Cobb's land.

National Archives RAIL 1057/1466

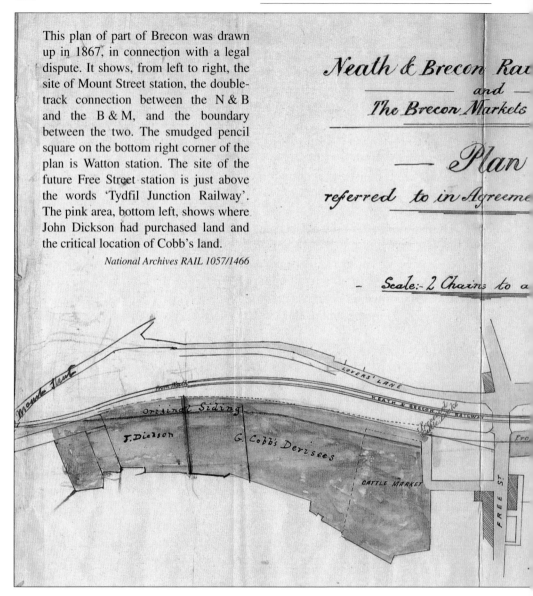

– where temporary timbers had been used on the Brecon viaduct they needed strengthening;
– the double line should be completed from Mount Street to the end-on junction with the B & M; (According to the B & M inspection the following day the double track appears to have been laid, but not provided with signals.)
– arrangements should be made for the use of Mount Street as a joint station.

Meanwhile the B & M were seeking approval to open from Heol Lladron to the end-on junction with the N & B and gave notice on 10 April. This line had a complex authorisation which casts interesting light on the way these things were

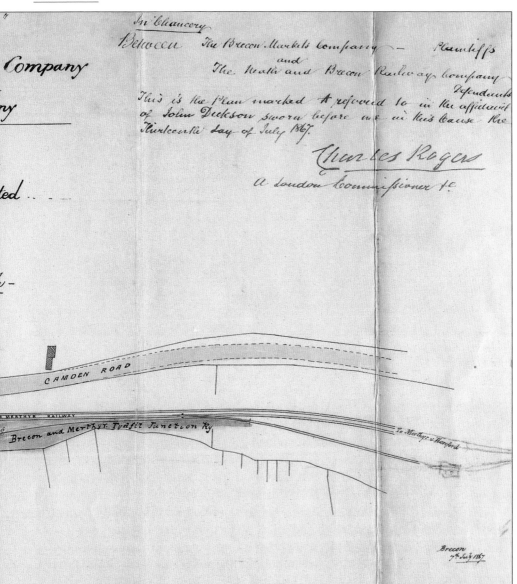

arranged at that time. The line in question, which was to be double track, diverged from the line into Watton at Heol Lladron, a road which ran under the railway east of Watton. The idea that there might be a line across the centre of Brecon, just north of the line into Watton, appeared for the first time in the plans included with the Brecon & Merthyr Act of 1861 which foresaw a junction east of Watton from which a line ran across the north of the town centre terminating at a point just to the north-west of the barracks and some way short of the eventual end-on junction. The first reference to that line having an end-on junction with the N & B was in the Vale of Crickhowell Act of 1866. This was a development of an earlier Act of 1864 which had authorised a railway from the MTA in Abergavenny to Crickhowell.

Watton station, on the right-hand side, the original terminus for the lines to Merthyr and mid Wales.

Courtesy Brecon Museum

This small town lies on the Usk between Brecon and Abergavennny, east of Talybont. The 1866 Act extended the 1864 line westward to Brecon to a junction with the N & B (no wonder they supported it) 'at or near the point where that railway is authorised to cross Free Street'. Authority to build that part of the railway lying west of the B & M, that is between Talybont and Brecon, was to be in suspense for one year to give the B & M time to implement the approval contained in their Northern Lines Act, also of 1866, to double their line from Talybont to Brecon and build 'an extension to and effect a junction with the N & B at Brecon'. This concession to the B & M was the price for the Vale of Crickhowell giving up the right acquired in their 1866 Act to build a line to Abergavenny from Talyllyn Junction. The line west from Heol Lladron was to form the vital link between Hereford and Swansea, but it could only function as a passenger line when the N & B had completed the link and provided a joint station suitable for all parties. It could, however, function as a through goods line and the first train over the 'connected system' was reported on 15 March 1867. Passenger trains were another matter and in view of the number of objections it is not altogether surprising that on 29 April 1867 Captain Tyler rejected the B & M application. Opening was to be postponed one month because:

– although the double track was now laid all the way into Mount Street station, the signalling and junction arrangements were not complete and there was no agreement on joint user of the station;

– the intended continuation of the Watton branch westward to a junction with the new
line needed agreement between the companies on methods of working;

– signals and points were needed at Heol Lladron Junction and at a location on the
Watton branch (probably to the turntable, as that is mentioned later).

The N & B engineer, Hans St. George Caulfield, acted quickly and only three
weeks after Tyler's critical report of 1 May produced a detailed confirmation of the
action taken. The Board of Trade said that Tyler was too busy to visit south Wales
but on the strength of Caulfield's report and subject to a satisfactory confirmation
of the method of working, the line could be opened from Neath as far as Mount
Street. On 27 May Banks signed a sealed undertaking. The go-ahead was given two
days later. The first passenger train ran from Neath on 3 June 1867, though regular
services appear to have started on 8 June.

On 18 June the B & M gave their second notice to the Board of Trade that the
line from Heol Lladron to the end-on junction was ready for passenger traffic. Tyler
came down again on 13 July and again rejected the line:

– the second line was now laid from the junction to Mount Street; (This description is
unclear as double track into Mount Street was reported laid on 29 April. More likely
it refers to the extension from Watton which was needed if Mount Street was to
become the joint passenger station, leaving Watton as the joint goods station.)

The N & B was principally a single-track railway, but the connecting line between their
system and the B & M was double track. In this photograph, looking west from Free Street
station, both lines are, somewhat unusually, in use. The boundary between the two systems
was just beyond the two trains. The locomotives featured are Nos 46519 and 8732. 7 July
1962.
John Davies

Another view from Free Street looking west towards Mount Street. August 1954.
GBJ Coll.

By 1964, the double track had been singled. In this view, looking west towards Mount Street, the site of the market is on the left.
GBJ Coll.

Free Street station from the west.   *GBJ Coll.*

– there was no way of getting B & M passengers into Mount Street for although a portion of one platform was allocated to the B & M and preparations had been made for bringing a line of rails to that platform, completion was delayed due to problems in acquiring the necessary land;

– proper passenger accommodation was needed at Mount Street.

The B & M were clearly intensely frustrated by this further refusal. Henshaw, the general manager, wrote to the Board of Trade in July desperate to open on 1 August, but on 14 August Tyler was still reporting that there was no accommodation at Mount Street. On 3 September the B & M blamed the N & B for having failed to put in the necessary siding at Mount Street and asked permission to open as far as the junction. (It is unclear what they would have done with the passengers there as there was not even a platform available.) Tyler replied that the portion of line between the junction and Mount Street had not been approved because Mount Street was not complete; this was because the N & B could not get hold of the land needed which was owned by Joseph Cobb, who besides being a prominent solicitor in the town happened also to be solicitor to the B & M. Tyler insisted that the B & M should withdraw their application and wait for the arrangements at Mount Street to be completed. The N & B, he reported, had wrongly believed that they had permisssion to open to the end-on junction. Their original permission was to Mount Street only. N & B passengers wanting to travel further east from Mount Street and needing to make their way to a train for Merthyr, Hereford or Llanidloes at Watton had no direct connection. Caulfield told a House of Lords Committee in 1869 that after their tickets had been taken at Mount Street, passengers were put on a locomotive and ferried across the Free Street bridge and then dumped at a point above Watton and left to make their own way down to the platform there. There was no such opportunity in the opposite direction and no passenger trains from the MWR, the HH & B or the B & M entered Mount Street.

On 6 September 1867 the B & M withdrew their request for inspection of the line from Heol Lladron to the end-on junction.

During these exchanges the B & M and the N & B had been discussing the lay-out of the proposed new Mount Street station, which was to be a joint station for all companies. In October 1866 a draft agreement was produced by the B & M. On 10 January 1867 a deputation from the B & M attended a board meeting of the N & B and they agreed the joint station should be located between Struet (the street parallel to the river Honddu, bridged by the viaduct), Mount Street, the end-on junction between the two companies, and a similar distance east of that junction. Watton was to be a joint goods station

On 15 March 1867 N & B shareholders were told that connection had been made with the B & M at Brecon. On 2 May it was reported that a committee of the companies interested in the joint station had been set up and had met at Ethelburga House until 'a late hour'. Negotiations, particularly between Banks and Cobb, were very strained. A draft of the contract exists in the National Archive with Banks' amendments and temperate comments in blue and Joseph Cobb's appropriately in red, accompanied by his acrimonious and tetchy remarks. Dickson produced a drawing of the proposed station and eventually the agreement between the B & M and the N & B was signed. Banks' signature appeared for both parties. The other N & B signatories were Layton, Cox and Dickson.

By this agreement the N & B was to accommodate both B & M and MWR passengers at Mount Street, the B & M sharing the cost of wages but not rent. The B & M was to accommodate the N & B local goods at Watton, the B & M receiving normal terminals charges, the N & B contributing to the wages bill. Neither company would charge the other for use of the new line between Mount Street and Watton but each would allow the other to charge for such use by other companies as if it were their own line. The N & B was to double the line between Mount Street and what was termed 'Heolrhyd Terminus'. (This refers to the end-on junction between the two companies just east of Free Street at a road under the line called Heol Rhyd. In fact, it looks as though this line was already double.)

In order to acquire sufficient land to extend Mount Street and make it suitable as a joint station, an undertaking had been given to Lord Camden who owned land at Cae Prior, just to the north of the centre of Brecon. Due to the failure to exercise the right to this land, to extend the station, the B & M was seeking a contribution towards a £10 p.a. penalty due to Lord Camden. The N & B considered the B & M should pay Lord Camden out of the 'terminals receipts' at Watton, but on 9 September 1867 the N & B agreed, after much delay, to pay half. Meanwhile, the B & M were still insisting on the access to Mount Street station granted under the

A troop train bound for Sennybridge passing the west end of Brecon Free Street station
c.1960.

John Davies

May agreement. John Dickson, who was still contractor to the N & B, explained that the B & M could not have the access to Mount Street while work was in hand on a siding required by Capt. Tyler. The B & M reiterated their demands and the N & B explained they were still waiting for Tyler to see the siding he had told them to put in. By 16 October 1867 the two parties had fallen out and in despair the B & M cancelled the May agreement.

There is then a most peculiar incident which is hard to understand and explain. On 5 December 1867, on receiving a complaint from the Brecon magistrates, the Board of Trade wrote to the N & B seeking explanation of the 'lawless manner' in which they were conducting their affairs. The fact that Dickson 'undertook to explain all' suggests that the problem lay with Dickson. In view of his financial plight it is reasonable to assume that he was using the land he had bought for the N & B, but which was surplus to the requirement of the railway, as collateral for loans on which he was slow to pay interest. Two local landowners, Messrs Wilts and Tippett, are recorded as being in this position. There is no evidence that this had any influence upon the Board of Trade inspectors, though on the 7 May 1868 the Board of Trade were still seeking an answer to the complaint of the Brecon magistrates. The only other dubious practice of which we are aware today was the carriage of passengers across Brecon on locomotives but Caulfield admitted that quite openly to the Committee of the House of Lords in May 1869 and it elicited no comment. The most likely source was Joseph Cobb, the B & M solicitor, who admitted he was bad tempered, and whom Cave censured with acting throughout with the intention of bringing the N & B down. Evidence of his attitude was revealed in another land dispute.

This arose just west of the end-on junction. Initially the Brecon Markets Co., which ran the market in the centre of Brecon, had been supplied with a siding off the N & B. In order to increase accommodation at Mount Street, it was now desired to have the siding come off the B & M line (see previous plan). The N & B were willing to make the change free of charge and the Market Co. was to give up land it did not need north of the railway. Unfortunately, one of the owners of the market and its solicitor was Joseph Cobb. He wrote in typically choleric vein to Caulfield on 21 June: 'I am exceedingly disgusted at the activity shown in getting me to pay for what I agreed to pay for, while the performance by Mr Dickson of what he has agreed to do is laughed at as an idle joke. Further the excessive beastliness of the men in the pathway reserved for use by myself and family which has now been going on unrestrained for upwards of 12 months is enough to ruffle the temper of a less irritable man than myself.' Cobb then took the matter to the Court of Chancery seeking Specific Performance by the N & B. His petition failed, largely because neither he nor his client owned the parcel of land on which he wanted Dickson to start work. The record states that a compromise was found.

The deal with Cobb took time to conclude and on 14 September 1868 when the N & B board met at the Castle Hotel in Brecon, Cave, now N & B chairman, reported that he had agreed with Cobb a redefinition of the boundaries where the line passed over Cobb's land, a right of way crossing from Lovers' Lane to

Clawdd-y-gaer, and a £16 p.a. rent for the land north of the railway line and between it and Lovers' Lane. A hint as to the reason for the delay in resolving the land issue lies in a comment by the B & M to the Board of Trade in September 1867 to the effect that Cobb was at that time ready to sell at a price to be agreed with the N & B provided the N & B would pay for it. Anyway, on 14 September 1868 it was reported that the N & B were preparing the siding accommodation 'for the joint service of passengers at Brecon Station over Cobb's land'.

Later that September, the N & B told the Board of Trade that the line from Mount Street to the end-on junction was ready. On receipt of this, McGregor the senior manager in the Railway Department wrote: 'What portion of railway is this? It does not appear to have been inspected or even a final notice given.' Tyler was sent to inspect. On 20 October he reported:

- it was 15 chains from Mount Street to the end-on junction just beyond Free Street bridge;
- the line could only be opened simultaneously with the B & M part. The reason for the N & B giving notice was in order to accommodate the Mid Wales who were keen to use Mount Street rather than Watton; (Presumably Watton was congested and interchange for passengers to and from Neath was difficult as it involved walking between Watton and Mount Street.)
- Mount Street was judged unfit for additional traffic. There were no arrangements for turning or watering engines. The station consisted of two lines of rail with a platform on either side and one dock line, but no sidings;

On 11 September 1951, the 8.25 a.m. train from Neath arriving at Brecon Free Street.

H.C. Casserley

- Tyler wrote: 'Opening of this portion of railway would under existing circumstances and by reason of the incompleteness of the works be attended with danger to the public using it.'
- he recommended the best solution would be an entirely new joint station on a new site.

On 12 November 1868 the N & B withdrew their request to open from Mount Street to the junction. What happened to the MWR is unclear as there is a surprising statement from the Board of Trade, dated 22 October 1868, authorising them to use Mount Street and this was confirmed in an Act of Parliament in 1869. However, Caulfield told a Committee of the House of Lords in May 1869 that no movements were made westward from Watton by any railway company and by that time the B & M, presumably to spite the N & B, had in any case taken out the points at the junction between the junction line and the Watton link. The result of this was that any goods train wanting to move from Mount Street to Watton had to proceed along the new junction line to Heol Lladron and then reverse down to Watton.

The idea of an entirely new site for the joint station seems to have been acknowledged by the parties for on 30 September 1868 joint discussions were being held between the N & B, B & M and MWR over the use of three Brecon stations, presumably Watton, Mount Street and a new one. As early as 14 February 1868 the B & M had reported to Tyler that, having failed to come to an agreement with the N & B over Mount Street, they had agreed with Lord Camden on a new site for a joint passenger station near the end-on junction and mid-way between Watton and Mount Street. This materialised as Free Street station.

Things must then have moved fairly quickly. By June 1870 the N & B felt matters had progressed so far that the Midland should be consulted. Allport was reported as saying that 'he thought it the proper course to be adopted'. By December that year the B & M were ready to open. There must have been some last minute hitches for on 19 December the B & M had to send a telegram to the Board of Trade saying 'not ready'. The next day a plan of the new station was despatched. On 11 January 1871 the B & M asked for an inspection to be held on 26 or 27 January. Tyler made it to Brecon on 8 February and rejected the application on the grounds that although the station was complete, there was a need for further signalling arrangements, new rails and better fencing between the new station (Free Street) and Mount Street. On 24 February the B & M asked if they could open as far as Free Street. Tyler agreed on the strength of an undertaking to have the interlocking signals at the end-on junction ready by the end of March. The B & M and the HH & B, which was now part of the Midland, started to use the new station on 1 March 1871. The MWR began using the new station on 1 May. The N & B and B & M signed the agreement over use of the joint station on 4 January 1872.

For a year the N & B was prevented by the Board of Trade from using the new station but eventually received clearance to start on 6 March 1872. The reason for the delay was given by Caulfield in a letter to the N & B board that day. He wrote that there had been a need for a signal-box to control the end of the double track section at Mount Street station. This section of line appears to have caused enormous difficulties for the N & B ever since it was constructed and it is hard at this distance to understand just why. There had clearly been a reluctance to spend money, and the availability of land was for a time a problem, but it remains a mystery why an apparently intelligent and able engineer like Caulfield had so much difficulty. Once Free Street was accessed, the N & B continued to use Ely Place for coal distribution and Mount Street for general goods. Passenger trains from Swansea to Brecon Free Street were operated until 2 July 1877. From that date these trains were taken over by the Midland. From the same date the Midland used Watton for goods.

The future of Mount Street proved another bone of contention as early as August 1877. At this date the Midland closed Mount Street to goods traffic. In July 1878 the N & B, having woken up to this, declared that the Midland had no right to do this and claimed a proportion of all receipts at Brecon as though Mount Street were still open. The Midland argued that Mount Street was quite inadequate, a simple platform and 'not a station at all' and that the N & B only kept it open to avoid the cost of sharing use of Watton. The N & B argued that the 'worked line' terminal at Watton became an intermediate as opposed to a terminal station if traffic was operated to Watton as it lay beyond the junction where the N & B and B & M met. Unfortunately, the N & B were unable to identify the value of their claim for damages without being told by the Midland how much terminal traffic they had lost, since the Midland was responsible for keeping the records. The outcome is not

A present-day view of Free Street (from left to right) and the site of the railway bridge. Beyond it, where the Fire Station now stands, lay Free Street station. The photographer was standing virtually on the track-bed.

DD

revealed but it looks as though the odds were stacked against the N & B. Although use of Mount Street was apparently discontinued, it took a long time to die and was still listed as a destination in the 1932 GWR Working Timetable and in the Western Region Working Timetable as late as September 1960.

Brecon provided a bone of contention again in 1889, this time involving not only the N & B and the Midland, who were by now on the same side, but the B & M, Pollitt of the MS & LR, and Phillips of the North Staffordshire Railway as an arbitrator. In all there were 53 written exchanges between 27 July 1889 and 28 October 1891 involving these parties on the issue of whether N & B local traffic between the junction and Watton was covered by the payments made by the Midland or whether, as contended by the B & M, it should be treated as separate and pay a further charge. The record, though immensely detailed, is tantalisingly silent on the outcome.

When the GWR took over the N & B line trains from the LMS in 1931 they continued to use Free Street and Watton, as did the diminishing service operated by British Rail. These services ceased on 15 October 1962 and the sites of the Brecon stations were gradually absorbed into the town. Free Street became a station of another kind, a fire station. Watton became a car park. Only Mount Street survives, but as a private house.

Opening dates for stations are notoriously imprecise. In the absence of a board minute or other official notice it is necessary to rely on company timetables or Bradshaw or the known date of the first passenger train. Closing dates are usually more precisely defined. Opening and closing dates for the stations on the N & B seem to have been as follows:

Neath Low Level	3 June 1867–1 August 1878
Neath N & B	2 August 1878–31 July 1889
Neath Low Level	1 August 1889–15 June 1964
Cadoxton Terrace Halt	18 March 1929–15 Oct. 1962
Penscynor	1 August 1929–15 Oct. 1962
Cilfrew	Dec 1888–15 Oct. 1962
Cefn Coed Colliery Halt	8 September 1929–15 Oct. 1962
Crynant	3 June 1867–15 Oct. 1962
Seven Sisters	before 11 March 1875–15 Oct. 1962
Pantyffordd Halt	2 September 1929–15 Oct. 1962
Onllwyn	3 June 1867–15 June 1964
Colbren Junction	10 Nov. 1873–15 Oct. 1962
Craig-y-nos (Penwyllt until 31 Jan. 1907)	3 June 1867–15 Oct. 1962
Cray	Feb. 1870–15 Oct. 1962
Devynock	3 June 1867–15 Oct. 1962
Abercamlais Halt	3 June 1867–15 Oct. 1962
Penpont Halt	3 June 1867–15 Oct. 1962
Aberbran	14 Sept. 1868–15 Oct. 1962
Cradoc	1 March 1877–15 Oct. 1962

Brecon Mount Street...3 June 1867–March 1872
Free Street..6 March 1872–15 Oct. 1962
Abercrave...….1882–12 Sept. 1932
Ystradgynlais...November 1873–12 Sept. 1932

SIGNALLING

The N & B was single track except for a short section between Mount Street and the B & M Junction in Brecon and between Neath signal-box and the junction with the VoN in Neath. It only had junctions at Onllwyn and Colbren. Elsewhere there were sidings and passing loops. Accordingly, signalling was not a complex part of the business. Nevertheless, or perhaps because of this, it was the provision of signalling, adequate in the eyes of a Board of Trade inspector, which, as we have just seen, caused such a delay in making progress at Brecon.

At its peak there were 15 boxes on the N & B, the earliest being at Colbren Junction, installed in 1873 when the Junction Line was completed. This was a McKenzie & Holland box. However, just over half the boxes were built around 1895 when interlocking was installed as a result of the 1889 Act and this work was awarded to Dutton. Signals were of the Dutton type with finials similar to those on the Cambrian and LNWR. Until 1917 they were painted red with a white spot but then they were changed to the more normal white bar on red. Distance signals were also red and were individually worked up to the Grouping. This was changed by the GWR.

The signal-boxes were in two colours, brown below and stone above. Window frames were red-brown below floor level and white above. The interiors had white ceilings with joints and trusses salmon. The upper walls were stone and the lower part brown.

Originally a staff and ticket line, by 1900 the whole line was converted to Tyer's No. 6 tablet. In 1903 the single line tablet sections were listed as:

Mount Street to Aberbran	Ystradgynlais to Ynisygeinon Junction
Aberbran to Devynock	Colbren Junction to Onllwyn
Devynock to Bwlch	Onllwyn to Crynant
Bwlch to Penwyllt	Crynant to Cilfrew Loop
Penwyllt to Colbren Junction	Cilfrew Loop to Neath Signal-box.
Colbren Junction to Ystradgynlais	

By 1957 they were:

Neath Yard to Cadoxton	Ynisdawley to Onllwyn
Cadoxton to Cilfrew	Onllwyn to Colbren
Cilfrew to Crynant	Colbren to Devynock and Sennybridge
Crynant to Ynisdawley	Devynock and Sennybridge to Brecon.

By 1960 the first section was from Neath Yard to Cilfrew. The rest were the same.

A GW pannier tank propels 7 loaded wagons up the junction line towards Colbren Junction; 1963.

Private Collection.

A Patti special train passes Onllwyn, *en route* to Penwyllt.

Chapter 6

THE TRAINS

Opening Dates:
Neath to Onllwyn *ad hoc* trains, 2 October 1864
Neath to Onllwyn regular goods trains, September 1865
Neath to Brecon first train, 13 September 1866
Neath to Brecon first regular goods train, 29 September 1866
Neath to Brecon first official passenger train, 3 June 1867
Neath to Brecon Free Street passenger train, 6 March 1872
Swansea to Brecon goods trains, 1 October 1873
Swansea to Brecon passenger trains, 10 November 1873
Swansea to Brecon Board of Trade authorisation, 29 November 1873
Swansea to Brecon Midland take over, 2 July 1877

The N & B was not a prestigious main line. Its traffic was mainly coal and that was over the southern end. Goods trains operated over the route to Brecon and beyond. As for passenger trains, it was at best part of a through route from the Midlands to Swansea, with trains operated by the Midland and for a time the LMS. For the most part it was a local line and much of its passenger trade was the carriage of colliers to and from the mines. For most of the nineteenth century the mines up the Dulais valley were manned by men who lived in or near Neath, so the N & B was a commuter line. For this and its other local trade the directors saw no need to provide luxury travel. Accordingly, the rolling-stock was second-hand, purchased from other railways, and not expected to travel at any speed or to provide anything more than the most basic accommodation.

The first trains ran from an uncertain and informal location in Neath from 2 October 1864. They ran up the Dulais valley as far as Onllwyn, a distance of just over 10 miles. The trains were mainly for goods though they may have had primitive accommodation for miners. From the available evidence it seems that until the line was extended to Brecon, trains were run on an informal and *ad hoc* basis. No evidence of a timetable survives and there were no official stations. There is no evidence that such passenger services as were offered were ever authorised by the Board of Trade. Furthermore, there is no evidence of properly recorded accounts of passenger and goods receipts for this period. They were probably lost in the confusion of Dickson's affairs. On 28 September 1864 the N & B board agreed to let Dickson run the trains 'prior to opening to general traffic and to appropriate profits against debenture interest'. On 27 September 1865 an engineer's report stated that the portion of line open to mineral traffic was 'fully answering expectations as to profitable results'. The fact that formal accounts show figures for passenger receipts starting only in June 1867 may be interpreted as evidence that there were none previously. Further confirmation of this comes from Morley telling a House of Lords Committee on 28 May 1869 that the N & B opened 'for goods and mineral traffic' in September 1865, though only as far as Onllwyn.

On 13 September 1866 the board recorded what would appear to be the first acquisition of rolling-stock. This consisted of three composite carriages, 10 third class carriages, 20 open goods trucks and two passenger vans to be hired or purchased from the Metropolitan Railway Carriage Co. but it was not until 3 June 1867 that the GWR started to hold the N & B liable for rent for the use of their station in Neath.

The first passenger trains as far as Onllwyn were fairly primitive and normally mixed. These trains were still in use in the early 1880s after the line to Brecon had been officially opened on 3 June 1867 but were confined to the original line from Neath to Onllwyn. They are described in a letter of complaint written to the Board of Trade in 1883 thus: '10 to 20 wagons in front of the engine, then a lot more wagons, then the unfortunate passengers, more wagons and a brake.' The writer felt this 'unusual, to say nothing of the inconvenience of having to hold on all the way up which takes from 1½ hours to 3 hours down'. The company, writing in defence to the Board of Trade from its office in Coleman Street in the City of London, defended its practice on the grounds of the layout of the sidings, and, as to the station, said, 'Accommodation afforded at Neath is quite sufficient to meet the requirements of the class of people using it.' Gross passenger receipts in 1882 were only £1-12-0 per mile a week so the London office were to some extent justified in placing a low priority on passenger convenience.

The Swansea Boy had already noted the operating practices of the N & B in 1879 when it wrote, 'The practice of running empty trucks on this line in front of a passenger train and "mixed" trains will also be discontinued so soon after an accident occurs as possible.'

More orthodox goods trains between Neath and Brecon began on 29 September 1866 and on 3 June 1867 passenger services were officially opened from Neath Low Level to Brecon Mount Street station. This changed to Free Street on 6 March 1872. Goods trains had the use of Ely Place, which was a coal depot on the western side of Brecon, while from the time Free Street became available, general goods were handled at Watton.

By 1870 there were three passenger trains a day taking about an hour and three quarters to cover the 33 miles from Neath to Brecon. In the opposite direction there were only two trains a day. Little attention seems to have been paid to the interchange time between stations at Brecon for passengers making their way to and from the Midlands as it varied between 10 and 50 minutes. Since it involved a circuitous route by road or a more direct climb over the intervening tracks, this would have been critical.

At this point it is interesting to pause and look in detail at a tour of inspection made by the Midland directors in July 1872. This was exactly four months after the

MIDLAND RAILWAY.

TIME TABLE OF SPECIAL TRAINS.

For the Information of the Company's Servants only.

DIRECTORS' TOUR of INSPECTION,

Wednesday, July 10th, Thursday, July 11th, and Friday, July 12th.

WEDNESDAY, JULY 10th.

DERBY	....	....	dep.	8 10 a.m.		
Whitacre	....	....	"	" " "		
BIRMINGHAM	....	arr.	9 30 "			
Do.	....	....	dep.	10 3 "		
BARNT GREEN	....	"	10 55 "			
*REDDITCH	....	"	11 15 "			
ALCESTER	..	"	11 40 "			
†EVESHAM	..	"	12 14 p.m.			
ASHCHURCH	....	arr.	12 55 "			
CHELTENHAM	....	dep.	1 20 "			
GLOUCESTER	....	arr.	1 40 "			
Do.	....	dep.	2 10 "			
STONEHOUSE	....	arr.	2 40 "			
Do.	....	dep.	2 46 "			

NAILSWORTH	....	arr.	3 5 p.m.	
Do.	....	dep.	3 10 "	
STONEHOUSE	....	..	3 26 "	
COALEY JUNC'ION	arr.	3 29 "		
Do.	....	dep.	3 40 "	
DURSLEY	....	arr.	3 50 "	
Do.	....	a p.	3 55 "	
COALEY JUNCTION	..	5 2 "		
YATE	....	....	arr	4 47 "	

Go over Thornbury Branch.

YATE	....	....	dep.	5 55 "
MANGOTSFIELD	....	arr.	6 10 "	
BATH	....	....	..	6 30 "

* Pass 9 50 a.m. from Ashchurch at Redditch.
† The 11.30 a.m. Goods from Evesham must not leave until after arrival of Special.

THURSDAY, JULY 11th.

BATH	..	dep.	8 0 a.m.	
MANGOTSFIELD	..	"	8 30 "	
BRISTOL (St. Philips)	..	arr.	6 40 "	
Do.	..	dep.	8 55 "	
Gloucester	..	"	9 48 "	
ASHCHURCH	..	ar.	10 20 "	
GREAT MALVERN	..	"	11 15 "	
MALVERN WELLS	..	dep.	11 20 "	
COLWALL	..	"	11 25 "	
*NORTH END of LEDB'RY TNL	11 30 "			
LEDBURY	..	"	11 35 "	
HEREFORD (Barton)	....	"	12 0 p.m.	
Do. (Morfield)	arr.	12 5 "		
Do. do.	dep.	12 35 "		
MOORHAMPTON	..	"	1 5 "	

†EARDISLEY	..	"	1 20 p.m.	
HAY	..	..	arr.	1 50 "
Do.	..	dep.	2 9 "	
THREE COCKS	..	"	2 30 "	
TALGARTH	..	"	2 37 "	
‡TALYLLYN	..	"	arr.	2 50 "
BRECON	..	arr.	3 0 "	
Do. (Neath & Brecon L.)	dep.	3 5 "		
DEVYNOCK	..	"	3 20 "	
¶PENWYLLT	..	"	3 40 "	
ONLLWYN	..	"	3 55 "	
NEATH	..	arr.	4 20 "	
Do. (Ordinary Train)	dep.	4 46 "		
SWANSEA (High Street)	arr.	5 0 "		

* Cross 10.20 a.m. Goods from Hereford at North End of Ledbury Tunnel.
†8 26 a.m. Goods from Brecon not to leave Eardisley until Special arrives.
‡ Cross 1.10 p m. Passenger Train from Brecon at Hay.
§ Cross 2.20 p.m. Mid Goods from Brecon at Talyllyn.
¶ Cross 3.0 p.m. Passenger Train from Neath at Penwyllt.

FRIDAY, JULY 12th.

SWANSEA, Wind St. (Ord. Trn.)	dep.	11 40 a.m.		
(after arr from Llanelly)				
NEATH,	Do.	arr.	12 2 p.m.	
Do.	....	dep.	12 10 "	
ONLLWYN	..	..	12 32 "	
*PENWYLLT	....	"	12 44 "	
DEVYNOCK	....	"	12 55 "	
†BRECON	....	arr.	1 15 "	
Do.	....	d p.	1 40 "	
‡TALYLLYN	....	"	1 57 "	
TALGARTH	..	"	2 7 "	
THREE COCKS	....	arr.	2 15 "	
HAY	....	"	2 25 "	
EARDISLEY	....	"	2 37 "	

MOORHAMPTON	....	..	2 47 p.m.	
HEREFORD (Moorfields)	..	3 5 "		
Do. (Barton)	..	3 10 "		
LEDBURY	..	..	3 35 "	
COLWALL	....	..	3 42 "	
MALVERN WELLS	....	..	3 48 "	
GREAT MALVERN	....	..	3 53 "	
WORCESTER	....	arr.	4 15 "	
Do.	....	dep.	4 20 "	
BROMSGROVE	....	..	4 40 "	
BARNT GREEN	....	..	4 50 "	
CAMP HILL	....	..	5 5 "	
SALTLEY	....	..	5 10 "	
DERBY	....	....	..	6 25 "

* Cross 11.45 a.m. Passenger Train from Brecon at Penwyllt.
† The 1 0 p m. Goods from Neath to wait at Brecon until Special arrives.
‡ Cross 11.30 a.m. Passenger Train from Llanidloes, and 12.30 p.m. Mid. Pass. Train from Hereford at Talyllyn.

Mr. Maxey to provide Saloon and Guard.

Derby, July 6th, 1872.

E. M. NEEDHAM.
Superintendent.

National Archives

through line to Free Street station in Brecon had been opened. One might have expected that they would have wanted to look at Mount Street and understand something of the difficult history of the arrangements at Brecon but they were only allowed five minutes stop-over at Free Street. The hour and twenty minutes allowed for the journey to Neath was considerably faster than the time the scheduled trains were taking. It is also surprising that they did not pause at Colbren Junction to have a look at progress on the Junction Line. This line must already have been of critical interest to them and was due to be opened on 1 November in the following year. They were already in discussion with the SV having in the previous March set up a sub-committee of the board to negotiate acquisition. All the more surprising therefore that they did not travel over this railway even in a local 'ordinary train'.

When this photograph was taken the interchange at Neath involved a road journey of almost a mile.

Courtesy Tudor Watkins

Once they reached Neath they would have had the short-lived benefit of an easy interchange from Low Level to High Level before taking a GWR train to Swansea High Street. High Level was a temporary station which suffered from being squeezed onto the bridge over the line of the S & N. They might have been able to see the change-over from broad to standard gauge at this point as this was carried out during 1872. Having reached Swansea, it would be surprising if they had not made a site visit to St Thomas station of the SV and it must be safe to assume that dinner that evening was in the company of Starling Benson.

The following morning it appears that they went on to Llanelly. This seems an odd thing to have done as, by this time, the LNWR had gained access to Swansea Victoria over lines it had recently acquired from the Llanelly, and the Llanelly Railway itself was about to be leased to the GWR. It is interesting to see that later that morning they left Swansea from Wind Street station. This former S & N station, which was used by VoN line trains from Hereford, had opened in 1863 and was about to be closed to passenger traffic in 1873. Its wooden platform was squeezed between the mixed-gauge tracks on a brick viaduct adjacent to the LNWR terminus at Victoria. Access to the track was from an entrance in one of the arches and up a flight of stairs. Their train from Wind Street might have been a through train to Hereford, a short-lived service which was cut short at Pontypool Road the following year. At Neath they would have been able to remain on the platform at Low Level for their saloon carriage to arrive from the sidings. Then there was another relatively quick journey to Brecon without stopping at Colbren Junction and, after a short stop, away towards Derby. A fascinating journey made at a particularly interesting time.

On 10 November 1873 the Junction Line was at last opened from Colbren Junction to an end-on meeting with the SV at Ynisygeinon Junction. The N & B now operated four passenger trains a day from Swansea to Brecon, taking 2 hours 10 minutes in each direction. Neath appears to have been relegated to branch line status from this time though R.E. Bowen recorded that one train a day ran from Neath up to Colbren and then down to Swansea St Thomas. This unlikely operation must have been of short duration. The SV which had reciprocal rights over the N & B operated through goods trains to Brecon. This was recorded in a board minute of 5 February 1874, but there is no record of any passenger trains. A typical N & B passenger train of the time is recorded in an accident report dated 29 March 1874. This covered a derailment at Ynisygeinon Junction. The N & B train from Brecon was hauled by a tender engine, either *Neath* or *Brecon*, and consisted of three four-wheeled coaches and six vans. On 29 January in the following year a similar train was derailed just outside St Thomas station, this time hauled by one of the 0-6-0STs built by Avonside.

According to *The Cambrian* there was, from the opening of the Junction Line in 1873, a daily MWR passenger train between Swansea and Llanidloes. Departure from Swansea was at 11.05 a.m. with arrival at Llanidloes at 3.30 p.m. According to Bradshaw, a similar train was still running in 1887, splitting at Three Cocks with the front portion for Llanidloes and the rear for Hereford.

Already in November 1874 the Midland was showing in its timetable three trains a day each way between Brecon and Swansea without any acknowledgement that they were operated by the N & B. They appeared under the heading 'Hereford, Hay and Brecon Branch'. In January of the same year, when the HH & B still existed as an entity, trains between Swansea and Brecon were mentioned in the table headed Hereford, Hay and Brecon Railway and credit was still being given to the N & B.

With effect from 1 April 1875 the Midland Working Timetable included one through Midland goods train a day in each direction between Brecon and Swansea. The same timetable gave instructions that these trains should be worked with two guards and two 'breaks'.

In spite of this incursion by the Midland, the traffic was increasing and this had some effect upon the N & B financial performance, even though it was insufficient to cover the cost of the debt. The growth can be seen in the increase in train mileage for the following half year periods:

Dec. 1869   46,417 (Passenger & Goods)
Dec. 1875   85,348 (of which Passenger 61,828)

TABLE 41] [FEBRUARY, 1870.

BRISTOL AND BATH BRANCH.

BRISTOL TO BATH.

Fares from Bristol: Single Journey 1st Class	Single 2nd Class	Single GOV	Return 1st Class	Return 2nd Class	Stations	Week-days 1 (1 2 GOV)	2 (1 2 GOV)	3 (1 2 Class)	4 (1 2 GOV)	5 (1 2 Class)	6 (1 2 Class)	7 (1 2 Class)	8 (1 2 GOV)	9 (1 2 GOV)	10	11	Sundays 1 (1 2 GOV)	2 (1 2 GOV)	3 (1 2 GOV)	4 (1 2 GOV)
..	..	..	..	..	BRISTOL dep.	7 10	9 15	10 25	11 55	1 35	3 45	B 5 10	6 10	7 35	..	..	9 40	..	4 45	7 [illegible]
0/7	0/5	0/3	1/0	0/9	Fish Ponds	7 19	..	10 35	..	1 4	..	5 19	6 20	..	..	..	9 49	..	4 51	..
1/0	0/8	0/5	2/0	1/3	MANGOTSFIELD	7 28	9 30	10 40	12 10	2 10	..	5 28	6 27	7 50	..	..	9 58	11 25	5 5	7 15
1/1	0/9	0/6	1/10	1/3	Warmley	7 34	9 36	10 46	..	2 16	..	5 33	6 31	7 56	..	..	10 4	11 31	5 11	7 21
1/2	0/9	0/6	2/0	1/3	Bitton	7 40	9 42	10 52	12 18	2 22	4 1	5 39	6 35	8 2	..	..	10 10	11 37	5 17	7 27
1/3	1/0	0/8	2/1	1/8	Kelston, for Saltford	..	9 48	..	..	2 28	..	..	6 41	..	..	..	..	..	..	..
1/11	1/4	0/11	3/3	2/3	Weston	7 50	9 55	11 2	12 27	2 35	4 10	5 48	6 48	8 12	..	..	10 20	11 47	5 27	7 37
2/2	1/6	0/11½	3/9	2/6	BATH arr.	7 55	9 58	11 5	12 30	2 38	4 15	5 51	6 53	8 15	..	..	10 25	11 50	5 30	7 40

BATH TO BRISTOL.

Fares from Bath: Single Journey 1st Class	Single 2nd Class	Single GOV	Return 1st Class	Return 2nd Class	Stations	Week-days 1 (1 2 GOV)	2 (1 2 GOV)	3 (1 2 Class)	4 (1 2 GOV)	5 (1 2 Class)	6 (1 2 Class)	7 (1 2 GOV)	8 (1 2 Class)	9 (1 2 Class)	10 (1 2 GOV)	11	Sundays 1 (1 2 GOV)	2 (1 2 GOV)	3 (1 2 GOV)	4 (1 2 GOV)
..	..	..	..	..	BATH dep.	7 40	8 15	9 20	10 42	1 15	2 40	4 15	6 30	7 25	8 15	..	10 45	4 25	6 30	8 15
0/3	0/2	0/1	0/6	0/4	Weston	7 43	8 18	9 23	10 45	1 18	2 43	4 18	6 33	7 28	8 18	..	10 48	4 28	6 33	8 18
0/10	0/7	0/4	1/5	1/0	Kelston, for Saltford	..	8 25	..	..	1 25	..	..	6 40	..	..	..	..	..	..	..
1/2	0/10	0/6	2/0	1/5	Bitton	7 53	8 31	9 33	10 55	1 31	2 53	4 28	6 46	7 38	8 28	..	10 58	4 38	6 43	8 28
1/6	1/2	0/8½	2/6	2/0	Warmley	7 58	8 37	9 39	11 1	1 37	..	4 34	..	7 44	8 34	..	11 4	4 44	6 51	8 34
1/10	1/5	0/10	3/3	2/5	MANGOTSFIELD	8 4	8 46	..	11 9	2 3	3 4	4 43	6 57	7 50	8 43	..	11 13	4 50	6 57	8 41
2/2	1/6	0/11½	3/9	2/6	Fish Ponds	8 10	8 52	..	11 15	2 11	3 10	4 49	7 3	..	8 49	..	11 27	..	..	8 48
2/2	1/6	0/11½	3/9	2/6	BRISTOL arr.	8 20	9 3	9 55	11 25	2 25	3 20	5 0	7 13	..	9 0	..	11 40	..	..	9 0

B Third Class to Fish Ponds.

BRISTOL MARKET.

CHEAP RETURN MARKET TICKETS are issued to BRISTOL EVERY THURSDAY, as under:

From	Times	Fares for the Double Journey: 2nd Class	3rd Class
From Bath	at 7.40, 8.15, and 10.42 a.m.	2s. 0d.	1s. 3d.
" Weston	" 7.43, 8.18, and 10.45 a.m.	1s. 6d.	1s. 0d.
" Kelston for Saltford	" 8.25 a.m.	1s. 3d.	0s. 9d.
" Bitton	" 7.53, 8.31, and 10.55 a.m.	10d.	7d.
" Warmley	" 7.58, 8.37, and 11. 1 a.m.	(as above)	(as above)
" Mangotsfield	" 8. 4, 8.46, and 11. 9 a.m.	9d.	6d

Available for returning from Bristol, on the day of issue only, to Mangotsfield at 5.10, 6. 10, & 7.35 p.m. To Bitton, Weston, & Bath at 3.45, 6.10, and 7.35 p.m. To Warmley at 5.10 and 7.35 p m., and to Kelston for Saltford at 6.10 p.m. only. If used by any other Trains the Tickets will be forfeited, and the Ordinary Fare charged.

Table 42.]

HEREFORD, HAY, & BRECON RAILWAY.

Miles from Brecon	Stations	Week-days 1	2	3	4	5	6
	NEATH (N. & B.) dep.	..	8 25	11 0	3 15	..	..
..	Penwyllt "	..	9 5	11 46	4 5	..	..
..	Devynock "	..	9 35	12 19	4 35	..	..
..	Brecon arr.	..	10 0	12 45	5 0	..	..
..	NEWPORT (Dock St.) dep.	..	7 35	..	..	..	..
..	Cardiff (T. V.) "	..	..	8 20	..	..	..
..	Merthyr (V. of N. Sta.) "	..	8 55	11 40	..	..	..
..	Dowlais "	..	9 10	11 50	..	..	..
..	BRECON (B. & M.) dep.	7 15	10 10	12 55	5 40	..	..
4	Talyllyn Junction "	7 30	10 20	1 10	5 50	..	..
9	Talgarth "	7 40	10 37	1 25	6 5	..	..
..	Mid Wales: Llanidloes dep.	..	7 0	11 30	4 30	..	..
..	Mid Wales: Rhayader "	..	7 30	12 10	5 5	..	..
..	Mid Wales: Builth (Wells) "	..	9 50	1 0	5 38	..	..
11¾	Three Cocks Junction dep.	7 47	10 42	1 35	6 15	..	..
12¾	Glasbury	7 52	10 55	1 40	6 20	..	..
17	HAY	8 2	11 5	1 50	6 30	..	..
20½	Whitney	8 11	11 15	1 59	6 39	..	..
24	Eardisley	8 19	11 24	2 7	6 45	..	..
25½	Kinnersley	8 25	11 29	2 12	6 50	..	..
29	Moorhampton	8 35	11 59	2 22	7 2	..	..
33½	Credenhill	8 45	11 49	2 32	7 12	..	..
37½	HEREFORD (Moorfields Stn.) arr.	8 55	12 0	2 45	7 25	..	..
..	Hereford (Barton Station) dep.	9 5	12 55	4 5	..	..	..
..	Ledbury arr.	9 30	1 20	4 30	..	..	..
..	Great Malvern "	9 45	1 36	4 46	..	..	..
..	Malvern Link "	9 49	1 59	4 50	..	..	..
..	Worcester "	10 5	1 55	5 10	..	..	..
..	BIRMINGHAM "	11 17	3 20	6 15	..	..	..
..	LEICESTER "	12 35	6 40	8 35	..	..	..
..	DERBY	12 45	6 5	7 35	..	..	..
..	Liverpool "	4 20	9 21	11 25	..	..	..
..	MANCHESTER "	3 0	8 5	10 0	..	..	..
..	Nottingham "	1 39	7 5	8 25	..	..	..
..	SHEFFIELD "	2 8	7 40	8 53	..	..	..
..	Wakefield (Westgate) "	3 10	9 12	..	..	..	..
..	Wakefield (L & Y.) "	3 10	9 10	9 55	..	..	..
..	LEEDS "	3 35	9 45	10 15	..	..	..
..	Bradford "	4 50	11 10	11 10	..	..	..
..	YORK "	4 15	10 10	11 50	..	..	..
..	Hull "	5 30	11 10	12 30	..	..	..
..	Scarboro' "	6 30	..	..	..	..	..
..	NEWCASTLE "	7 55	12 35	..	..	..	..

Miles from Hereford	Stations	Week-days 1	2	3	4	5	6
	NEWCASTLE dep.	..	11 23	..	8 30	..	..
..	Scarboro' "	..	..	..	9 20	..	..
..	Hull "	..	..	..	10 40	..	..
..	YORK "	..	2 10	..	11 45	..	..
..	Bradford "	..	..	5 0	12 0	..	..
..	LEEDS "	..	2 40	5 40	12 45	..	..
..	Wakefield (L. & Y.) "	..	..	6 5	1 7	..	..
..	Wakefield (Westgate) "	..	..	6 5	1 8	..	..
..	SHEFFIELD "	..	4 7	8 5	2 12	..	..
..	Nottingham "	..	6 5	9 25	2 40	..	..
..	MANCHESTER "	..	..	7 10	1 0	..	..
..	Liverpool "	..	..	..	11 42	..	..
..	DERBY "	..	7 0	10 20	3 35	..	..
..	LEICESTER "	..	7 0	9 40	2 55	..	..
..	BIRMINGHAM "	..	9 0	12 50	4 50	..	..
..	Worcester "	..	10 10	1 30	6 0	..	..
..	Malvern Link "	..	10 26	2 4	6 14	..	..
..	Great Malvern "	..	10 35	2 8	6 18	..	..
..	Ledbury "	..	10 50	2 25	6 35	..	..
..	Hereford (Barton Station) arr.	..	11 15	2 59	7 0	..	..
..	HEREFORD (Moorfields Stn.) dep.	9 35	12 20	3 10	8 0	..	..
4¼	Credenhill	9 45	12 30	3 20	8 12	..	..
8¾	Moorhampton	9 55	12 42	3 32	8 22	..	..
11¾	Kinnersley	10 3	12 52	3 42	8 32	..	..
13¾	Eardisley	10 8	12 58	3 48	8 42	..	..
16¾	Whitney	10 16	1 6	3 56	8 50	..	..
20¼	HAY	10 26	1 16	4 6	9 3	..	..
24¼	Glasbury	10 36	1 26	4 16	9 15	..	..
26	Three Cocks Junction arr.	10 42	1 30	4 21	9 25	..	..
..	Mid Wales: Builth (Wells) arr.	11 50	2 [illegible]	6 10	..	..	..
..	Mid Wales: Rhayader "	..	3 6	6 45	..	..	..
..	Mid Wales: Llanidloes "	..	3 25	7 20	..	..	..
28½	Talgarth arr.	10 50	1 40	4 29	9 32	..	..
33½	Talyllyn Junction "	11 5	1 55	4 45	9 50	..	..
37½	BRECON (B. & M.) "	11 20	2 5	4 55	10 0	..	..
..	Dowlais arr.	..	3 7	6 3	..	..	..
..	Merthyr (V. of N. Stn.) "	..	3 15	6 15	..	..	..
..	Cardiff (T. V.) "	..	4 35	8 5	..	..	..
..	NEWPORT (Dock St.) "	..	..	7 40	..	..	..
..	Brecon dep.	11 55	..	5 45	..	..	..
..	Devynock arr.	12 19	..	6 9	..	..	..
..	Penwyllt "	12 54	..	6 39	..	..	..
..	NEATH (N. & B.) "	1 43	..	7 20	..	..	..

The Trains are all First, Second, and Third Class between HEREFORD and BRECON.

NOTE.—Passengers travelling locally between Brecon and Talgarth and Three Cocks, or between Talyllyn and Talgarth or Three Cocks are not conveyed by these Trains.

A MARKET TRAIN for HAY and INTERMEDIATE STATIONS leaves HEREFORD (Moorfields Station) at 4.30 p.m. on WEDNESDAYS.

NOTE.—The Times from Noon to Midnight are distinguished by the Thin Line, see Cover.

February 1870 Midland Timetable includes the N & B. *National Archives*

TABLE 51.　HEREFORD, HAY, & BRECON RAILWAY.

Miles from Brecon	STATIONS		WEEK-DAYS 1	2	3	4	Miles from Hereford	STATIONS		WEEK-DAYS 1	2	3	4
	N. & B. SWANSEA	dep.	..	8 0	11 5	3 20		NEWCASTLE	dep.	7 8	11 23	2 15	8 30
	Neath	,,	..	8 15	11 5	3 40		Scarboro'	,,	7 0	..	..	9 10
	Penwyllt	,,	..	9 15	12 16	4 36		Hull	,,	8 50	..	5 45	10 30
	Devynock	,,	..	9 45	12 43	5 6		YORK	,,	9 38	2 10	6 50	11 45
	BRECON	arr.	..	10 10	1 5	5 32		Bradford	,,	9 15	10 30	6 55	11 55
								LEEDS	,,	10 5	2 40	7 45	12 40
	B. & M. NEWPORT (Dock St.)	dep.	..	8 5	..	12 40		Wakefield (L. & Y.)	,,	8 53	11 15	8 15	1 0
	Cardiff (T. V.)	,,	..	8 20	11 0	..		Wakefield (Westgate)	,,	..	..	8 12	12 10
	Cardiff (Rhymney Rly.)	,,	..	..	..	9 0		SHEFFIELD	,,	11 26	4 7	9 50	2 15
	Swansea	,,	..	7 45	..	..		Nottingham	,,	11 35	..	10 10	2 40
	Merthyr (V. of N. Sta.)	,,	..	9 5	12 20	..		MANCHESTER	,,	6 15	..	9 45	1 0
	Dowlais	,,	..	9 15	12 15	2 10		Liverpool (Brunswick)	,,	4 45	..	8 15	8 40
								DERBY	,,	12 35	6 55	11 35	3 40
4½	BRECON	dep	7 10	10 30	1 10	5 50		LONDON { Moorgate St.	,,	..	..	6 15	11 27
9½	Talyllyn Junction	,,	7 12	10 45	1 25	6 0		{ St. Pancras	,,	..	..	..	11 45
	Talgarth	,,	7 33	10 58	1 38	6 15		Leicester	,,	..	..	8 40	2 55
								BIRMINGHAM	,,	2 45	9 5	12 40	4 50
	Mid Wales ABERYSTWITH	dep.	..	8 0	12 30			Worcester	,,	7 35	10 20	2 0	6 10
	{ Llanidloes	,,	..	6 40	11 30	4 37		Malvern Link	,,	8 0	10 46	2 20	6 31
	{ Rhayader	,,	..	7 35	12 8	5 10		BRISTOL (via Malvern)	,,	..	7 45	..	3 25
	{ Builth (Wells)	,,	..	10 5	1 0	5 46		Bath (via Malvern)	,,	..	7 30	..	3 5
								Great Malvern	,,	8 5	10 52	2 27	6 40
11½	Three Cocks Junction	dep.	7 41	11 10	1 55	6 25		Ledbury	,,	8 27	11 16	2 44	6 59
13½	Glasbury	,,	7 47	11 14	1 59	6 30		Hereford (Barton Station)	arr.	..	11 55	3 28	7 35
17½	HAY	,,	7 57	11 24	2 9	6 40							
21½	Whitney	,,	8 6	11 33	2 18	6 49		HEREFORD (Moorfields Stn.)	dep.	9 25	12 30	3 40	8 0
24½	Eardisley	,,	8 15	11 40	2 25	6 56	4½	Credenhill	,,	9 35	12 39	3 50	8 10
26	Kinnersley	,,	8 21	11 45	2 30	7 2	8½	Moorhampton	,,	9 43	12 47	3 58	8 20
29½	Moorhampton	,,	8 30	11 52	2 37	7 9	11½	Kinnersley	,,	9 50	12 55	4 5	8 28
33½	Credenhill	,,	8 39	12 0	2 45	7 18	13½	Eardisley	,,	9 55	1 0	4 11	8 34
37½	HEREFORD (Moorfields Stn.)	arr.	8 50	12 10	2 55	7 30	16½	Whitney	,,	10 3	1 8	4 19	8 44
							20½	HAY	,,	10 13	1 17	4 27	8 54
	Hereford (Barton Station)	dep.	9 52	12 35	3 40	7 45	24½	Glasbury	,,	10 23	1 32	4 39	9 4
	Ledbury	arr.	10 40	1 15	4 10	8 24	26	Three Cocks Junction	arr.	10 27	1 37	4 45	9 9
	Great Malvern	,,	11 5	1 40	4 33	8 44							
	BRISTOL (via Malvern)	,,	2 30	..	..	..		Mid Wales { Builth (Wells)	arr.	11 50	2 19	6 18	..
	Bath (via Malvern)	,,	2 7	..	12 20	..		{ Rhayader	,,	..	6 5	6 31	..
	Malvern Link	,,	11 10	1 45	4 38	8 49		{ Llanidloes	,,	..	3 30	7 30	..
	Worcester	,,	11 35	2 3	5 0	9 10		ABERYSTWITH	,,	6 24	..	..	..
	Leicester	,,	1 23	3 25	6 40	10 18							
	BIRMINGHAM	,,	3 50	6 15	7 48	..	28½	Talgarth	arr.	10 34	1 52	4 56	9 16
	LONDON { St. Pancras	,,	6 40	8 55	10 0	4 30	33½	Talyllyn Junction	,,	10 45	2 5	5 9	9 32
	{ Moorgate St.	,,	7 4	9 10	13 0	..	37½	BRECON	arr.	11 5	2 20	5 20	9 45
	DERBY	,,	2 45	6 0	8 7	12 38							
	Liverpool (Brunswick)	,,	6 27	9 31	11 25	..		M. Dowlais	arr.	..	3 10	6 27	..
	MANCHESTER	,,	5 20	8 15	10 0	..		& Merthyr (V. of N. Stn.)	,,	..	3 17	6 30	..
	Nottingham	,,	3 50	7 10	9 8	1 40		B. Swansea	,,	..	..	8 20	..
	SHEFFIELD	,,	4 11	7 44	9 37	1 43		Cardiff (Rhymney Rly.)	,,	..	..	..	..
	Wakefield (Westgate)	,,	..	9 0	..	..		Cardiff (T. V.)	,,	..	4 0	7 55	..
	Wakefield (L. & Y.)	,,	..	..	..	..		NEWPORT (Dock St.)	,,	..	4 35	8 2	..
	LEEDS	,,	5 10	..	..	5 50							
	Bradford	,,	6 15	10 15	..	3 0		BRECON	dep.	11 25	2 30	5 55	..
	YORK	,,	6 40	10 16	..	3 55		Devynock	arr.	11 47	2 56	6 19	..
	Hull	,,	7 50	11 10	..	4 32		Penwyllt	,,	12 16	3 26	6 48	..
	Scarboro'	,,	9 10	..	..	7 45		Neath	,,	1 15	3 57	7 5	..
	NEWCASTLE	,,	11 20	12 35	..	5 58		SWANSEA	,,	1 35	4 40	8 2	..

NOTE.—The Times from Noon to Midnight are distinguished by the Thin Line see Cover.

A year later, Swansea has been added but as part of the N & B and, presumably, using the Swansea & Neath from Wind Street.

National Archives

When finally, on 2 July 1877, the Midland took over all passenger services between Swansea and Brecon, the N & B was confined to operating a branch line service between Neath and Colbren Junction. The Midland continued to operate three trains a day in each direction between Brecon and Swansea. The journey time was reduced by five minutes to 2 hours 5 minutes in both directions. A through Birmingham/Swansea carriage was provided on the 12.40 p.m. from Birmingham to Swansea and the 8.00 a.m. and 11.00 a.m. from Swansea. The Working Timetables reveal that variations were made in the arrangements for these through carriages over the years. Thus in 1893 there were still through carriages from Swansea to Birmingham at 8.00 a.m. and 11.00 a.m. and now one to Worcester at 7.15 p.m. In the opposite direction, through carriages were available from Worcester at 7.40 a.m. and 2.15 p.m. There were also through carriages from Birmingham as far as Brecon at 8.45 a.m. and 5.10 p.m. The journey time between

Swansea and Birmingham was seven hours, and, hardly surprisingly, this service ceased on 31 December 1916 during the First World War and was never revived. In its last year there was only one through carriage from Swansea to Birmingham at 8.30 a.m. and one back from Worcester at 2.22 p.m. A footnote in the 1893 Working Timetable stated that passengers wanting a taxi on arrival at Swansea should alert the stationmaster at Brecon. Presumably, taxi drivers did not expect much custom from the normal users of St Thomas station.

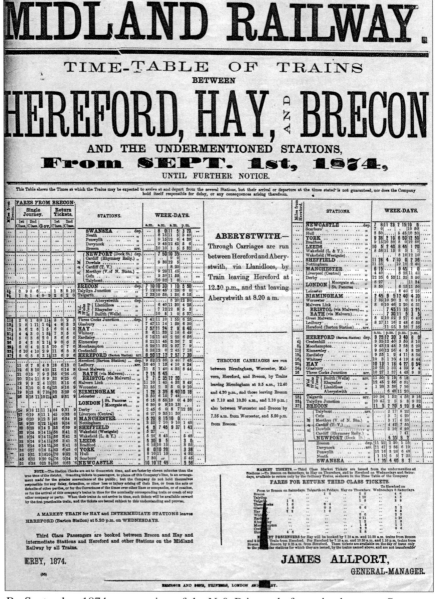

By September 1874, no mention of the N & B is made for trains between Swansea and Brecon via Neath.

National Archives

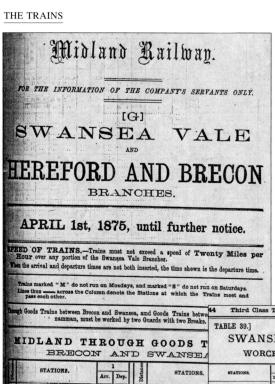

April 1875, the Midland Railway Working Timetable includes Brecon to Swansea goods trains over the Junction Line.

National Archives

Midland Timetable for 1877 includes Swansea to Brecon as part of the Midland. Neath is mentioned as a N & B connection.

National Archives

The 1902 N & B Working Timetable mentioned in small print that traffic on the main line was worked by the Midland Railway but otherwise only distinguished between the Main Line and Neath Branch Line. All reference to train operating was as though it were all N & B. There were passenger trains from Swansea to Brecon at 8.05 a.m., and 11.05 a.m. and 3.35 p.m. timed at just under two hours. From Brecon there were the 8.10 a.m., 11.20 a.m. and 5.55 p.m. On a Friday, which was market day in Brecon, there was an afternoon train to Devynock returning the same afternoon.

The carriages in use on the N & B were not the most up-to-date. For the colliers' trains it was not felt necessary to provide anything other than an absolute minimum of accommodation on four wheels. The only larger carriages appear to have been six-wheelers, all purchased second-hand from the LSWR. Four-wheelers were supplied by the MS & LR, North London, and Hull & Barnsley in particular. On the N & B, until about 1910, all were painted cream above and brown below, similar to the GWR colour scheme. Thereafter they were brown all over.

The Midland also used four-wheelers until the 1880s. A typical train immediately after the take-over would have consisted of a set of three vehicles, two 20ft brake/thirds, and a 24ft first/second composite. Thereafter a typical set was composed of a Clayton 31ft. brake/third, a 31ft composite, a 31ft third, and a 40ft brake/composite. This type of train lasted until the LMS days. The through coach for Birmingham, which ran until 1916, was a 33ft 6 inch clerestory composite. During the LMS period ex-Midland six-wheeled clerestory carriages were used, typically two brake/thirds, a lavatory third, and a lavatory composite. Towards the end, former LNWR carriages began to appear. Efforts were made to stimulate

An example of the LSWR six-wheeler carriages purchased by the N & B. This example is thought to be N & B No. 48, which was a 34ft composite. At the time of the photograph, the vehicle was in use on the Bishop's Castle railway.   *Tudor Watkins Coll.*

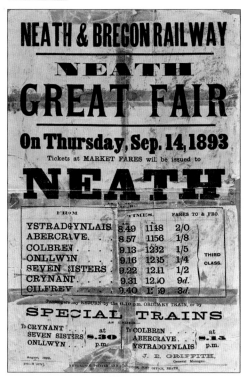

The N & B generated additional funds by running special trains, even over the 'worked line' as demonstrated by this poster from 1893. *TW Coll.*

Another example of N & B promotions, again including the 'worked line'. *TW Coll.*

passenger traffic and there were a number of excursions and special trains offered. One particularly interesting attempt was included in the Summer Timetable of 1908 in the form of a through carriage from Swansea St Thomas to Aberystwyth, leaving at 11.00 a.m. and running by way of Brecon to Moat Lane, where it was attached to a south express from Welshpool at 3.15 p.m. It arrived at its destination at 5.30 p.m. The return journey took from 1.00 p.m. to 7.40 p.m. It only lasted for one summer. The GWR alternative, by way of Carmarthen and Lampeter, was quicker and more frequent.

The other trains were all goods, but operating all round the clock. For instance, in 1902 a general goods train left Swansea at twenty-five minutes after midnight and reached Brecon at 4.20 a.m. later that morning. It was due to pass another in the opposite direction which left Brecon at 1.45 a.m. and was due at Swansea at 5.30 a.m. The passing place was Penwyllt. It passed another train for Swansea, which left Brecon at 3.00 a.m., at Devynock. Two mineral trains and four goods trains occupied the line in each direction for the rest of the day. One of these from Brecon was scheduled to take 11 hours over the journey, pausing for lengthy shunting at every station.

Passenger traffic at
Brecon station,
1906.
Brecon Museum

General view of
Brecon Free
Street in 1905.
Little change
took place over
the years.
Brecon Museum

A delightful picture of Brecon youngsters 'on parade' for a Sunday School trip, at Free
Street station *c*.1915.

Brecon Museum

The line was expensive to operate due to the gradients. For example, freight trains had to be banked in both directions up to Bwlch. Once there the banker would run round and couple onto the front of the train in order to assist in holding the train on the descent. Between Brecon and Ynisygeinon all freight trains had to be provided with two guards and two 10 ton brake vans. With single engine trains both vans were to be at the rear of the train, but in cases where two engines were employed one brake van had to be in the middle of the train and the other at the back.

Goods traffic was normally exchanged at Brecon where the Midland was allowed 45 minutes for marshalling the traffic. At Colbren the approach to the exchange siding on the Neath branch was on a heavy gradient and guards were required to exercise great care. At Ynisygeinon Junction there was no space for interchange sidings and so this was carried out half a mile down the valley at Ynisygeinon sidings on the Midland's Brynamman branch. Here, betwen 1890 and 1910, there was a considerable traffic in coal from Brynamman to the Midlands.

N & B goods vehicles were often purchased second-hand. In 1899 a report identified a stock of 29 goods and cattle wagons, 14 covered wagons, 4 timber trucks, and 3 brake vans. This was considered at the time to be inadequate and led to purchases over the following years of 12 ballast wagons, 2 brake vans, 6 covered vans and a Great Eastern horse box. Most of the mineral traffic would have been carried in private owner wagons as was the general practice in south Wales. The livery of company owned vehicles was lead-grey with black ironwork and white lettering

David James 'Mr N & B' poses with Col. Bevan at Seven Sisters Colliery in 1922.

Tudor Watkins Coll.

The N & B began to prosper towards the end of the century because there was a healthy development in the production of coal in the Dulais valley. In 1875 the Evans Bevan family opened the colliery at Seven Sisters. Annual production from this and other pits along the line increased steadily up to the time of the First World War. The coal traffic in tons carried by the N & B tells part of the story:

1881......................................	114,112
1890......................................	243,827
1900......................................	500,692
1905......................................	599,413
1907......................................	861,356
1910......................................	1,045,883
1913......................................	1,322,576
1920......................................	873,631
1921......................................	611,851

During the First World War the Midland hauled trainloads of coal and minerals from the Swansea valley to the Midlands and the north of England and, after the armistice, loads of scrap munitions back in the opposite direction. D.T.H. Price, who lived at Defynnog and whose grandmother lived on a farm known as Blaentwyni, near the head of the Swansea valley, recalled the pungent smell of red-hot locomotive brake blocks, and the speed achieved on the fish trains by some of the Midland enginemen on the winding run down from Bwlch to Devynock. That was in the days before the GWR took over and imposed an overall speed limit of 30 m.p.h. He also recalled the arrival at Devynock of an 0-6-0 on a goods train with safety valves roaring thunderously and the whistle shrieking to celebrate 11 November 1918.

He described a blizzard in the early 1920s when one Sunday morning his father took him by the 9.00 a.m. train from Devynock up the line to visit his grandmother. The four- or five-coach train of red six-wheeled carriages was headed by an 0-4-4T in Midland red. The train made the usual stop at Cray and then proceeded up to Bwlch. There a platelayer who had struggled up from Craig-y-nos reported deep drifts of snow lower down. Progress was initially good over the winding line and across the many bridges over the culverts leading off the side of the mountain. Rounding the last bend before the only straight stretch of line in this area the train was confronted by deep drifts of snow which had formed in the cutting and rose to the level of the train windows. After the train came to a gentle stop, they clambered out and floundered throught the snow to see the engine. It had come to a halt with the front wheels some 12" to 18" above the track. A vast hummock of snow had accumulated in front of the engine as she struggled over the last 100 yards. In addition, the fireman reported that so much snow had been rammed into the bottom of the firebox that he doubted whether he would be able to keep the fire alive. Nevertheless, the line was cleared quickly enough for them to be able to catch a train back to Devynock at 5.20 p.m. that day, no doubt reinvigorated by grandmother's Welsh cakes and hot tea.

Similar conditions returned in March 1947 and the depth of the snow near Craig-y-nos was pictured well above the top of the locomotives in the first two *Railway Magazine* editions of 1948.

By way of contrast, the Neath Branch was unexciting though fairly busy with a mixed train from Neath to Onllwyn in the early morning, returning immediately, then five passenger trains in each direction and seven goods, and buoyant coal production along the line. A reasonable interchange time was allowed for passengers at Colbren Junction whose trains were normally hauled by the 4-4-0T No. 5, but also by the 2-4-0T No. 6.

After 1903 the N & B took over the operation of mineral trains over the Junction Line between Ynisygeinon and Colbren. For the purpose, two 0-6-2 tank engines were acquired from the Port Talbot Railway. This unusual movement against the lie of the land was occasioned by the fact that the GWR had better dock facilities in Swansea than the Midland. It was therefore worth hauling the coal up to Colbren Junction and down the Dulais valley, rather than what would appear to be the more obvious and simple route straight down the Tawe valley, downhill all the way to Swansea. The Working Timetables do not differentiate between companies. However, as a result of this extra traffic, there was an immediately obvious change in the N & B train mileage reported in the half-yearly accounts. There was also an unexplained increase in passenger traffic, due no doubt to the N & B operating some excursion trains and specials of the type illustrated on the accompanying bills advertising special trains for the Neath Great Fair and boating on the Usk (see p. 143):

N & B TRAIN MILES		
	Main Line	Neath Branch
JUNE 1890	31	21,761
DEC. 1898	161 (Goods 12)	43,544
DEC. 1902	51	43,219
DEC. 1903	4,283 (Pass. 221)	46,452
DEC. 1912	6,754 (Pass. 119)	69,427

By 1914, which is generally regarded as being near the peak of activity on the Welsh railways, the following pattern of trains had emerged on the main line. From Swansea, passenger trains to Brecon were at 8.30 a.m., 11.05 a.m., 4.06 p.m., and 8.25 p.m. On Saturdays there was a late night extra at 9.25 p.m. ariving at Brecon at 2.10 a.m. in the morning. There was a marked increase in the variety of goods activity with a 'through freight' at 5.00 a.m., a 'stopping freight' at 12.15 p.m., a train of empties at 3.25 p.m., a 'through freight to Worcester' at 6.23 p.m., an 'express freight to Birmingham' at 8.45 p.m. and another 'through freight to Worcester' at 9.50 p.m. The direction of travel of the empties is surprising as it might have been supposed that there would be a significant movement of goods from Swansea to the Midlands but it seems to have been the other way. The

Local Rifle Club Volunteers welcome home a Boer War veteran at Devynock, 1902.

Brecon Museum

A Midland Railway goods train at Devynock *c.*1902. The footplate men and the two shunters appear to be Midland men; the two porters N & B. The affiliations of the dog are not known. 0-6-0T No. 1106A.

Tudor Watkins Coll.

'stopping freight' was allowed 8½ hours to reach Brecon whereas the Birmingham train took only 3 hours 20 minutes. If it had minerals on board it was allowed an extra 20 minutes. In the opposite direction the pattern was similar.

The signalman at Bwlch at the summit of the line, at an altitude of 1,267ft, would have had to cope with the following in the course of 24 hours:

12.15 a.m. ..... Saturdays only passenger train from Swansea
12.32 a.m. ..... Through freight to Worcester
 2.40 a.m. ..... Through freight from Worcester
 3.10 a.m. ..... Through freight from Brecon
 6.18 a.m. ..... Through freight from Birmingham
 9.01 a.m. ..... Passenger train from Brecon
 9.02 a.m. ..... Through freight from Swansea
 9.35 a.m. ..... Passenger train from Swansea
12.07 p.m. ..... Passenger train from Brecon
12.21 p.m. ..... Passenger train from Swansea
Unspecified time p.m. Stopping freight from Swansea
 3.18 p.m. ..... Passenger train from Brecon. Half minute stop only
 4.20 p.m. ..... Stopping freight from Brecon
 5.11 p.m. ..... Passenger train from Swansea
 6.42 p.m. ..... Passenger train from Brecon
 7.08 p.m. ..... Empties from Swansea
 9.31 p.m. ..... Through freight to Worcester
 9.32 p.m. ..... Passenger train from Swansea
11.13 p.m. ..... Express freight to Birmingham

After the absorption of the N & B into the GWR in 1922, the arrangement between the N & B and the Midland was continued by the GWR and LMS for eight years, though the LMS began routeing freight over the CWR. From 1 January 1931 passenger trains to and from Brecon were routed exclusively to Neath and the Junction Line became a branch, operated by the GWR between Colbren Junction and Ystradgynlais. From 12 September 1932 passenger trains ceased to operate on the Junction Line and it became exclusively a goods line. All former LMS traffic to and from Swansea and the Midlands was routed over the GWR or over the CWR.

The removal of Swansea from the timetable after 1932 seriously reduced the importance of the whole line. By summer 1938 the GW had three passenger trains a day from Brecon to Neath at 8.30 a.m., 11.25 a.m. and 4.10 p.m. In the opposite direction they were at 8.25 a.m., 11.25 a.m. and 4.10 p.m. It still operated the Friday afternoon return trip from Brecon to Devynock and there were still no trains on Sundays. The train consisted of a pannier tank locomotive hauling three corridor bogie carriages. There were no officially announced through trains beyond Brecon, but it has been said that sets of carriages would often work all the way from Neath as far as Whitchurch. If anyone had wanted to travel from Neath to, say, Hereford the 11.25 a.m. from Neath Riverside would have taken them to Brecon by 1.06

p.m. where a quick change on to the 1.10 p.m. would have landed them at Three
Cocks Junction at 1.40 p.m. Ten minutes later the 1.50 p.m. would depart for
Hereford where it arrived at 2.57 p.m., a total of some three and a half hours from
Neath. With this speed and intensity of traffic it is surprising that the line survived
until June 1964, almost exactly 100 years after the first train from Neath to
Onllwyn.

A Brecon-bound
train approaching the
summit of the line at
Bwlch. The main
road used to curve
sharply beneath the
railway at this point.
Engine No. 8751.

R.M. Casserley

Another view of the
summit, showing the
level of the road already
beginning its descent and
a Neath-bound train, on
12 June, 1962.
*H.B. Priestley/
Tudor Watkins Coll.*

This useful photograph
of a Brecon-bound train
at Bwlch clearly shows
the narrow, tortuous
carriageway at this
location, the scene of
several road accidents.

DD Coll.

COLBREN JUNCTION AND YNISYGEINON JUNCTION.

Down Trains.   **Week Days.**

Distance from Colbren Jct.	STATIONS.	Station Number.	Gradient 1 in ●	8.20 a.m. Brecon to Swansea (St. Thomas) L.M.S. Passenger.		11.25 a.m. Brecon to Swansea (St. Thomas) L.M.S. Passenger. SO		11.25 a.m. Brecon to Swansea (St. Thomas) L.M.S. Passenger. SX		Swansea (St. Thomas) L.M.S. Passenger. SO	
M. C.				arr.	dep.	arr.	dep.	arr.	dep.	arr.	dep.
— —	**Colbren Junction**			A.M.	A.M.	P.M.	P.M.	P.M.	P.M.	P.M.	P.M.
— —	Colbren Junction			9 16	9 22	12 22	12 29	12 22	12 29		3 32
1 29	Cwmtawe Colliery Siding										
1 71	Abercrave Colliery Siding										
2 5	Abercrave			9 26	9 27	12 33	12 34	12 33	12 34	3 36	3 37
2 8½	International Colliery Siding										
2 37	Gwaunclawdd Colliery Siding										
3 40	Penrhos Brick Works Siding										
4 46	Ystradgynlais Colliery Siding										
4 63	**Ystradgynlais**				9 32		12 41		12 41		3 44
5 64	Varteg Brick Works Siding										
6 11½	Ynisci Colliery Siding										
6 64	Ynisygeinon Colliery Siding										
7 22½	Ynisygeinon Junction				9 39		12 45	12 46	12 54		3 48

STATIONS.			1.0 p.m. Brecon L.M.S. Goods.		6.0 p.m. Brecon to Swansea (St. Thomas) L.M.S. Passenger.		L.M.S. Light Engine.				11.0 p.m. Craig-y-nos L.M.S. Empty Coaches to Swansea (St. Thomas). SO	
			arr.	dep.	arr.	dep.	arr.	dep.			arr.	dep.
			P.M.	P.M.	P.M.	P.M.	P.M.	P.M.			P.M.	P.M.
Colbren Junction			4 20	4 55	6 57	7 1					11 7	11 10
Cwmtawe Colliery Siding							9 33					
Abercrave Colliery Siding ..												
Abercrave			5 5	5 15	7 5	7 6						
International Colliery Siding												
Gwaunclawdd Colliery Siding												
Penrhos Brick Works Siding												
Ystradgynlais Colliery Siding												
Ystradgynlais			5 30	5 52		7 13	9 46					11 20
Varteg Brick Works Siding												
Ynisci Colliery Sidings												
Ynisygeinon Colliery Siding			6 4	6 7								
Ynisygeinon Junction ..						7 18	9 53	9 54				11 25

NEATH (RIVERSIDE) AND BRECON.

Up Trains.   **Week Days.**

STATIONS.	B Passenger. SO		B Passenger. SO		B Passenger. SX			B Passenger. SO		E Goods. SX		9.35 p.m. Swansea (St. Thomas) L.M.S. Passenger. SO	
	arr.	dep.	arr.	dep.	arr.	dep.		arr.	dep	arr.	dep.	arr.	dep.
	P.M.	P.M.	P.M.	P.M.	P.M.	P.M.		P.M.	P.M.	P.M.	P.M.	P.M.	P.M.
Neath (Riverside) ..	—	8 15	—	9 15	—	9 40		—	10 15				
Neath Yard Signal Box											11 45		
Cadoxton Terrace Halt	8 18	8 20	9 18	9 20	9 43	9 45		10 18	10 20	11 47	12 10		
Penscynor Halt.. ..	8 22	8 24	9 22	9 24	9 47	9 49		10 22	10 24				
Cilfrew	8 26	8 28	9 26	9 28	9 51	9 53		10 26	10 28				
Cilfrew Colliery													
Cilfrew Loop	8 33		9 33		9 54					12 20	12 30		
Llwynon Colliery													
Crynant	8 38	8 41	9 38½	9 41	10 3	10 6		10 58	10 40	12 40	12 55		
Crynant Colliery North	—	—	—	—	—	—		—	—				
Crynant Colliery New Siding	—	—	—	—	—	—		—	—				
Dillwyn Colliery	—	—	—	—	—	—		—	—				
Dillwyn and Brynteg Platform	—	—	—	—	—	10 13		—	—				
Brynteg Colliery	—	—	—	—	—	—		—	—	1 15	1 20		
Ynisdawley	8 47		9 47										
Seven Sisters	8 50	8 52	9 50	9 52	10 16	10 17		10 49	10 51				
Seven Sisters Colliery North	—	—	—	—	—	—		—	—				
Dulais Colliery South	—	—	—	—	—	—		—	—				
Pantyffordd	8 56	8 58	9 56	9 58	10 21	10 23		10 55	10 58				
Onllwyn Colliery South	—	—	—	—	—	—		—	—				
Dulais Colliery North	—	—	—	—	—	—		—	—				
Onllwyn	9 0	9 4	10 1	10 6	10 25	10 29		11 0	11 5				
Onllwyn Colliery North	—	—	—	—	—	—		—	—				
Colbren Exchange Siding	—	—	—	—	—	—		—	—				
Colbren Junction	9 6		10 8		10 31	—		11 7				10 26	10 32
Craig-y-nos												10 40	—
Bwlch													
Cray													
Devynock and Sennybridge ..													
Aberbran													
Cradoc													
Brecon Ely Place													
Brecon Mount Street													
Brecon Passenger													
Brecon Goods													

The GW Working Timetable for July 1930 openly describes all operations between Colbren Junction and Ynisygeinon Junction, both goods and passenger, as part of a still existing LMS route from Brecon to Swansea.

National Archives/Rail 937/154

HEREFORD, THREE COCKS, BRECON, NEATH AND SWANSEA. 115

Week Days only.

Miles								
	Hereford ... dep.							
	Credenhill							
	Moorhampton							
	Kinnersley		For complete Service					
	Eardisley		between Three Cocks					
	Whitney-on-the-Wye		Junction and Brecon					
	Hay		See page 205.					
	Glasbury-on-Wye							
	Three Cocks Junction { arr. dep.							
	Talgarth							
	Trefeinon							
	Talyllyn Junction arr. dep.							
	Brecon arr. dep.							
	Cradoc							
	Aberbran							
	Devynock & Senny Bridge							
	Cray							
	Craigynos (Penwyllt)							
	Colbren Junction arr.							
	Colbren Junction dep.							
	Onllwyn							
	Pantyffordd Halt							
	Seven Sisters							
	Crynant							
	Cilfrew							
	Penscynor Halt							
	Cadoxton Terrace Halt arr.							
	Neath (Riverside)							
	Colbren Junction dep.							
	Abercrave							
	Ystradgynlais							
	Brynamman							
	Cwmllynfell							
	Gwys							
	Ystalyfera							
	Pontardawe dep.							
	Glais							
	Clydach-on-Tawe							
	Morriston							
	Upper Bank							
	Swansea (St. Thomas) arr.							

	Swansea (St. Thomas) dep.							
	Upper Bank							
	Morriston							
	Clydach-on-Tawe							
	Glais							
	Pontardawe							
	Ystalyfera dep.							
	Gwys							
	Cwmllynfell							
	Brynamman arr.							
	Ystradgynlais dep.							
	Abercrave							
	Colbren Junction arr.							
	Neath (Riverside) dep.							
	Cadoxton Terrace Halt							
	Penscynor Halt							
	Cilfrew							
	Crynant							
	Seven Sisters							
	Pantyffordd Halt							
	Onllwyn							
	Colbren Junction arr.							
	Colbren Junction dep.							
	Craigynos (Penwyllt)							
	Cray							
	Devynock & Senny Bridge							
	Aberbran							
	Cradoc							
	Brecon arr. dep.							
	Talyllyn Junction arr. dep.							
	Trefeinon							
	Talgarth							
	Three Cocks Junction { arr. dep.							
	Glasbury-on-Wye							
	Hay							
	Whitney-on-the-Wye							
	Eardisley							
	Kinnersley							
	Moorhampton							
	Credenhill		For Complete Service					
	Hereford arr.		between Brecon and Three Cocks Jn. See page 205.					

J—Calls on Fridays only to pick up passengers for Brecon. Notice to be given to the Guard.   K—Calls on Wednesdays only.   L—Calls only when required to set down passengers.   R—Calls at Pontardawe at 9.55 p.m. to pick up passengers only.   S—Saturdays only.   *—About ¼ mile from Swansea (High Street) G.W. Station.   †—Adjoins G.W. Station.   ¶—About ¼ mile from Neath (General) Station.

On the other hand, already in July 1930, the GW public timetable makes no reference to the LMS between Colbren Junction and Ystradgynlais but, presumably, a connection was available for Swansea (St Thomas).

National Archives/Rail 936/64

HEREFORD AND BRECON, GREAT WESTERN AND SWANSEA VALE LINES.

Week Days.

Bradford (Forster Sq.) dep.		9R 5		1 38		8 15		2b 2
Leeds (Weilington) ,,		10 0		3 6		8 50		2b45
Sheffield ,,		11 18		4 42		9 52		3b45
Manchester { Victoria ,,			1145		0 33		
Central ,,		7825		12) 0		9 55		1 45
Buxton ,,		8815				10 35		2 25
Nottingham ,,		11R50		5 4		10 35		3 30
Derby ,,		12 40		6 50		11 55		4 40
Leicester ,,		12R45		6 30		11 7		4 5
Birmingham ,,		2 48		8 45		1 10		5 46
Worcester (S.H.) ,,		7 5		10R25		3 2		7 12
Malvern Link ,,		7 30		11 10		3 48		7 28
Great Malvern ,,		7 37		11 16		3 20		7 42
Ledbury ,,		8 2		11 40		3 15		3 5
Hereford arr.		8 40		12 0		3 55		8 33
Hereford dep.		9 20		12 45		4 0	3 20	2 45
Credenhill ,,		9 32		12 58		4 12	3 32	8 57
Moorhampton ,,		9 41		1 7		4 21	3 41	9 6
Kinnersley ,,		9 49		1 15		4 29	3 49	9 14
Eardisley ,,		9 54		1 20		4 34	3 54	9 19
Whitney-on-Wye ,,		10 1		1 27		4 41	6 1	9 28
Hay ,,		10 11		1 38		4 50	6 10	9 30
Glasbury-on-Wye ,,		10 21		1 46		5 0	6 20	9 45
Three Cocks arr.		10 25		1 50		5 4	6 24	9 49
Builth Wells arr.		11D47		2 22		6 13		10G920
Rhayader ,,		1 21		2 52		6 45		
Llanidloes ,,		1 57		3 20		7 17		
Newtown ,,		2 45		3 54		8 4		
Welshpool ,,		3 12		4 28		8 35		
Oswestry ,,		3 51		5 16		9 15		
Aberystwyth ,,		3 55		5 6				
Aberdovey ,,		3 45		4 53				
Dolgelley ,,				6 17				
Barmouth ,,		4 20		5 31				
Portmadoc ,,		4 53		6 25				
Aberystwyth dep.				7 50		12 55		2 40
Three Cocks dep.	7 5	10 28		1 58		5 6	6 28	9 50
Talgarth ,,	7 10	10 34		2 4		5 12	6 34	9 56
Trefeinon ,,	7 17	P		U		U	6 40	
Talyllyn Junction arr.	7 25	10 45		2 15		5 23	6 47	10 7
Talybont-n-Usk arr.	9 2	12 25		2 37		6 28		
Dowlais (Central) ,,	9 14	1 32		3y35		7 45		
Merthyr ,,				3 45		7 0		
Cardiff (Queen St.) ,,	11 22	2 56		5 9		9 0		
Newport ,,	10 21	2 41		5 9		8 44		
Talyllyn Junction dep.	7 30	11 0		2 25		5 28	6 49	10 9
Brecon arr.	7 40	11 10		2 35		5 38	6 59	10 13
Brecon dep	8 20	11 25			3 30	6 0		
Cradoe ,,	8 26	11 31			3 36	6 6		
Aberbran ,,	8 32	11 37			3 41	6 12		
Devynock & Sennybridge ,,	8 42	11 48			3 50	6 23		
Cray ,,	8 52	11 58				6 33		
Craig-y-nos (Pen't) ,,	9 12	12 15				6 50		
Colbren Junction ,,	9 16	12 22	3 32			6 57		
Neath (Riverside) { arr.	10 6	1 12				7 47		
dep.	8 25	11 20				6 15		
Abercrave ,,	9 26	12 34	3 37			7 6		
Ystradgynlais ,,	9 33	12 41	3 44			7 13		
Pontardawe ,,	9 45	12 3	3 56			7 27		
Glais ,,		10 19	4 2			7 33		
Clydach-on-Tawe ,,		10 15	4 7			7 38		
Morriston ,,		1028	4 14			7 41		
Upper Bank ,,		1028	4 20			7 44		
Swansea (St. Thomas) arr.	10 5	1035	4 25			7 50		

Swansea (St. Thomas) dep.	8 11		8 30	11 0	2 26	3 50	3 52	4 5	9 35
Upper Bank ,,	8 16			11 5	2 30	3 54	3 56		
Morriston ,,	8 22		8 38	11 12	2 36	3 58			
Clydach-on-Tawe ,,	8 29		8 43	11 19	2 42	4 5	4 4	4 6	4 16
Glais ,,	8 33		8 47	11 23	2 46	4 10		4 10	4 20
Pontardawe ,,	8 40		8 52	11 32	2 52	4 16	4 18		4 26
Ystradgynlais ,,	Stop		9 6	11 48	3 10			Stop	4 39	
Abercrave ,,			9 15	11 57	3 18				4 48	20
Neath (Riverside) { arr.			10 6	1 12					5 37	
dep.			8 25	11 20					4 10	9
Colbren Junction ,,			9 2	12 4	3 24				4 55	10
Craig-y-nos (Pen't) ,,			9 31	12 14					5 4	4 10
Cray ,,			9 47	12 30					5 20	
Devynock & Sennybridge ,,			9 57	12 39					5 30	
Aberbran ,,			10 6	12 48				4 14	5 39	
Cradoc ,,			10 13	12 55				4 20	5 46	
Brecon arr.			10 18	1 0				4 26	5 51	
Brecon dep.	7 0	8 50	10 30	1 10				6 0	
Talyllyn Junction arr.	7 10	9 0	10 40	1 20				6 10	
Newport dep.			8 5	10 55					2 45	
Cardiff (Queen St.) ,,			8 20	10 50					1850	
Merthyr ,,			9 30	12 16					4 0	
Dowlais (Central) ,,			9 35	12 15					4 10	
Talybont-on-Usk ,,			10 29	1 10					4 59	
Talyllyn Junction dep.	7 11	9	10 50	1 23				6 11	
Trefeinon ,,	U	9	9 U						
Talgarth ,,	7 23	9	11 1	1 26				6 22	
Three Cocks arr.	7 29	9 20	11 6	1 41				6 27	
Aberystwyth ,,	11 40		3 55	5 5					
Portmadoc dep.			6 40					11 2	
Barmouth ,,			7 30					12 23	
Dolgelley ,,			7 0					11 35	
Aberdovey ,,			8 10					1 3	
Aberystwyth ,,			7 50					12 55	
Oswestry ,,	3 31		8 20					10 35	
Welshpool ,,	4 25		9 3					11 41	
Newtown ,,	5 32		9 32					12 14	
Llanidloes ,,			8 0	10 18					3 7	
Rhayader ,,	6 0		8 30	10 49					3 38	
Builth Wells ,,	6 36		9 23	1 10					4 10	
Three Cocks dep.	7 30	9 21	11 8	1 50				6 25	
Glasbury-on-Wye ,,	7 34	9 26	11 13	1 57				6 32	
Hay ,,	7 45	9 30	11 23	2 7				6 43	
Whitney-on-Wye ,,	7 52	9 45	11 34	2 16				6 51	
Eardisley ,,	7 59	9 45	11 49	2 23				6 58	
Kinnersley ,,	8 3	9 69	11 54	2 28				7 3	
Moorhampton ,,	8 10	10 6	12 1	2 35				7 10	
Credenhill ,,	8 26	10 15	12 10	2 45				7 20	
Hereford arr.	8 31	10 27	12 24	2 56				7 31	
Hereford dep.		11 15	12 50	3 30				7 42	
Ledbury ,,	10R36	11 33	1 42	4 4				8 15	
Great Malvern ,,	10 30	12 48	1 25	4 22				8 30	
Malvern Link ,,	11 6	12 43	1 30	4 43				8 39	
Worcester (S.H.) ,,	10 42	12X 8	1 45	4 53				8 56	
Birmingham ,,	1 39		3 54	6 46				10 17	
Leicester ,,	3 0		5 55	8 56				1 K40	
Derby ,,	5a 12		5 28	8 8				12 0	
Nottingham ,,	4 20		6 7	8 47				1 45	
Buxton ,,	5a 55		7 1	10 0					
Manchester { Central ,,	6 25		8 46	10 28				5 15	
Victoria ,,								6 7	
Sheffield ,,	4a 23		6 36	9 17				1 5	
Leeds (Wellington) ,,	5a 55		7 58	10 7				3 27	
Bradford (Forster Sq.) ,,	6a 0		8 27	10 24				4R55	

A—Foregate Street Station depart 10.59 a.m.
a—On Saturdays due Derby 3.49, Buxton 6.1, Sheffield 4.55, Leeds 6.0 and Bradford 6.35 p.m.
B—Leaves Portmadoc 11.20 a.m., on Mondays, Fridays and Saturdays.
b—Leaves Bradford 2.23, Leeds 2.55 and Sheffield 3.10 p.m. on Saturdays.
D—Arrives Builth Wells 10.58 a.m. on Mondays.
E—Monday mornings excepted. 11.12 p.m., Sunday nights via Derby; also on Friday, August 2nd.
G—Leaves Pontardawe 12.55, Glais 1.2, Clydach-on-Tawe 1.6, Morriston 1.11, Upper Bank 1.17, and arrives Swansea at 1.22 p.m. on Saturdays.
H—2.30 p.m on Saturdays.
J—Stops at 9.54 p.m. to take up Passengers.

K—Via Derby. Season Tickets are not available by this Service unless so routed. Arrives on Sundays at 12.10 a.m. (via Hinckley).
L—Foregate Street Station. Arrives Shrub Hill at 11.32 a.m.
N—5.5 a.m. on Sundays.
P—Stops at Trefeinon on Fridays to take up Passengers for Brecon.
Q—Hereford depart 10.2 a.m.
R—On Sundays leaves Bradford 9.25 p.m., Manchester (Central) 10.40, Buxton 7.10, and Nottingham 11.55 p.m.
S—Saturdays excepted. SO—Saturdays only.
U—Stops at Trefeinon on Wednesdays only. V—Hereford dep. 1.0 p.m.
X—Foregate Street Station. Arrives Shrub Hill 1.31 p.m.
y—Arrives Dowlais (Central) 3.57 p.m. on Fridays.

SWANSEA AND BRYNAMMAN.

WEEK DAYS.

Swansea (St. Thomas) dep.	8 11	3 30	11 0	1 0	2 26	3 50	3 52	4 5	5 25	6 0	6 30	7 40	9 5	9 20	9 20	9 50	10 15	11 0
Upper Bank ,,	8 16		11 5	1 5	2 30	3 54			5 29			7 44	9 9	9 24	9 24		10 19	11 4
Morriston ,,	8 22	8 33	11 12	1 11	2 36	3 59			5 34			7 49	9 16	9 31	9 31		10 26	11 11
Clydach-on-Tawe ,,	8 29	8 43	11 19	1 17	2 42	4 4		4 16	5 41			7 55	9 23	9 38	9 38		10 33	11 18
Glais ,,	8 33	8 47	11 23	1 21	2 46	4 8		4 20	5 45			7 59	9 27	9 42	9 42		10 37	11 22
Pontardawe ,,	8 40	8 52	11 32	1 29	2 52	4 16		4 26	5 52			8 7	9 35	9 50	9 50		10 45	11 30
Ystalyfera ,,	7 10	8 56		11 49	1 44		4 31	4 50		6 1	6 23	8 22		10 4	10 19	10 19		11	
Gwys ,,	7 18	9 4		11 57	1 52		4 38	4 57		6 8	6 32	8 29		10 11	10 26	10 26			
Cwmllynfell ,,	7 26	9 12		12 5	2 0		4 45	5 4		6 15	7 30	8 35		10 18	10 33	10 33			
Brynamman arr.	7 33	9 19		12 12	2 7		4 52	4 57		6 21	7 36	8 42		10 39	11 7	11 7			

Brynamman dep.	7 43		9 35		12 23	2 17		5 0	5 7	7 34	7 52	11 30
Cwmllynfell ,,	7 50		9 42		12 30	2 24		5 6	5 14	7 41	7 59	11 37
Gwys ,,	7 58		9 50		12 38	2 32		5 12	5 22	7 48	8 6	
Ystalyfera ,,	8 10	9 0	10 1		12 48	2 42	4 5	5 20	5 55	8 0	8 15	
Pontardawe ,,	8 21	9 10	9 45	10 13	12 56	1 2	2 56	3 24	4 31	5 52	7 27	8 15	8 35	8 48	11
Glais ,,	8 27	9 16	10 20	1 8	3 10	3 30	4 35	5 58	7 33	8 20	8 31	8 54	
Clydach-on-Tawe ,,	8 31	9 19	10 24	1 11	3 6	4 7	4 31	5 41	6 1	7 36	8 24	8 35	8 59	
Morriston ,,	8 37	9 24	10 29	1 18	1 22	3 12	4 0	4 40	5 46	6 7	7 41	8 32	8 43	9 5	
Upper Bank ,,	8 43	9 29	10 35	1 22	3 16	4 40	5 51	6 12	7 46	8 37	8 49	9 10	
Swansea (St. Thomas) arr.	8 49	9 35	10 5	10 40	1 22	1 33	3 21	4 25	4 52	5 58	6 12	7 50	8 42	8 50	9 15

LMS Timetable for 1931, showing the 'Junction Line' served by the GWR.

National Archive/Rail 937/155

SWANSEA, NEATH, BRECON, THREE COCKS AND HEREFORD. 115

Week Days only.

	a.m.	a.m.	a.m.	a.m.		p.m.	p.m.	p.m.	p.m.		p.m.	p.m.		p.m.		p.m.		p.m.
Swansea (High Street) dep.			7 40	10 55		12 48			3 10		5 38	7 5		8 25		9 10		9 55
Neath (General) ¶ arr.			7 58	11 13		1 10			3 30		5 57	7 33		8 47		9 28		10 2
Swansea (East Dock) dep.				10M45		12M55			3M25									
Neath (Riverside) arr.				11M5		1M15			3M44									
Neath (Riverside) dep.		8 25	11 25			1 35			4 10		6 25	8 15		9 15		9 40		10 18
Cadoxton Terrace Halt		8 29	11 29			1 39			4 14		6 29	8 20		9 20		9 44		10 20
Penscynor Halt		8 32	11 32			1 42			4 17		6 32	8 24		9 24		9 47		10 24
Cilfrew		8 36	11 36			1 46			4 21		6 36	8 29		9 29		9 51		10 29
Cefn Coed Colliery Halt		8 45	11 38			1 53			4 28		6 43	8 36		9 36		9 58		10 36
Crynant		8 49	11 47			1 57			4 32		6 47	8 41		9 41				10 41
Seven Sisters		8 58	11 56			2 6			4 41		6 56	8 51		9 51		10 13		10 51
Pantyffordd Halt		9 2	12 0			2 10			4 45		7 6	8 56		9 57		10 17		10 57
Onllwyn		9 5	12 3			2 13			4 49		7 4	9 2		10 4		10 22		11 4
Colbren Junction arr.		9 7	12 5			2 15			4 52		7 6	9 5		10 6		10 24		11 6
Ystradgynlais dep.	8 50								4 35									
Abercrave	8 58								4 43									
Colbren Junction arr.	9 7								4 48									
Colbren Junction dep.	9 10	12 7							4 54									
Craigynos (Penwyllt)	9 20	12 17							5 3									
Cray	9 36	12 33							5 19									
Devynock & Senny Bridge	9 45	12 42				4 15			5 28									
Aberbran	9 54	12 51				4 24			5 37									
Cradoc	10 1	12 58				4 30			5 44									
Brecon arr.	10 6	1 3				4 35			5 49									
Brecon dep.	7 1	8 51	10 41	1 10			5 10	6 1										
Talyllyn Junction dep.	7 9	8 59	10 49	1 19			5 17	6 9										
Trefeinon	7 10	9 0	10 52	1 25			5 21	6 10										
Talgarth	K	9 7	K				5 27											
Three Cocks Junction arr.	7 23	9 13	11 3	1 36			5 33	6 21										
Three Cocks Junction dep.	7 29	9 18	11 8	1 41			5 40	6 26										
Glasbury-on-Wye	7 30	9 21	11 10	1 44				6 28										
Hay	7 34	9 26	11 15	1 57				6 32										
Whitney-on-the-Wye	7 45	9 36	11 23	2 7		5 26		6 43										
Eardisley	7 52	9 45	11 36	2 16		5 32		6 51										
Kinnersley	7 59	9 55	11 49	2 23		5 39		6 58										
Moorhampton	8 3	9 59	11 54	2 28		5 46		7 3										
Credenhill	8 10	10 6	12 1	2 35		5 52		7 10										
Hereford arr.	8 20	10 15	12 10	2 45		6 1		7 20										
	8 31	10 27	12 24	2 56		6 15		7 31										

For complete Service between Brecon and Three Cocks Jn. See page 210.

	a.m.		a.m.	a.m.	p.m.	p.m.				p.m.	p.m.		p.m.		p.m.	p.m.
Hereford dep.			9 20	12 46					4 7	5 30				8 45	10 15	
Credenhill			9 32	12 58					4 19	5 52				8 57	10 27	
Moorhampton			9 41	1 7					4 28	5 41				9 6	10 36	
Kinnersley			9 49	1 15					4 36	5 49				9 14	10 44	
Eardisley			9 54	1 20					4 41	5 54				9 19	10 53	
Whitney-on-the-Wye			10 1	1 27					4 48	6 1				L	10 58	
Hay			10 11	1 35					4 57	6 10				9 35	11 4	
Glasbury-on-Wye			11 21	1 46					5 7	6 20				L		
Three Cocks Junction arr.			10 25	1 50					5 13	6 24				9 40		
Three Cocks Junction dep.		7 5	10 28	1 55					5 13	6 24				9 50		
Talgarth		7 10	10 34	2 2					5 18	6 34				9 56		
Trefeinon		7 17	J	K					K	6 40						
Talyllyn Junction arr.		7 25	10 47	2 13					5 35	6 47				10 7		
Talyllyn Junction dep.		7 30	10 50	2 17					5 48	6 48				10 9		
Brecon dep.		7 37	10 57	2 25					5 46	6 57				10 17		
Cradoc		8 30	11 25				3 50		6 0							
Aberbran		8 36	11 31				3 56		6 6							
Devynock & Senny Bridge		8 41	11 37				3 41		6 12							
Cray		8 52	11 48				3 50		6 23							
Craigynos (Penwyllt)		9 1	11 57						6 28							
Colbren Junction arr.		9 20	12 16						6 49							
		9 27	12 23						6 56							
Colbren Junction dep.		9 30							7 10					9 30		
Abercrave		9 35							7 15					9 35		
Ystradgynlais arr.		9 41							7 21					9 41		
Colbren Junction dep.	8 10	9 31	12 27			3 5	5 0		6 58	7 8				9 30		
Onllwyn	8 13	9 34	12 30			3 8	5 4		7 0	7 3				9 34		
Pantyffordd Halt	8 16	9 37	12 33			3 12	5 8		7 6	7 10				9 37		
Seven Sisters	8 19	9 45	12 41			3 22	5 12		7 10	7 18				9 40		
Crynant	8 27	9 49	12 45			3 26	5 21		7 18	7 22				9 44		
Cefn Coed Colliery Halt	8 31	9 55	12 51			3 34	5 25		7 22	7 32				9 50		
Cilfrew	8 36	9 59	12 55			3 38	5 31		7 31	7 35				9 58		
Penscynor Halt	8 43	10 1	12 57			3 40	5 35		7 32	7 38				9 59		
Cadoxton Terrace Halt	8 45	10 4	1 0			3 43	5 38		7 35							
Neath (Riverside) arr.	8 48						5 41		7 38							
Neath (Riverside) dep.	8M53	10M15														
Swansea (East Dock) arr.	9M12	10M34														
Neath (General) ¶ dep.	9 2	10 38	1N34			4 30		5P55	7 49				10 21		
Swansea (High Street) arr.	9 25	11 1	1N57			4 52		6P18	8 4				10 44		

J—Calls on Fridays only to pick up passengers for Brecon. K—Calls on Wednesdays only. L—Calls only when required to set down passengers.
Notice to be given to the Guard. M—Rail Motor Car, one class only. N—On Saturdays, Neath (General) depart 1.29 p.m., Swansea (High Street)
arrive 1.52 p.m. P—On Saturdays, Neath (General) depart 5.53 p.m., Swansea (High Street) arrive 6.8 p.m. ¶—About ⅜ mile from Neath
(Riverside) Station.

SWANSEA, PONTARDAWE AND BRYNAMMAN. (L.M. & S. Rly.)

Week Days only.

	a.m.	a.m.	a.m.		a.m.	a.m.	p.m.	p.m.	p.m.	p.m.	p.m.			p.m.	p.m.	p.m.
Swansea (St. Thomas') * dep.		8G10	8S 10		11G 0	11S 0					0			8S 50	10S15	11S 0
Upper Bank		8G15	8S 15		11G 5	11S 5					0				10S20	11S 5
Morriston		8G19	8S 19		11G 9	11S 9					0				10S24	11S10
Ynydach-on-Tawe		8G24	8S 24		11G15	11S15					0				10S29	11S16
Glais		8G28	8S 28		11G19	11S19					0				10S33	11S21
Pontardawe	7 10	8G40	8S 40		11G40	11S40					0			10S15	10S40	11S33
Ystalyfera	7 16	8G45	8S 45		11G47	11S47					0			10S41	10S46	11S38
Gurs	7 22	9G 1	9S 6		11G53	11S53					0			10S47		
Gwaun-cae-Gurwen																
Cwmllynfell	7 25	9G 8	9S 18													
Brynamman ‡ arr.	7 28	9G 7	9S 18											10S56		

	a.m.	a.m.	p.m.	p.m.	p.m.	p.m.	p.m.	p.m.	p.m.	p.m.			p.m.	p.m.
Brynamman ‡ dep.	7 43	9G35	12S22		4G 5	6 7				7 55			11 30	
Cwmllynfell	7 45	9G38	12S25		5G10	6 12				7 48			11 56	
Gurs	7 53	9G44	12S32		5G17	6 22				8 0				
Ystalyfera	8 4	9 1	12S40		5G20	6 27				8 10			8 55	
Pontardawe	8 14	9 10	12S50		5G24	6 33				8 19			8 46	
Glais	8 20	9 16	12S58		5G29	6 39				8 27			8 52	
Ynydach-on-Tawe	8 25	9 20			5G33	6 43				8 29			8 56	
Morriston	8 31	9 25			5G38	6 49				8 34			9 1	
Upper Bank	8 36	9 30			5G41	6 53				8 37			9 8	
Swansea (St. Thomas') * arr.	8 43	9 37			5G46	6 59				8 40			9 13	

G—Saturdays excepted. S—Saturdays only. *—About ½ mile from Swansea (High St.) G.W. Station. ‡—Adjoins G.W. Station.

The GW public timetable for July 1932 includes a Third Class only service between Colbren Junction and Ystradgynlais. No mention is made of any connection for Swansea (St Thomas); a passenger from Brecon to Swansea would have to change at Neath Riverside and travel to Swansea East Dock.

National Archives/Rail 936/66

The main reason for the line's survival was the coal handling on the southern end. During the first half of the 1920s there was a boom in Welsh coal exports with 95% of coal from the N & B going to export at Swansea. Demand was sustained because the coal was an anthracite type for which the export demand was steady. But after the depression and collapse of 1929, decline set in. By 1938 there were only some nine coal trains a day each way between Neath and Onllwyn. A further four or five operated beween Ynisygeinon and Neath. Most of the surviving collieries were owned by the Amalgamated Anthracite Collieries Ltd, formed in 1923 by Sir Alfred Mond. These included Diamond, Gurnos, Ystradgynlais and Ynysgedwyn in the Tawe valley, whose production was still being hauled uphill to Colbren and then down the Dulais valley to Neath.

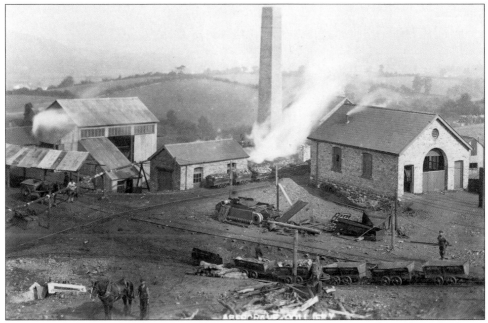

An early photograph of Abercrave Colliery.   *Tudor Watkins Coll.*

Seven Sisters
Colliery, before
construction of the
new station building.
Tudor Watkins Coll.

A variety of
coals at
Abercrave
Colliery
*c.*1910.
Courtesy R.H.
Marrows
Collection

Dulais Higher Pit
at Onllwyn, 1920.
John Cornwell

A 1910 view of
Ystradgynlais
Colliery, in the
foreground, with
a rake of
Ynysgedwyn and
Ystradgynlais
wagons extended
across the centre
ground.
Tudor Watkins Coll.

After 1945 the production remained fairly constant due to the opening of open-cast mines between Onllwyn and Abercrave, and this continued to grow in volume from the end of the Second World War. There were still collieries at Cefn Coed, Crynant, Dillwyn, Seven Sisters and Abercrave, while at Onllwyn, besides the washery, there were three collieries and an open-cast site. Cefn Coed was a disappointment for, in spite of being modern and at the time having the deepest shaft in Britain, the best of the seam had been missed and production was well below planned capacity. However, the 1950s saw a decline with pits closing one after the other:

1953 Onllwyn	1964 Onllwyn No. 1
1954 Seven Sisters	1967 Abercrave
1956 Crynant	1968 Ynysgedwyn
1962 Onllwyn No. 3	1968 Cefn Coed
1963 Seven Sisters	1990 Blaenant

A panoramic view of Ystradgynlais Colliery *c.*1930.   *Cenydd Nickel*

Two panniers at Cefn Coed Colliery on 11 April 1950.   *DD Coll.*

In 1945 goods trains left Neath yard at 4.00 a.m., 6.05 a.m., 7.20 a.m., 9.35 a.m., 10.05 a.m. and 11.35 a.m., and 2.00 p.m., 5.00 p.m. and 6.55 p.m. By 1961, in spite of the pit closures, these had been increased by three with only some 40% of the coal produced going for export via Swansea. The operation was surprisingly complex, partly because the line was single with crossing places only at Neath, Cilfrew, Crynant, Ynisdawley (near Seven Sisters) and Onllwyn. On the Ynisygeinon branch there was a crossing at Colbren Junction. On the main line there was also a crossing at Devynock. The crossing at the summit at Bwlch was taken out in the 1930s and that located at Craig-y-nos was taken out in the 1950s. But the movement of trains was also complex consisting of:

    1. Washed coal from Onllwyn to Neath;
    2. Empties from Neath to the collieries;
    3. Unwashed coal from collieries to Onllwyn washing plant;
    4. Pit-props from Neath to the collieries;
    5. Military traffic to and from Devynock;
    6. Goods to Craig-y-nos and Devynock.

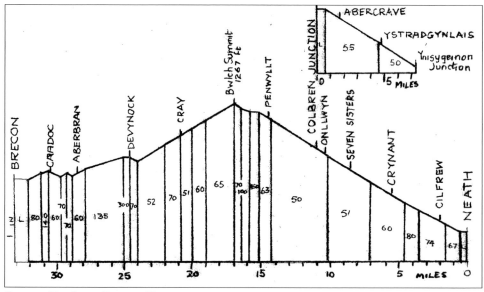

Brecon–Neath gradient profile.   *Courtesy of Tudor Watkins*

    A further source of operating complexity was the gradient profile, exacerbated by the location of the washery at Onllwyn at nearly the highest point. All coal had to be moved there prior to moving down to Neath and the markets. The maximum load of empties for the standard locomotive on the line, a '5700' Class pannier tank, was 33, but only 12 for the haul up from Crynant to Onllwyn and from Ynisygeinon to Colbren.

    A gradual run-down of the passenger service was the main characteristic of nationalisation, though this coincided with what was probably the first regular appearance of bogie carriages. After 1947 the 11.25 a.m. from Brecon and from Neath were only run on Saturdays. On weekdays there were thus only two trains a day each way.

From 1954 there was a re-scheduling to save operating costs. In order that the trains could be operated by only one locomotive based at Neath, the times were modified as follows:

Brecon Free Street station decorated for the visit of HM The Queen in August 1955.

Brecon Museum

8.25 a.m. and 4.10 p.m. from Neath, with 11.05 a.m. and 6.20 p.m. from Brecon.

After 1958, on weekdays there was only one train a day in each direction and only on Saturdays were there two. The scene, as described in the *Railway Observer*, in 1960 was of decay all around. The writer of the article took the only train of the day, the 11.25 a.m. from Neath, a train of two corridor carriages and one non-corridor, hauled by locomotive No. 9746 of the '5700' Class. In many places the station name-boards could no longer be read and there was grass up to two feet high growing on the platforms, even in the month of November. Sennybridge was the only station in good order, probably because it served a significant military need. The train reached Brecon twenty minutes late.

By the time of the winter timetable for 1961/2, besides the one train a day in each direction between Brecon and Neath, there were three from Colbren to Neath. There was also a workmen's train early in the morning from Neath to Colbren. On 15 October 1962 passenger services were closed between Brecon and Onllwyn.

An 11-coach empty coaching stock special returns towards Brecon after conveying military personnel to Sennybridge.
Tudor Watkins Coll.

A returning Porthcawl–Crynant excursion, hauled by 0-6-2T No. 6686 and pannier No. 3652. 2 June 1962.

John Davies

The 11.25 a.m. Neath to Brecon service manages to attract a respectable clutch of passengers for the journey north. 29 April 1961.

R.M. Casserley

The last train from Brecon to Neath was so popular that a relief train was required. Since it was run on a Saturday evening, the handling of two trains from Neath caused a serious problem for the relief stationmaster at Brecon where all four platforms were in use.

A service between Neath and Onllwyn continued until 15 June 1964, but the intermediate stations were all closed on 15 October 1962.

Until about 1954 there was a general goods train service from Brecon to Colbren Junction but by 1961 this was cut back to Devynock and was not expected to survive for any length of time. Mineral traffic was confined to the line between Neath and Onllwyn, sustained by the existence of the coal washery at Onllwyn. On 31 March 1970 the line was reopened from Onllwyn to Craig-y-nos in connection with the reopening of the limestone quarries there. This resulted in trains of 27 ton tipper waggons running down to Jersey Marine once a day *en route* to Llanwern steelworks. This lasted until 28 November 1977 but the section down to Onllwyn survived until 1981. The Junction Line out-lived much of the main line as it was not closed to goods traffic until 20 February 1967.

In 1983 there were up to four freight trains a day in each direction between Neath and Onllwyn. In addition, there were trains from Blaenant Colliery to Aberthaw power station. Class 37 locomotives were used double-headed to haul trains of 35 wagons from Blaenant.

At the time of writing this part of the line remains in regular use for coal trains.

The 4.10 p.m. train from Neath, due at Brecon at 5.51 p.m., drifts into the distance. 27 September 1960.

H.C. Casserley

NEATH & BRECON RAILWAY TICKETS – notes by David Geldard

Nothing is known of the arrangements made by the company for the supply of their tickets; it is most unlikely that they printed their own. For a time the serial numbers were printed in the negative type (018). These were characteristic of a machine manufactured by John B. Edmondson & Co. of Manchester, but by the mid-1890s all tickets had positively printed serial numbers.

Ordinary singles were 1st class white, 2nd class blue and 3rd class buff. Tickets 018, 859 and 277 are local singles dating respectively from the early 1890s, the 1910s and the early 1920s. The term Revised Fare on 277 indicates a fare calculated on the scale in force from 6 August 1920. Singles for foreign journeys (i.e. to stations on other companies' lines) were of similar format on the front, but had extensive conditions of issue printed on the back. Of the examples shown, 074 is from the early 1890s, 027 from the 1910s and 3899 from 1920. Blue card was used for 3rd class child singles, 1st class were on white card with a central longitudinal red band.

Specially printed child tickets were not used for all journeys and, for any journey for which they were not held, a cut adult ticket was issued to a child. During the 1890s a snip was taken from the lower edge of the ticket. On ticket 018, for example, this would remove the small number 6 and a repeat of the destination station. The cut-out snips were returned to the audit office as evidence of the lower fare paid. The number in the snip enabled the issuing station to be verified, the stations being numbered as follows:

1 Neath	6 Colbren	11 Devynock
2 Cilfrew	7 Abercrave	12 Aberbran
3 Crynant	8 Ystradgynlais	13 Cradoc
4 Seven Sisters	9 Penwyllt	14 Brecon
5 Onllwyn	10 Cray	

The adult snip system was discounted for single tickets around the turn of the century, single tickets were thereafter vertically bisected for child issue and re-designed (058) so that the class and journey details were repeated in full on each half.

All return tickets had the outward half on the right-hand side, coloured as for singles of the corresponding class. The return halves were 1st class yellow, 2nd class pink and 3rd class green. Ticket 020 is from the 1890s; note the station number in the audit snip. Tickets 060 and 496 are from the 1910s; by then the audit snip had been modified to show the two station names. All three tickets illustrated are for local journeys and have conditions of issue on the back of each half; foreign returns had the same longer conditions as foreign singles.

The railway catered extensively for leisure travel and tickets 008, 016, 955 and 063 reflect some of the reduced fare facilities that were available. A wide range of colours was used. Pleasure party tickets were only issued when a minimum number of passengers travelled together, and advance notice of the journey and its purpose had to be given to the booking-office. Tourist tickets were issued during the 'summer' season (usually from April to September) and were available for a longer period than other tickets. They also allowed the passenger to break the journey at intermediate stations.

In common with other railways the N & B allowed their employees and their families reduced rate travel at one quarter of the ordinary fares. Privilege order forms were issued to the men and were exchanged at the booking-office for the necessary privilege ticket. Ticket 437 is a 3rd class example. Concessionary fares were also available for other groups, including soldiers, sailors and police (744).

Neath & Brecon Railway tickets

Courtesy of Roy F. Burrows, Midland Collection Trust

The Dulais valley, to the south of Colbren, was coalfield country. Special colliers' trains were run and miners were able to book day, half weekly or weekly tickets. Both the day shift and the night shift workers were catered for and tickets 1920, 1050 and 491 represent some of the many colours used to differentiate journeys and periods of availability.

Passengers did not have to travel alone. Dogs, bicycles and other articles were also conveyed by railway and required their own tickets (133, 063).

Courtesy of Roy F. Burrows, Midland Collection Trust

This demolition contractor's train was noted at Bwlch: August 1963.

Progress, the world's first Fairlie locomotive, portrayed near Cilfrew, c. 1866.

Chapter 7

LOCOMOTIVES

As has emerged from the previous chapter, the demands for motive power were not complex. The locomotives were required primarily for the relatively short distance haulage of coal. Due to a weight restriction, heavy gradients and short sidings, with much manoeuvring of loaded and empty wagons, the tank engine was preferred and, except on some Midland and GW trains, the tender engine was a rarity. In spite of this or perhaps because of it, there was an interesting and, especially in the early days, quaint assortment of locomotives. Although both the Midland and LMS and later the GWR used a variety of locomotives, by the time BR took over the pannier tank had achieved a hegemony.

Management of the locomotives and rolling-stock was initially under the engineer, Hans St George Caulfield. He engaged Henry Appleby, the locomotive superintendent of the Monmouthshire Railway on a part-time basis. He retired in 1875 when the GW took over the Monmouthshire, and J. Whigham took his place for two years. However, when the Midland took over most of the operations, it was decided to dispense with the services of a locomotive superintendent. By 1880 it was decided that perhaps it would after all be a good idea to have a permanent superintendent and J.E. Medley was appointed from a similar post on the Felixstowe Railway & Dock Co. However, he only lasted four years and there was another gap until 1896 when S.W. Allen took charge. He had been in charge of the locomotives of the Marquis of Bute. He survived in post until his death in 1920.

It is not clear what was used for the first operations between Neath and Onllwyn. It is probable that locomotives were hired from the VoN as the first passenger train, the special from Neath to Brecon which was run on 13 September 1866, was hauled by a locomotive hired from them. The VoN had been in the market for standard-gauge locomotives as the strategic decision had been made to put in a third rail so that standard-gauge trains could be operated from Swansea to the Midlands. They may therefore have had some surplus capacity.

The first N & B locomotive was supplied by Dickson under his contract to run the railway for its first year. He also supplied the rolling-stock. In January 1867, as financial problems hit Dickson, the company agreed to buy all the rolling-stock but it had difficulty in finding the cash. Accordingly, in September, it was all transferred to one T.B. Forwood and already in October he was pressing the company for payment of the hire charges.

The first locomotive was a Fairlie 0-4+4-0 with two boiler barrels and a single fire-box, named *Progress*, built by Cross & Co. of St Helens and completed at the end of 1865. It was the first locomotive in the world built to Fairlie's patent.

0-4+4-0 *Progress*, delivered to the N & B in 1865, was the world's first Fairlie locomotive but its career in the Dulais valley was short-lived; there is no evidence that it ever reached Brecon.
Tudor Watkins Coll.

0-4+4-0 *Mountaineer*, delivered in 1866, displayed the same weakness as *Progress* and lasted on the N & B for an even shorter period.
Tudor Watkins Coll.

Employed almost exclusively on mineral trains, it proved less than satisfactory so, in September 1868, it was advertised for sale. It was handed over to George England of Hatcham Ironworks in payment of some earlier debts. It finally left the N & B in 1869 and was subjected to trials on the Midland Railway. From February to June 1870 it was in use on the B & M, whereupon it was transferred to the Monmouthshire Railway & Canal Co. and thence into oblivion. A similar locomotive called *Mountaineer* was also built by Cross and delivered in 1866. Both locomotives suffered from a loss of steam in the flexible connections. A board minute of 10 May 1869 mentions an enquiry about a Fairlie locomotive from the Norwegian Trunk Railway but as with so many items in board minutes, there was no follow-up. The thought of a locomotive that was hard pressed in Wales struggling with conditions in Norway leads one to suppose that, one way or another, the Norwegians managed to avoid a problem. *Mountaineer* was taken out of service in 1868 and after standing unused for over 10 years was eventually sold in 1880 to Briton Ferry Ironworks who dismantled it.

For passenger trains Dickson ordered two 2-4-0 tender engines, No. 1 *Neath* and No. 2 *Brecon*. According to the Railway Correspondence and Travel Society, whose account is an authoritative source of information on the N & B locomotives, they had been built by George England & Co. and had almost certainly been intended for the Somerset and Dorset Railway. Financial problems prevented fulfilment of this order so they became available in late 1867. They hauled the passenger trains betwen Neath and Brecon until these operations ceased in 1877. They then languished in Cadoxton Yard until 1884 when they were cut up.

The fifth locomotive appears to have come from the Anglesey Central Railway which was also run by Dickson. It was named *Anglesey*, mis-spelt 'Anglesea' in the board minutes of October 1867. This was a well-tank engine, an 0-6-0, built by Hawthorns of Leith in 1862. Its wheels were of only 3' 6" diameter and it was thus suitable only for shunting. However, it received a new name, *Miers*, after the N & B's first chairman. It was up for sale by 1876 and in 1882 was sold and eventually appeared on the Waterford & Limerick Railway where Appleby had become superintendent the same year.

The locomotive availability was therefore very stretched and for a railway principally built to move coal it was especially inadequate. For mineral trains it is probable that locomotives were hired from neighbouring railways such as the MWR. In 1870 a locomotive was hired from the Midland, presumably for freight movements, for in the same year, instead of acquiring a new engine of their own for mineral trains, they ordered a passenger train tank engine similar to one already in

4-4-0T No. 4 arrived on the N & B in 1871 and for some fifty years hauled the passenger trains between Neath and Onllwyn. There is no record of it reaching Brecon in normal service.
P.Q. Treloar Coll.

use on the Monmouthshire. This 4-4-0T was built by the Yorkshire Engine Co. of Sheffield and was destined to become a key member of the N & B's passenger fleet for the next 50 years. In 1871 the locomotive fleet was allocated numbers and consisted of the following:

> No. 1. *Neath* 2-4-0
> No. 2. *Brecon* also 2-4-0
> No. 3. *Miers* 0-6-0WT
> No. 4. 4-4-0T.

From 1873, with the opening of the Junction Line, the N & B had to be able to run passenger and goods trains between Brecon and Swansea and mineral trains between Ynisygeinon Junction and Colbren and so a four-coupled saddle tank was acquired from the North Staffordshire Railway. This cannot have been a great success as it was sold in 1877 to the Hoylake & Birkenhead Railway.

The management at the same time acted more seriously to provide capacity for hauling the growing mineral traffic and early in 1873 acquired two Avonside-built double-framed 0-6-0STs. These were similar to locomotives introduced by Appleby on the Monmouthshire. In April they ordered two more and then a further pair making six altogether, numbered initially Nos 5-10. It was one of these which was involved in the derailment which occurred in July 1889, during the period when the Midland had withdrawn its support and the N & B was dependent on its own resources and assistance from the MS & LR.

Late in 1873 they bought another passenger tank, a 2-4-0 well-tank from Budd & Holt, at one time believed to have been in use on the Monmouthshire. It was not a success and was sold again in 1877. Thus in 1877 they had:

> No. 1. *Neath* 2-4-0
> No. 2. *Brecon* 2-4-0
> No. 3. *Miers* 0-6-0WT
> No. 4. 4-4-0T
> Nos 5-10. 0-6-0ST
> Un-numbered 2-4-0WT

This was more than was needed once the Midland had taken over the lion's share of operations and so Nos 7 and 8 were sold to the B & M where they were most successful and indeed survived beyond the First World War. Early in the 1880s, the N & B disposed of *Neath*, *Brecon* and *Miers* and took the opportunity to renumber what they had left as follows:

> No. 1. 0-6-0ST formerly No. 5 Avonside
> No. 2. 0-6-0ST formerly No. 6 Avonside
> No. 3. 0-6-0ST formerly No. 9 Avonside
> No. 4. 0-6-0ST formerly No. 10 Avonside
> No. 5. 4-4-0T formerly No. 4

In the early 1880s, No. 4 was renumbered No. 5 and at some stage received a covered cab.

P.Q. Treloar Coll.

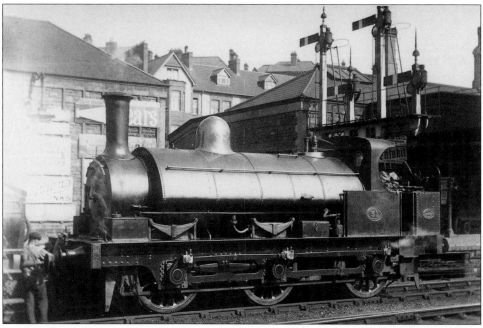

N & B No. 8 of the Avonside-built group of six locomotives, two of which became redundant after the Midland take-over and were sold to the B & M, where it became No. 31, here photographed at Newport.

Ken Nunn/Tudor Watkins Coll.

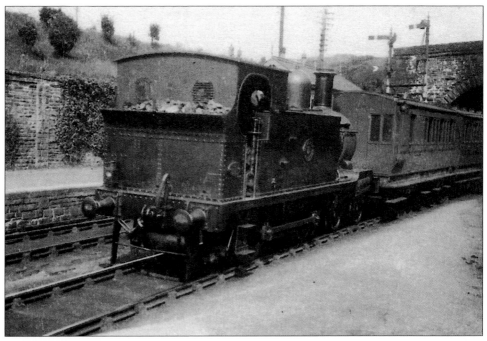

No. 5 running bunker-first into Neath Riverside in the later years of the N & B when the carriage livery had become brown all over.
P. Q. Treloar Coll.

A more unusual view of No. 5 about to depart from Riverside for Colbren, also during the later years of the N & B.

Tudor Watkins Coll.

This fleet was adequate until 1892 when a 2-4-0 tank engine was ordered from Sharp Stewart similar to the Class 'C' on the Barry Railway. This was delivered the following year and was the first N & B engine to have continuous brake fittings. It became No. 6.

In 1898 it again became apparent that more capacity was needed as the mineral traffic was continuing to expand and so two 0-6-0 saddle tanks were ordered from Nasmyth Wilson. They were delivered in 1899 and became Nos 7 and 8.

In 1903 the company took over again the operation of mineral trains between Ynisygeinon and Colbren and to meet this demand bought two Robert Stephenson-built 0-6-2 tank engines from the Port Talbot Railway (PTR). These became Nos 9 and 10. They were so successful that a further three were ordered from Stephensons of the same wheel arrangement and almost identical to the 'M' Class on the Rhymney Railway. These were numbered 11, 12 and 13. They then purchased from the GW four 0-6-0 saddle tanks which became Nos 3, 14, 15 and 16.

In 1892, a 2-4-0T was ordered from Sharp Stewart. It became No. 6. *Tudor Watkins Coll.*

A broadside view of No. 6. *Real Photographs/P.Q. Treloar Coll.*

0-6-0ST No. 8
as delivered by
Nasmyth Wilson
in 1899. The
signal-box, at
Ynisdawley,
appears newly-
built. *c*.1903.
R. Grant Coll.

In 1916, No. 8
was rebuilt by
the GW. It was
photographed
in the yard at
Neath, a
location used
for the
following four
photographs.
*Tudor Watkins
Coll.*

No. 9, an 0-6-2T,
was built by Robert
Stephenson and
purchased second-
hand from the PTR
in 1903. This was
necessitated by the
resumption of coal
haulage from
Ynisygeinon.
*Real Photographs/
Tudor Watkins Coll.*

No. 10 was acquired from the same source and at the same time as No. 9.   *Tudor Watkins Coll.*

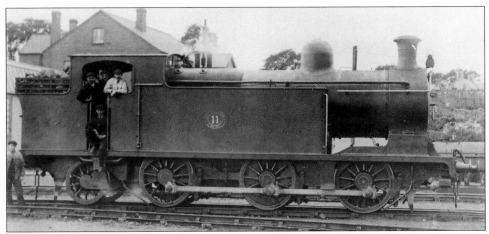

No.11 was one of three slightly larger locomotives acquired direct from Robert Stephenson in 1904.   *Tudor Watkins Coll.*

No. 3 was an ex-GW saddle tank locomotive purchased in 1908.   *Tudor Watkins Coll.*

No. 14, ex-GW outside-framed Buffalo Class 0-6-0ST, purchased 1911.

Tudor Watkins Coll.

Thus when the N & B was absorbed into the GWR in 1922 it had the following locomotives:

    No. 1. 0-6-0ST Avonside
    No. 2. 0-6-0ST Avonside
    No. 3. 0-6-0ST ex-GW
    No. 5. 4-4-0T
    No. 6. 2-4-0T Sharp Stewart
    No. 7. 0-6-0ST Nasmyth Wilson
    No. 8. 0-6-0ST Nasmyth Wilson
    No. 9. 0-6-2T Stephenson ex-PTR
    No. 10. 0-6-2T Stephenson ex-PTR
    No. 11. 0-6-2T Stephenson
    No. 12. 0-6-2T Stephenson
    No. 13. 0-6-2T Stephenson
    No. 14. 0-6-0ST ex-GW
    No. 15. 0-6-0ST ex-GW
    No. 16. 0-6-0ST ex-GW

By 1933 only the ex-GW engines survived. The rest suffered the fate of other non-standard types.

N & B locomotives were painted a rich red/brown. This was a popular colour in south Wales, something similar having been used by both the Barry and the B & M. The locomotives were lined in black with fine yellow lining. Buffer beams were vermilion lined in yellow.

When the Midland took over operations in 1877 there is no evidence as to the locomotives they employed immediately, but by 1886 there is an accurate record from the sheds in use at the time. At Brecon a shed was shared with the MWR and in Swansea the shed was at Upper Bank, just outside St Thomas. There was also a subsidiary shed at Gurnos near Ystalyfera.

At Brecon were stabled six 0-4-4T passenger tanks. This type hauled the passenger trains throughout the Midland's existence, some having enlarged tanks and boilers to cope with the task. In 1886 the following of this type were at Brecon: 1734, 1735, 1736, 2020, 2235 and 2236, the latter two being of the enlarged type.

There were seven of the Kirtley double-framed '700' Class 0-6-0 tender engines, Nos 700-706, and 24 Neilson 0-6-0Ts built in 1874 and split between Brecon and Swansea, most of them being at Swansea. These were of the '1102' Class, Nos 1102A-1107A and Nos 1109A-1115A, 1116-1120, 2253 (ex-1121) and 1125-1130 built in 1895 at Derby. For a short time at Brecon there was also a 2-4-0 No. 192A built by Beyer Peacock in 1867.

At Swansea, no doubt for dock working, there were nine 0-4-0ST engines Nos 1323A-1326A and 1116A-1120A.

We next have a snapshot of the allocations in 1914. By then there were only four of the 0-4-4T type, all the enlarged variant, Nos 1421-1424. There were now only two double-framed Kirtley 0-6-0s, No. 2465 of the '480' Class and 2599 of the '700' Class and only two of the 0-4-0ST dock engines, Nos 1523 and 1524. There was also one Johnson 0-6-0 No. 3207 built in 1890 by Neilson. The rest were all of the 0-6-0T type. Fourteen of the 1874 '1102' Class were still in use, Nos 1620-1623 and 1625 at Brecon and 1629, 1632-1638 and 1648 at Swansea.

This stock was now supplemented by 11 of the '1377' Class Nos 1676, 1677, 1775-1779 and 1816-1819, all built at Derby and No. 1832 built at the Vulcan Foundry. There were also eight of the '1121' Class Nos 1850, 1851 and 1852, and 1860-1864 and two of the '2441' Class 1930 and 1931. All these were stabled at Swansea. They were augmented at Brecon in 1907 with two of the '2241' Class Nos 1955 and 1956 built by Vulcan in 1902 and initially used in the Manchester area. This allocation was little altered until the Grouping.

The next source of information on locomotive allocations is the signal-box register at Penwyllt during June, July and August 1929. From this we find the following ex-Midland locomotives were still in use:

    1F 0-6-0T Nos 1676, 1725, 1730-1732, 1771, 1775, 1777, 1778, 1816, 1817, 1819, 1855, 1857 and 1864;
    3F 0-6-0T Nos 1906, 1930, 1950, 1958 and 1959;
    2F 0-6-0 Nos 3154, 3156, 3209 and 2409;
    3F 0-6-0 Nos 3207, 3259, 3398, 3410, 3575 and 3600.

In addition, some ex-LNWR engines were being used:

    5' 6" 2-4-2T Nos 6601, 6602, 6604, 6755, 6756 and 6757;
    5' 0" 0-6-2T Nos 6869 and 6884 which were in use on the Hereford to St Thomas passenger trains.

The first of the LMS 'Jinties' had just appeared, Nos 16006 and 16007, later re-numbered as 7523 and 7524. They were later joined by others.

By this time the line was maintained under contract by the GW and the following GW locomotives had started to appear: Dean double-framed 0-6-0 No. 2372 and Nos 947, 1629, 1704, 1738 and 1906.

Once the services from Swansea to Brecon had ceased, the GW flavour became total. By 1933, when the only passenger services were between Neath and Brecon, all the N & B locomotives had been withdrawn with the exception of No. 3 and No. 16 and the allocation of locomotives at the Neath (N & B) Shed on 1 January 1934 was:

    '1076' Class Nos 1608, 1611 and 1630;
    '1854' Class 1715, 1721 and 1882;
    '2721' Class Nos 2756 and 2796;
    '5700' Class 5702, 5720, 5734, 7739 and 7757.

On 6 September 1936 there is a photographic record showing six Dean's goods engines and two ex-Cambrian 0-6-0s at Brecon shed. These may have been used primarily east of Brecon, but three '5700's Nos 5738, 8781 and 9792, together with No. 1531 may well have been in use on the N & B.

By 1947 the '5700' Class was supreme on the N & B and the allocation at Neath was Nos 3621, 3757, 3774, 4621, 5746, 5778, 7701, 7739, 7743, 7799, 8782, 9627, 9779, 9786 and 9792. This was two more locomotives than before the war. The '5700' Class became so dominant because there was a weight limit over the line up from Ynisygeinon to Colbren and although the popular south Wales 0-6-2 tank engines of the '5600' Class were within the weight limit on what was now the main line, they were too heavy for the old Junction Line, and it would no doubt have been less efficient to have to switch locomotives at Colbren. Under British Rail the '5700' Class continued its dominance, right to the end of steam, though for the last two years two or three '4200' Class 2-8-0T locomotives were used on the line.

Early BR diesels also found their way onto the N & B as evidenced by this 1965 view of D6891 at the later shed at Neath.

R. Grant

Views of N & B goods stock are limited but this related pair of timber wagons was carefully photographed by the Gloucester Railway Carriage & Wagon Company in January 1913.

Gloucestershire Record Office

Hardly amongst the most exciting of rolling-stock photographs, but included here because of the paucity of views of N & B stock.

Tudor Watkins Coll.

Admittedly not N & B wagons, but indicative of the traffic on the more northern, rural section of the line at Devynock, looking towards Brecon.

Tudor Watkins Coll.

Chapter 8

THE PERSONALITY AND PERSONALITIES
OF THE RAILWAY

Ordinarily, railways are constructed slowly and painstakingly but when they have served their purpose they are dismantled with little finesse and their disappearance can be rapid. Generally, their histories are usually chronicled in detail – with the possible exception, perhaps, of due acknowledgement of the contribution of ordinary working staff. The human element often attracts little attention.

Although only a comparatively short railway and undoubtedly less important than some, the N & B still managed a full quota of colourful characters and stories. Most regrettably, few have endured but some of the survivors may be exemplified here by the tale of the young Sennybridge man who regularly rode up to Cray to visit friends and released his horse to return home on its own, that he might travel down on the footplate of the last train of the day; or the woman (young or mature, beautiful or plain is not recorded) who entered a signal-box in the dead of night and

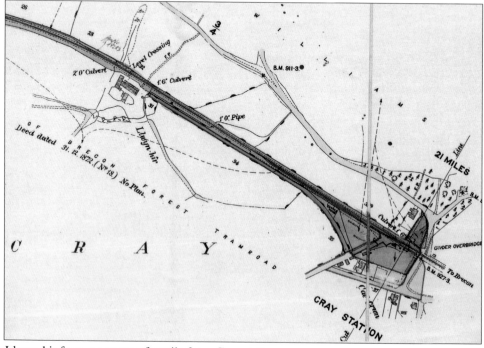

Llwyn-hir farm, a quarter of a mile from Cray station.

GWR Property Plans 1925/Tudor Watkins Coll.

lay down on the lockers. Less dramatic, but possibly of greater significance, are the memories of local people who can still recall the importance of the railway to daily life, particularly in the more remote regions north of Onllwyn. The Powell family, for instance, farmed land on either side of the main line at Llwyn-hir, near Crai; they rapidly learned how best to live with the railway. Stock had to be moved with extra care if the manoeuvre involved crossing the track and all members of the family knew the regular timetable by heart, additionally having a good grasp of when extra trains might be slotted into the pattern. Although against regulations, use of the railway line frequently provided a better route between farm, station and school than the often muddy farm track alongside – the younger members being particularly adept at 'walking the rails'. Livestock was regularly moved into and out of the region by train and on such occasions the station yard at Cray became a hive of activity. During the 'tacking' season, for example, sizeable trains of around twenty wagons left the pens with lambs for winter pastures and John McTurk, who owned vast tracts of the uplands between Coelbren and Sennybridge, additionally despatched a similar number of vans of wool from Cray. Whereas many central Wales farmers then sent their wool to Lancashire, McTurk patriotically sent his to Scotland and on at least one occasion is known to have imported prize rams from Dumfries, which arrived at Cray in a special 'double-deck' Highland Railway wagon. The thought of sending such traffic by road was inconceiveable before the Beeching era; the railway was the only viable lifeline for rural communities before the mid 1960s and at times of crises, natural disasters or other emergencies it was the railway which sustained those in the more remote and isolated parts of the country.

Local staff appear to have turned out to make a start at clearing the track at Craig-y-nos on 11 March 1947, although elsewhere, the line remained blocked between Colbren and Sennybridge.   *National Museums & Galleries of Wales*

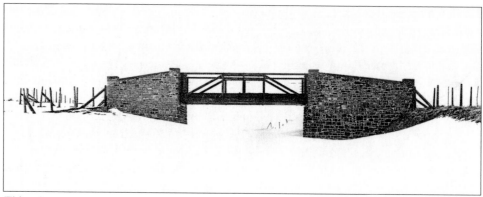

This view, facing Colbren, of the bridge at Upper Glyn-llech, at 12 miles 19½ chains, possesses a surreal quality. 11 March 1947.

National Museums & Galleries of Wales

Former Cambrian Railways 0-6-0 No. 844 and GW pannier tank No. 3706 trapped at 13 miles 40 chains, near Craig-y-nos. 11 March 1947.

National Museums & Galleries of Wales

Brynmigelyn bridge, together with the photographer's case of spare plates on the snow in the middle distance. The section of track beyond the bridge, on a low embankment, was exposed to the wind and bereft of snow. 11 March 1947.

National Museums & Galleries of Wales

The great snows of early 1947 serve to illustrate this point, for they caused problems throughout the country. Trains, including rescue locomotives, were trapped at several locations in Wales and the N & B did not escape. The approaches to the summit at Bwlch were impassable during most of February and March and when the Great Western's official photographer visited Craig-y-nos to record the locomotives trapped in the vicinity, the snow had already been lying for over four weeks. Areas where the fall appeared less, due to the effect of high winds, had begun to clear at this time, but the depth of snow remaining in the cuttings was awesome. Locomotives sought to batter their way through from Neath and Brecon but were baulked by heavy drifts; rescue locomotives initially fared no better, becoming embedded themselves and frequently derailed in the process. Conditions were atrocious. Matters were even more serious on the roads, which were completely impassable – snow was hedge-high for mile upon mile. It was left to the railway eventually to provide a path for essential supplies.

The close relationship which existed in the more rural parts of Wales between agricultural and permanent-way workers served the isolated communities well at such times. Most of the Cray Permanent Way Gang, for example, occupied small-holdings in the vicinity and augmented their regular railway wage by keeping some chickens, a cow or two, or maybe a few pigs or sheep. The practice was established at the dawn of railway construction when navvies were frequently recruited directly from the areas served by a new railway. An interesting variation on this theme occurred during the period following the Second World War when Italian Prisoners of War awaiting repatriation, who were granted special dispensation to help out at local farms in the late 1940s, were also used to relay stretches of the main line in the vicinity of Cray and Sennybridge.

Midland 0-6-0T No. 1107 on a ballast train near Penwyllt. The suggestion has been made that the figure with his foot on the crossing (right-hand foreground) may be John Dickson but since the Midland are unlikely to have been involved with permanent-way work when Dickson was around, this seems unlikely.
Tudor Watkins Coll.

A tale of more recent times is recalled when penguins escaped from the Pensgynor Bird Sanctuary and roamed along the track towards Cilfrew. Having been alerted, control warned enginemen of the situation, only to receive a retort from one particular driver who claimed he was well aware that it was a climb up to Onllwyn but he had no idea it was that close to the Arctic Circle. Sadly, such quips and tales – which must have been legion over the years – went largely unrecorded. Conversely, official reports had a better chance of survival and when they featured accidents or disasters, were often the only accounts to dwell on staff who actually worked the line.

During a heavy thunderstorm on the afternoon of Sunday, 21 July 1907, a large portion of the Byfre embankment, opposite the company's small reservoir near Craig-y-nos station (which supplied water to Colbren Junction) was washed away for a distance of about 50ft. A large culvert under the embankment at this point was virtually destroyed and similar culverts in the vicinity were also damaged or blocked; large quantities of ballast were swept away over a three-mile stretch of line.

Fate decreed that a N & B Permanent Way train was in the vicinity that day. It approached the Byfre embankment during the height of the storm when one of the men on the footplate noticed a part of the bank slipping away, leaving the rails suspended. The train was brought to an immediate halt and Inspector Morgans, in charge of Permanent Way operations that afternoon, at once set the men to repairing the void beneath the track. Fortunately, he had both men and materials at his disposal but the process of infilling was slow as only one wagon at a time could approach the slip to discharge its load. Resourcefully, heavy timber baulks were used to shore up the track, eventually permitting three or four wagons to be propelled simultaneously over the spot, accelerating the work considerably. The Midland and Great Western companies were urgently contacted by telegraph for additional ballast. Again, an element of luck favoured the work, for loaded trains were located near at hand. The N & B men were thus able to remain on site and dedicated to unloading and repair work. The Midland Railway supplied 25 trucks of ballast, the Great Western 9, and 26 were supplied from the nearby brickworks yard. The full count of wagons discharged at the scene of the disaster was not known at the time, but it was then estimated that there could have been 'no less than 160 to 170 discharged at the spot'.

By Monday morning, with the work still incomplete, arrangements were made with the Midland to work passenger trains to the location from both Swansea and Brecon. A narrow strip of embankment survived here, enabling passengers to walk from one train to the other. Such a manoeuvre would be quite impossible today, with our excessive and possibly stifling restrictions safeguarding health and safety. But in 1907, the ploy was successful and Midland goods traffic was resumed sometime after midnight on Monday, in time to avoid any need to divert traffic to other routes.

Although appropriate materials were readily accessible, this rapid and satisfactory repair was due in no small part to the excellent work of the men at the breach, who worked from Sunday, through that night until Monday mid-day, some even staying longer to join the relief gang which had been formed.

Griffiths reported to his directors on 25 July 1907;

> Considering the heavy character of the work which had to be continued through many hours and on Monday afternoon during a violent thunderstorm which drenched the men to the skin, I feel I cannot speak too highly of the expeditious manner in which they carried out a most difficult and laborious task, and I have felt confident that it would be your wish that a gratuity should be given to each man who in such extremely trying circumstances rendered the Company the most valuable service.

Writing to W. B. Partridge two days later, Griffiths recorded the following:

> Altogether there were about 50 men continuously working almost 40 hours at a stretch and about 22 men for nearly 24 hours, during part of which a terrible thunderstorm raged and a downpour of rain drenched them to the skin. If you approve of £20 to £25 being distributed amongst the men, kindly fill in the accompanying cheque accordingly.

By to-day's financial standards, a sum of £25 per man for heavy labour above and beyond the call of duty, in such circumstances, would seem grossly inadequate, but this was 1907 and the £25 was intended for distribution among the men. Griffiths continued:

> Mr Harris, who visited the scene of the disaster and saw the excellent work performed by the men in such a short time, considered that a gratuity of 10/- (50p) per man had been well merited but that sum runs into rather a big figure [£36] though I do not hesitate for a moment in agreeing with Mr Harris that such a gratuity is well deserved.

It could well be that each man received an additional 10/- in his pay packet that week – a final figure is not recorded – but the episode demonstrates the readiness of the N & B workforce to undertake emergency work in extremely trying conditions without debate or prevarication regarding payment.

Believed to be two young N & B ticket collectors at the start of their railway careers.

Courtesy Wil Davies Collection

If the above account focusses briefly on the loyalty of the N & B Permanent Way staff, no such spotlight fell on others who daily performed routine tasks with efficiency and courtesy. Passenger guards would be high on the list in this context. These were prominent figures, by nature of their work and the Midland men, particularly, appeared to have a special aura of their own. They were tall men of imposing stature, always courteous, helpful and smart in appearance; they made a lasting impression which has endured.

In terms of individuals no one, it would seem, could have been more faithful to the N & B than David James of Coelbren. He started his career as a lad-porter at Craig-y-nos in 1918, progressing to Seven Sisters as a porter/signalman in 1921. When the GWR took over at the Grouping, he was transferred to Bryn, on the former PTR, before returning to the N & B as signalman at Aberbran. A second brief period was spent on the PTR before he returned as signalman at Onllwyn in 1924; Craig-y-nos again in 1926, then Colbren from 1935 until 1941, when he became a relief signalman for the N & B section.

David James' whole life was devoted to the railway. He lived alone in a corrugated-iron bungalow, used originally for accommodation during the construction of Crai reservoir (1907) but later relocated just outside Coelbren. Entrance to the property was through a narrow gateway flanked by a pair of GW signal finials, hinting that an

A 1920 portrait of Cilfrew station master, Mr H. Lewis and his family.

Courtesy Brian King Coll.

Life for the signalman and his family, at Bwlch, was difficult. They were remote from shops and at 1,254ft the weather was harsh. The need to be self-sufficient led to the keeping of chickens and the breeding of goats at this place.

Tudor Watkins Coll.

A group of
station staff at
Craig-y-nos
in 1908.
*Tudor Watkins
Coll.*

A similar
group at
Devynock.
*Tudor Watkins
Coll.*

David James, on
the right, during a
period spent at
Seven Sisters.
Tudor Watkins Coll.

enthusiast lived beyond but without providing any real indication of the fervour and depth of that individual's enthusiasm. Once inside, progress was confined to very narrow passages between head-high stacks of magazines and newspapers bound with string. These suggested trenches in northern France during the First World War or perhaps some secret passage in Tutankhamen's tomb (to someone who had visited neither) before they suddenly opened to form a chamber, crammed with all manner of railway treasures. Every available space seemed occupied, whilst the centre area was almost entirely taken by model trains. When activated, these looped around on a multitude of circuits. No attempt was made to portray a particular stretch of line with any fidelity; indeed, not even the scale was constant, but as one might expect of a former signalman, an array of signals was much in evidence, together with a host of full-size instruments 'saved' from redundant signal-boxes. Had such a title existed, David James would undoubtedly have been 'Mr N & B' although his enthusiasm and superior knowledge of rule-books did not always endear him to his fellow workers.

In contrast, the name of the Revd Garmons [sic] Williams held no place in the story of the N & B until he penned a letter on 21 February 1900 to the Midland and Neath & Brecon companies. Now at the PRO in Kew, this most unusual missive reads as follows:

> I hereby request the Midland Railway Company to throw from their 8.5 a.m. and 3.55 p.m. trains from Swansea as they pass through the Abercamlais Private Station of the Neath & Brecon Railway Company all parcels of newspapers not exceeding 6lbs in weight that may be sent by those trains addressed to me or to my residence, and I hereby undertake to indemnify the Midland Railway Company and the Neath & Brecon or either or both of them against any losses, costs, damages or expenses that they may suffer or be put to by any reason of accident, damage, or injury whatever that may arise from the papers being thrown from the said trains, and I also undertake to hold the aforesaid Railway Companies indemnified against any damage to or loss of such parcels arising from being thrown from the trains, and against all claims for compensation for delay or inconvenience caused from the overcarrying of such parcels beyond the said Private station of Abercamlais.

The request was rejected but not before the Revd Garmons Williams had carved a special niche for himself in the annals of the N & B.

Few railways, particularly small rather impecunious concerns such as the N & B, can have benefitted from the patronage of a single individual as did the N & B – and the Midland – from Adelina Patti. Nowadays largely neglected outside the circle of those interested in operatic history, Adelina Patti (1843–1919) was then a glamorous and talented soprano whose fame encompassed the whole globe; she was an international star even before that term had been coined. Born of Italian parents in Madrid, Patti's career developed during an era when operatic singers enjoyed a status which today relates more with Hollywood film stars of the 1930s and '40s, or contemporary pop or television personalities.

An early portrait of Adelina Patti which she used throughout her life.   *Cardiff Central Library*

She enjoyed public adulation on a grand scale throughout a long and successful career, from the moment she first appeared on stage in New York in 1851 at the age of eight, to the early years of the twentieth century. She earned record-breaking fees throughout her career and amassed enormous wealth from extensive tours.

In addition to her vocal attributes, Patti was petite, attractive and attracted by men of wealth, power or talent; she was feted by royalty and presidents across Europe and by the rich and famous wherever she went. She could have chosen to live anywhere in the world but for over forty years, between 1878 and 1919, she made her home midst the Brecon Beacons, at Craig-y-nos castle.

Adelina married three times. Her first husband was the Marquis de Caux, whom she married in 1868 when she was 25. This proved unsuccessful and within three years she was consorting with Ernesto Nicolini, a French tenor, and consequently sought a retreat away from the full glare of social speculation and condemnation. It was during a visit to Sir Hussey Vivian (later Lord Swansea) at Cadoxton Lodge, Neath, that Patti and Nicolini first saw the house at Craig-y-nos. Patti immediately fell in love with the rather wild and romantic location, whilst Nicolini was attracted by the prospect of life as a country squire. The property was for sale and in 1878 was purchased by Patti for £3,500. In the ensuing years the pair collectively spent approximately £100,000 on improving the estate and the house, which was always referred to as a castle; in their heyday, they employed around forty servants. During this time De Caux steadfastly refused to grant Patti a divorce, until 1885, when she married Nicolini.

This was the first sight of Craig-y-nos castle for those who arrived by train; it may still be enjoyed by any who visit Patti's station.

Courtesy Knight Frank, Hereford

Notice for Driver Richards

NEATH & BRECON RAILWAY.

31, 24690.
Cir. No. 456

GENERAL MANAGER'S OFFICE,

NEATH, January 18th, 1899.

Madam Patti Nicolini's Wedding,

AT BRECON, 25th INSTANT.

On this occasion SPECIAL PASSENGER TRAINS for the conveyance of Madame PATTI NICOLINI and Party will be run as follows:—

UP.	Empty Train.		Passenger.		DOWN.	Passenger.	
	Arr.	Dep.	Arr.	Dep.		Arr.	Dep
	a.m.	a.m.	a.m.	a.m.		a.m.	a.m.
Neath Low Level		8.30			Brecon Pass. Station		11.33
Signal Box		8.32			„ Mount Street		11.34
Cilfrew Loop		8.40			Aberbran		11.44
Crynant		8.54			Devynock		12.5
Onllwyn		9.10			Bwlch (a)		12.21
Colbren	9.13	9.19			Penwyllt	12.26	12.35
Penwyllt	9 27	—		9.32	Colbren		12.42
Bwlch				9.43	Onllwyn		12.45
Devynock				10.0	Crynant (b)		12.57
Aberbran				10.10	Cilfrew Loop		1.3
Brecon Mount Street				10.19	Neath Signal Box		1.7
„ Pass. Station			10.20		„ Low Level		1.8

(a) Cross 11.0 a.m. Passenger ex. Swansea. (b) Cross 12.20 p.m. Goods ex. Neath.

The 1.0 p.m. Goods ex. Neath to be kept back at Neath until arrival of Special.

The Up Train to be formed at Neath as follows:—1 Third, 1 Saloon, 1 Brake Van. The Return Train, Brecon to Penwyllt, to consist of the same Coaches marshalled in like manner.

At Penwyllt the Party will change from the Saloon into a Corridor Train of 8 Coaches, both Trains being there combined, and worked to Neath.

The Corridor portion only will be worked through to London, by G.W.R. Special appointed to leave Neath at 1.15p.m.

Great Western Company's Stock willbe used.

Every effort must be made by the Station Agents to keep the line clear of all ordinary Trains so that these Special Trains may be run to their booked time.

J. E. Griffith

A time-worn copy of the official notice handed to the N & B's 'Top-link' engineman, Driver Richards, outlining the timing and general railway arrangements regarding Patti's third wedding, in 1899. *TW Coll.*

Adelina Patti Nicolini, as she became known at this time, was one of the first stars to exploit fully the advantages of rail travel. Her ability to tour extensively in luxury and privacy – the very foundation of her success – would have been impossible without the railway. Good lines of communication were essential and in this respect the location of Craig-y-nos was better suited to her requirements than might at first be supposed. With the railway just over a mile from the castle, a journey south via Neath offered access to London and the continent whilst to the north via Brecon, Hereford and Shrewsbury, she had ready access to Liverpool, at that time the principal port for America. Thus, the rural isolation and tranquility which she desired, far from hindering her career, gave her a base which provided beneficial periods of rest away from the stress and strain of public appearances.

Patti's diary for 1885 demonstrates her phenomenal work-rate and underlines the importance of travel to her career. January to the end of April was spent completing a tour of North America, which had started early November the previous year; the diva returned to Craig-y-nos to spend the spring in Wales before leaving for the Royal Opera season at Covent Garden, from 20 June to the end of July. The summer break that year was spent relaxing at Craig-y-nos, which Patti simply adored ('All the time I spend away from Craig-y-nos seems to me time lost' – Patti, 1886). During the autumn, she undertook her usual concert tour of the UK, visiting some fourteen centres, Glasgow, Edinburgh, Liverpool and Manchester amongst them. On 23 November, after a brief sojorn at Craig-y-nos, she left for opera appearances at Antwerp, Amsterdam, Pest and Prague, spending Christmas in Vienna.

These journeys were all undertaken by train; the advantages of rail travel were unsurpassed. Whilst Patti acknowledged her dependance on the train, the railway

The signalman's bungalow and passing loop at Bwlch.   *Tudor Watkins*

companies, equally, were careful to protect and foster her patronage, for not only was she a great supporter of rail travel but over the years she attracted a great many prominent and influential figures to Craig-y-nos; royalty, financiers and men of letters, as well as theatrical figures and musicians. The Prince of Wales, who had befriended Patti from the time of their first meeting as teenagers in Montreal in 1860, is widely believed to have visited Craig-y-nos although documentary confirmation is lacking. But all Patti's famous guests used the railway. Initially, this meant using the little station at Cray, the nearest convenient stop for the castle, for a road connection with Penwyllt was non-existent at that time; only a steep and difficult path then linked the castle and station.

Patti initially sought the construction of a small station at Bwlch, the summit of the line, which was nearer to her home. Her request was forwarded to the Midland company through no less a person than her friend and adviser Baron Alfred de Rothschild, who wrote,

> Madam Patti wishes to be allowed to direct your attention to the great inconvenience she is now put to in reaching her chateau in South Wales by having to use a station called 'Pennwilt' [sic] the road to which is so bad that her horses cannot accomplish it at all . . . whereas if a little station of the name Bwlch Siding which is now only for merchandise were made a passenger station, she would be able to reach her house in a quarter of an hour.

The reply from the general manager's office in Derby suggested this was more a matter for the N & B and de Rothchild's letter was passed on to them. It was estimated that the cost of a wooden platform 80ft by 10ft with a covered room 7ft wide by 12ft long would be £150. No agreement was reached; no station was built at Bwlch. Nonetheless, the N & B found justification for more serious expenditure at Penwyllt, acknowledging the fact that

> Madam Patti and her friends and visitors were the main sources of revenue and in order to retain the patronage of the great songstress it was essential that a palatial waiting room should be erected at Penwyllt Station for the diva's convenience.

The resultant building can hardly be described as 'palatial' but, of limestone and with a slate roof, it was certainly more substantial than the proposed '7ft wide by 12ft long' room at Bwlch which would probably have been constructed of wood.

Patti demonstrated her willingness to share some of the costs of the improvements at Penwyllt by paying for the construction of a new stretch of roadway to allow horses and carriages to reach the station. This was first used in April 1889, in good time for the intensive traffic later associated with the opening of the new theatre at the castle in 1891. The importance of the station to Patti is further emphasised by her willingness to meet the cost of furnishing her private waiting-room and also erecting a telephone line (1892) between castle and station. This included an annual wayleave charge of 'not less that 5/- [25p] and not more than 10/-'; by 1921, two years after Patti's death, this had risen to £2. 2s. 0d per annum.

Madam Patti's waiting-room, possibly at the time of the announcement of the closure of the line to passenger traffic.   *DD Coll.*

Amongst the many world-famous visitors who arrived at Penwyllt to pay homage to Patti were recording engineers despatched by one of the pioneers of sound recording, The Gramophone & Typewriter Co. (later HMV of Hayes, Middlesex). They wished to record the diva's voice, even though it can then only have reflected a fraction of the vocal brilliance of Patti's heyday; she was 62 at the time. Nonetheless, the record company was most anxious to secure the recording, whilst Patti herself was decidedly uncertain as to the wisdom of such a venture. She declined to travel to Hayes to the recording studio but the company persevered and the brothers Fred and Will Gaisberg, the chief engineers, travelled to Penwyllt to make test recordings at Craig-y-nos. Fred Gaisberg later recalled in his autobiography *Music on Record*, first published in 1942, that he and his brother travelled 'by a narrow-gauge railway to Penwylt [*sic*]'. This late reference to Stephenson's gauge as the 'narrow' gauge may be unique but it must have seemed perfectly natural to Gaisberg, who possibly relied on contemporary notes; he was obviously familiar with the broad gauge and might even have had memories of the GW main line at Hayes.

No other railway – certainly in Wales – could include amongst its regular clientele an international figure of Patti's stature. The N & B basked in the reflected glory; the GW took pride (and profit) in providing the great lady with luxurious saloon carriages and special trains and used her name to endorse the safety of the new Severn Tunnel, which had suffered problems and adverse publicity during its construction. Initially, only coal trains were allowed to use the bore, but a contemporary magazine (*By-gones*, of 15 June 1887) reported:

The Midland exploited its distinguished resident – and the remoteness of the N & B – in this inspired poster published in France. *National Museums and Galleries of Wales*

Madame Patti, in returning to Craig-y-nos castle, had the honour of opening the Severn Tunnel route to [*sic*] London. Madame Patti and party left London by special train, along the new route, this being the first passenger train to pass through the tunnel. The whole distance from Paddington to Neath was accomplished in 4 hours 20 mins. Madame Patti was received with loud cheers on emerging from the tunnel and was presented with a bouquet of flowers.

The Midland were equally proud to be associated with Patti. Well aware that their lines to Swansea were not at the forefront of their express passenger services, they nonetheless were quick to take advantage of Patti and the location of Craig-y-nos. It must be more than a mere coincidence that a Midland Railway poster, circulated in France where Patti was equally famous, emphasised a bold connection from the Midlands into Wales and featured the prominent figure of a single, attractive and obviously well-travelled lady. The Patti connection seems quite intentional.

The luxury of space afforded by rail travel appealed strongly to the diva, especially as she was always accompanied by an entourage of friends, servants and musicians, particularly in America, where vast mileages were covered between engagements. During her 1883 tour of the United States, a private car was especially constructed for her at a cost of £12,000; it contained a magnificent Steinway grand piano and a solid silver bath. The key of the outer door was of 18ct gold. During her tour of 1890, the car bore her name emblazoned on its side and by 1903 it proudly carried the name *Craig-y-nos*. In the UK, her party was of more modest proportions, but still warranted the hire of special trains, which included luggage vans. The lady did not travel 'light' and, on the American tours particularly, her wardrobe would have required between forty and fifty trunks and other items of luggage. When she embarked on her honeymoon in 1899, she was accompanied by 200 pieces of luggage.

Official specimen tickets especially printed for Patti's suite.

National Archives RAIL 1005/123

Identification of vehicles hired by Patti, particularly during the early years of her residency at Craig-y-nos, has not been possible. Private saloons used for her UK concert tours and journeys to and from London were provided mainly by the Great Western and were probably examples of that company's six-wheel saloon stock in the earlier years. It is difficult now to learn more of this fascinating era but by 1895, we know that the GW had constructed a special bogie saloon which became closely associated with Patti for the remainder of her life. This vehicle was to *Diagram G2*, running No. 248 as built, later No. 9004. It survives in private ownership at the premises of Mr Bill Parker, The Flour Mill, Bream, Forest of Dean, although it is not on general display.

Saloon No. 9004, used by Patti during her final years.   *GBJ Coll.*

The interior of 9004, showing one of the saloons.   *GBJ Coll.*

Surprisingly, not a single engine number has been recorded in connection with the Patti journeys; specific engine or carriage identification does not feature. References are to 'special trains' but these, at least, demonstrate Patti's exclusive approach to travel. There are other gaps in our knowledge: was her private saloon, for example, provided on a daily 'as-required' basis, or was the hire contract for longer periods – and what special arrangements did she have with the GWR? Again, the question of the saloon's storage between journeys becomes intriguing; Swindon may have been too distant whereas the Carriage & Wagon Department at Neath was undoubtedly more convenient and could possibly have offered covered accommodation. In any event, the diva's private saloon would hardly have been left to the vagaries of the weather at Penwyllt for anything but the briefest of periods. When Nicolini was recuperating from an illness at Langland Bay, Swansea, during the summer of 1897, Patti (who disliked the sea air intensely) chose to travel daily to visit him for a period of at least six weeks. This entailed a rail journey between Penwyllt and Swansea (Midland) station at St Thomas and a carriage drive to and from Langland. For this period, at least, it appears that Patti's saloon, most likely GW No. 248 at this time, might have been kept overnight at Penwyllt although it is equally possible that it travelled to and from Brecon each day. When Nicolini had later to be moved to Brighton to continue his treatment, he travelled in a special invalid carriage.

Patti occasionally placed her saloon at the disposal of others. In 1904, a Welsh singer living in Swansea, Mr Moss Joseph, was summoned to sing for Patti at the castle and privileged to use her saloon between Swansea (Midland) and Penwyllt, suggesting that the saloon (again, GW No. 248 in 1904) was conveniently stabled within easy reach at the time, possibly at Neath.

Nicolini's travels and treatment, however, had been unsuccessful and he died at Pau, France, in January 1898. Almost within a year Patti had acquired a third husband, a Swedish nobleman, Baron Cederstrom. They were married on 25 January 1899 at St Mary's Roman Catholic Church, Brecon. Yet again, the railway played a prominent role in Patti's life, for in addition to the journeys to and from the ceremony at Brecon (by GW non-corridor saloon carriages) the stations at Penwyllt and Brecon were gaily decorated, carpeted and beflagged again, rather surprisingly, by the GWR. In a letter of 30 January, J.E. Griffiths, ever mindful of controlling expenditure, reported to his directors: 'Except for the wages and expenses of the man I do not think any charge will be made', and adding 'The arrangements made at the stations were such as to afford the wedding party the highest satisfaction.'

On returning to Penwyllt, the Brecon saloons were attatched to a waiting GW corridor train, to which the wedding party transferred for the remainder of the journey to London; the non-corridor saloons were detached at Neath. The wedding breakfast was served during the journey, in a special saloon used previously by the Prince of Wales and reportedly placed at Patti's disposal on the instigation of the Prince himself. Although not recorded specifically, this vehicle would appear to have been No. 233 (later renumbered 9002), a saloon from the Royal Jubilee train favoured by the Prince of Wales. Built as recently as 1897, to celebrate Queen Victoria's Diamond Jubilee, this carriage would have been in pristine condition. It was hardly two years old, during which time it would have received only limited and very careful use, but the gesture reflected the friendship between the Prince of Wales and Patti. When saloon No. 9002 ended its service in the GW Royal Train in 1935, it was sold for £30 and served as a holiday home at Aber-porth in west Wales. Here it lay, overlooking the sea, until rescued and restored by Resco Railways in 1982, for display in the Madame Tussaud Railway exhibition at Windsor station.

A saloon built by the Great Western, which formed part of Queen Victoria's Royal Train, was withdrawn from service in 1935 and conveyed by rail to Newcastle Emlyn for transfer to road, in order to reach its final destination at Aber-porth.   *Ifor Higgon Coll.*

Patti died in 1919; her body lay at rest in her private chapel at the castle and later at the Roman Catholic Chapel, Kensal Green, for a total of eight months before burial, finally, at the Peré La Chaise Cemetery in Paris. Little is known of Patti's last journeys by rail. Did her closest servants and friends from the castle accompany her to the station for the last journey? Which vehicle carried her coffin and how was it dressed? It is inconceivable that her body would have been loaded without ceremony into an ordinary van, but an opportunity was missed to question David James. He was stationed at Craig-y-nos at the time and would surely have retained personal memories of the final departure from the little station which had served Patti so faithfully as her gateway to the world.

Patti's waiting-room remained locked for a period after her death, until the private furniture had been removed; it was opened for general use *c.*1921. It survived thus until closure in 1964 but was given a new lease of life by the directors of Hobbs Quarries who had taken over the quarry and at that time, moved large tonnages of stone by rail via Colbren. The little station was used for some years for company meetings and as a weekend retreat and some items of Patti's furniture were returned from Swindon. The quarry traffic has now ceased and although Patti's waiting-room still exists it appears little used; its survival now

The Craig-y-nos area was not all pomp and romance but also an important stone-quarrying locality. This was sufficient to cause the line to be re-opened after initial closure. Final closure took place in 1981.

Tudor Watkins Coll.

The other side of the coin at Penwyllt/ Craig-y-nos in 1959.
DD Coll.

GW Society's No. 1466 armour-plated for the film 'Young Winston' in 1971.

Courtesy of the Great Western Society

must be questionable. An ideal solution would be to transfer it to the National Museums & Galleries of Wales Museum of Welsh Life at St Fagans, Cardiff, where there is a notable lack of railway-related buildings to remind visitors of the rail industry's vital role in the development of modern Wales.

The old N & B undoubtedly lost some colour and appeal with the passing of Patti. It reverted to a more prosaic, mundane existence, although it had one final flirtation with 'theatrical' matters when location scenes for the film 'Young Winston' were shot in the vicinity of Craig-y-nos in June 1971. Film-makers, with the help of rolling-stock and volunteers from the Great Western Society at Didcot, succeeded in re-creating an episode on the high veldt in South Africa, when the young Winston Churchill was in an armoured train ambushed by the Boers. This was the last occasion for the old N & B to attract any headlines and although the route from Onllwyn to Neath still carries heavy tonnages of coal traffic, no stations have survived and the truncated line bears little resemblance to the Neath & Brecon of old.

When Tennyson wrote 'Our little systems have their day . . . they have their day and cease to be', he obviously had no knowledge of railways, but his melancholy words have a poignant ring even in this context.

The pristine condition of ballast and track of a still operating railway, contrasts with remnants of an earlier age at Cilfrew.
DD.

BIBLIOGRAPHY

Barnsdale, A.F.N. 'The Neath & Brecon Railway', *Railway Magazine*, v. 85, 1939

Barrie, D.S.M. *The Brecon and Merthyr Railway*, Oakwood, 1991

Bowen, R.E. 'Some Notes on Railway Development in the Neath and Brecon Areas', 1977

Davies J. B. *Neath and Brecon: A Comprehensive Survey*, West Glamorgan Railway Society. 1962

Hughes, Stephen *The Brecon Forest Tramroads*. Royal Comm. on Ancient and Historical Monuments Wales, 1990

House of Commons and House of Lords Committee proceedings 1862-1869

Jennings, Paul *Just a Few Lines*, Guinness Superlatives Ltd, 1969

Jones, G.B and Dunstone, D. *The Origins of the LMS in South Wales*, Gomer, 1998

Jones, G.B. and Dunstone, D. *The Vale of Neath Line*, Gomer, 1996

Kidner, R. *The Mid Wales Railway*, Oakwood, 2003

Low, A.C.W. 'The Neath & Brecon Railway', *The Locomotive*, v. 46, 1940

Mitchell, V. and Smith, K. *Brecon to Neath*, Middleton Press, 2004

Morgan, H. *South Wales Branch Lines*, Ian Allan, 1984

National Archives documents mainly in the RAIL 505 and 1057 series

Railway Correspondence and Travel Society, *GWR Locomotives Part 10*, RCTS, 1966

Rattenbury, G. and Cook, R. *The Hay and Kington Railways*, Royal Comm. on Ancient and Historical Monuments Wales, 1996

Reynolds, P. R. 'The Brecon Forest Tramroad', 1979

Richards, S. 'Neath and Brecon Railway', 1977

INDEX

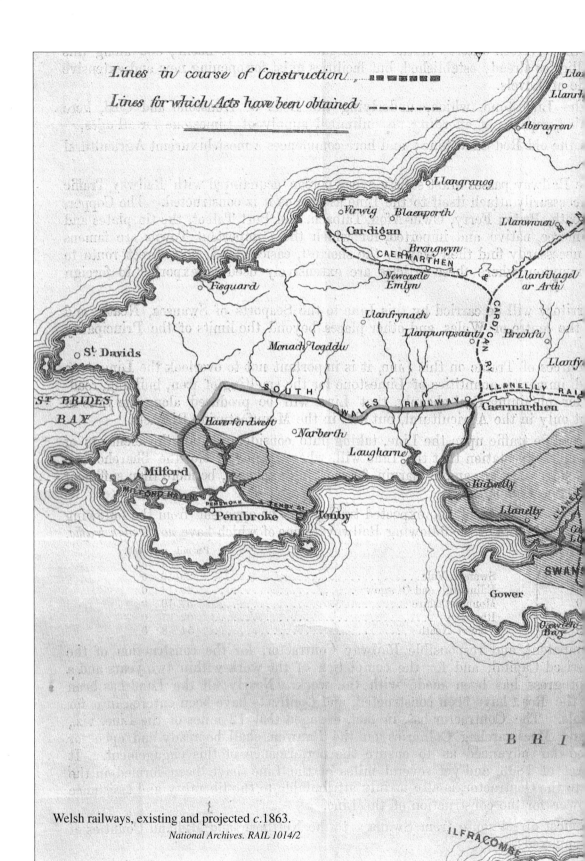

Lines in course of Construction

Lines for which Acts have been obtained

Welsh railways, existing and projected c.1863.

National Archives. RAIL 1014/2